SHURI

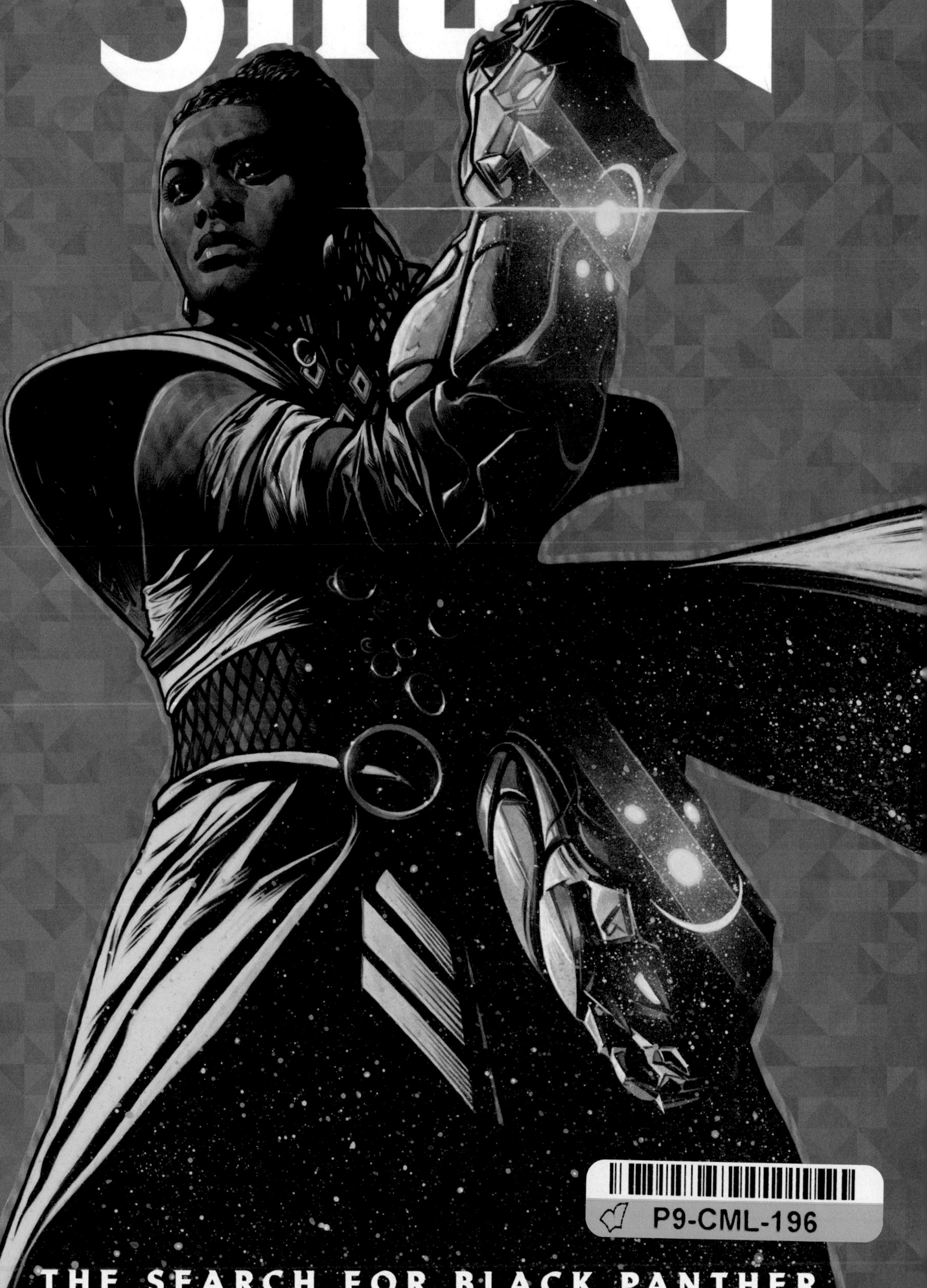

THE SEARCH FOR BLACK PANTHER

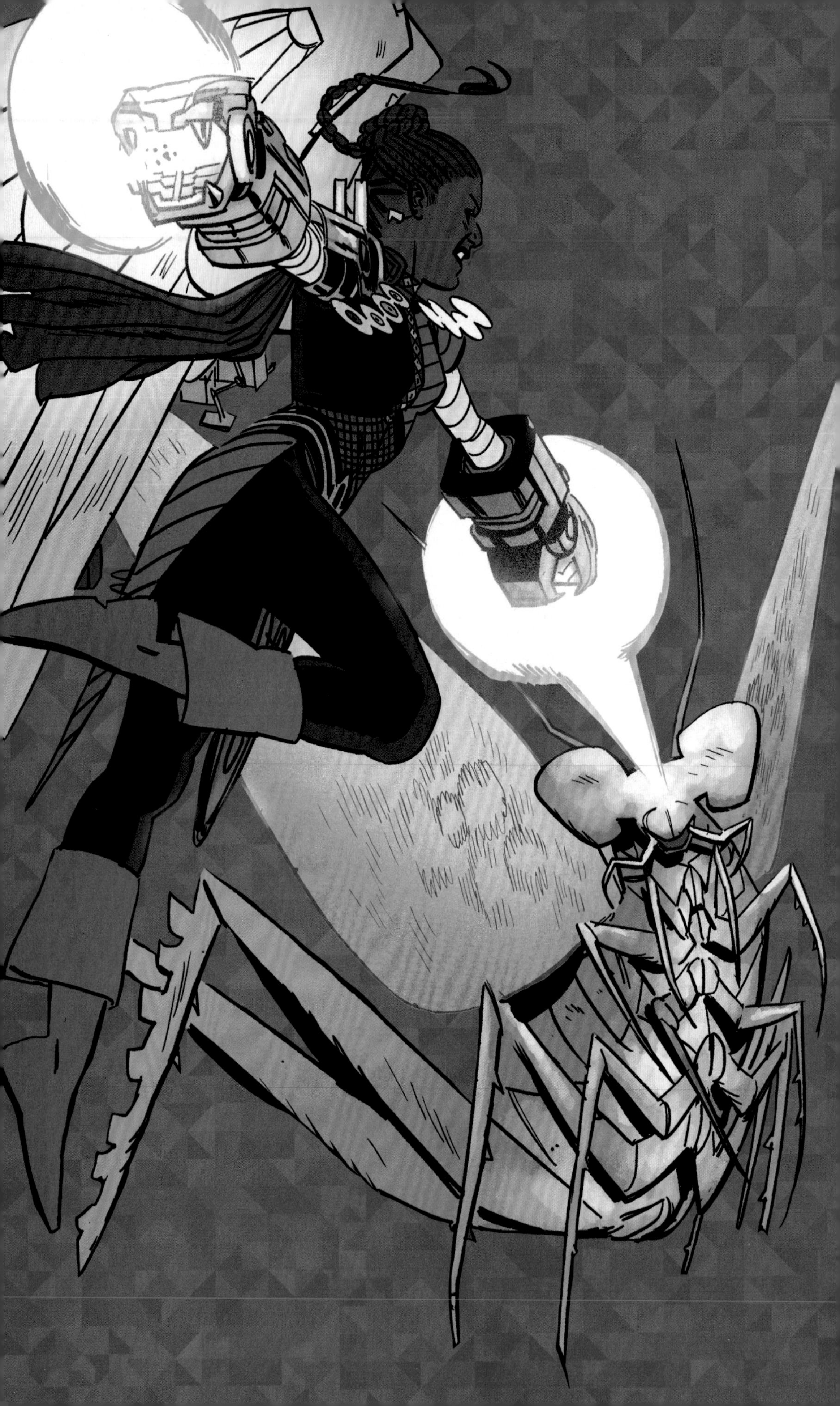

SHURI

THE SEARCH FOR BLACK PANTHER

Nnedi Okorafor
WRITER

Leonardo Romero
ARTIST

Jordie Bellaire
COLOR ARTIST

VC's Joe Sabino
LETTERER

Sam Spratt
COVER ART

Sarah Brunstad
ASSOCIATE EDITOR

Wil Moss
EDITOR

Tom Brevoort
EXECUTIVE EDITOR

COLLECTION EDITOR JENNIFER GRÜNWALD
ASSISTANT EDITOR CAITLIN O'CONNELL
ASSOCIATE MANAGING EDITOR KATERI WOODY
EDITOR, SPECIAL PROJECTS MARK D. BEAZLEY
VP PRODUCTION & SPECIAL PROJECTS JEFF YOUNGQUIST
SVP PRINT, SALES & MARKETING DAVID GABRIEL

BOOK DESIGNER STACIE ZUCKER

EDITOR IN CHIEF C.B. CEBULSKI
CHIEF CREATIVE OFFICER JOE QUESADA
PRESIDENT DAN BUCKLEY
EXECUTIVE PRODUCER ALAN FINE

SHURI: THE SEARCH FOR BLACK PANTHER. Contains material originally published in magazine form as SHURI #1-5. First printing 2019. ISBN 978-1-302-91523-0. Published by MARVEL WORLDWIDE, INC., a subsidiary of MARVEL ENTERTAINMENT, LLC. OFFICE OF PUBLICATION: 135 West 50th Street, New York, NY 10020. © 2019 MARVEL No similarity between any of the names, characters, persons, and/or institutions in this magazine with those of any living or dead person or institution is intended, and any such similarity which may exist is purely coincidental. **Printed in Canada.** DAN BUCKLEY, President, Marvel Entertainment; JOHN NEE, Publisher; JOE QUESADA, Chief Creative Officer; TOM BREVOORT, SVP of Publishing; DAVID BOGART, Associate Publisher & SVP of Talent Affairs; DAVID GABRIEL, SVP of Sales & Marketing, Publishing; JEFF YOUNGQUIST, VP of Production & Special Projects; DAN CARR, Executive Director of Publishing Technology; ALEX MORALES, Director of Publishing Operations; DAN EDINGTON, Managing Editor; SUSAN CRESPI, Production Manager; STAN LEE, Chairman Emeritus. For information regarding advertising in Marvel Comics or on Marvel.com, please contact Vit DeBellis, Custom Solutions & Integrated Advertising Manager, at vdebellis@marvel.com. For Marvel subscription inquiries, please call 888-511-5480. **Manufactured between 3/1/2019 and 4/2/2019 by SOLISCO PRINTERS, SCOTT, QC, CANADA.**

10 9 8 7 6 5 4 3 2 1

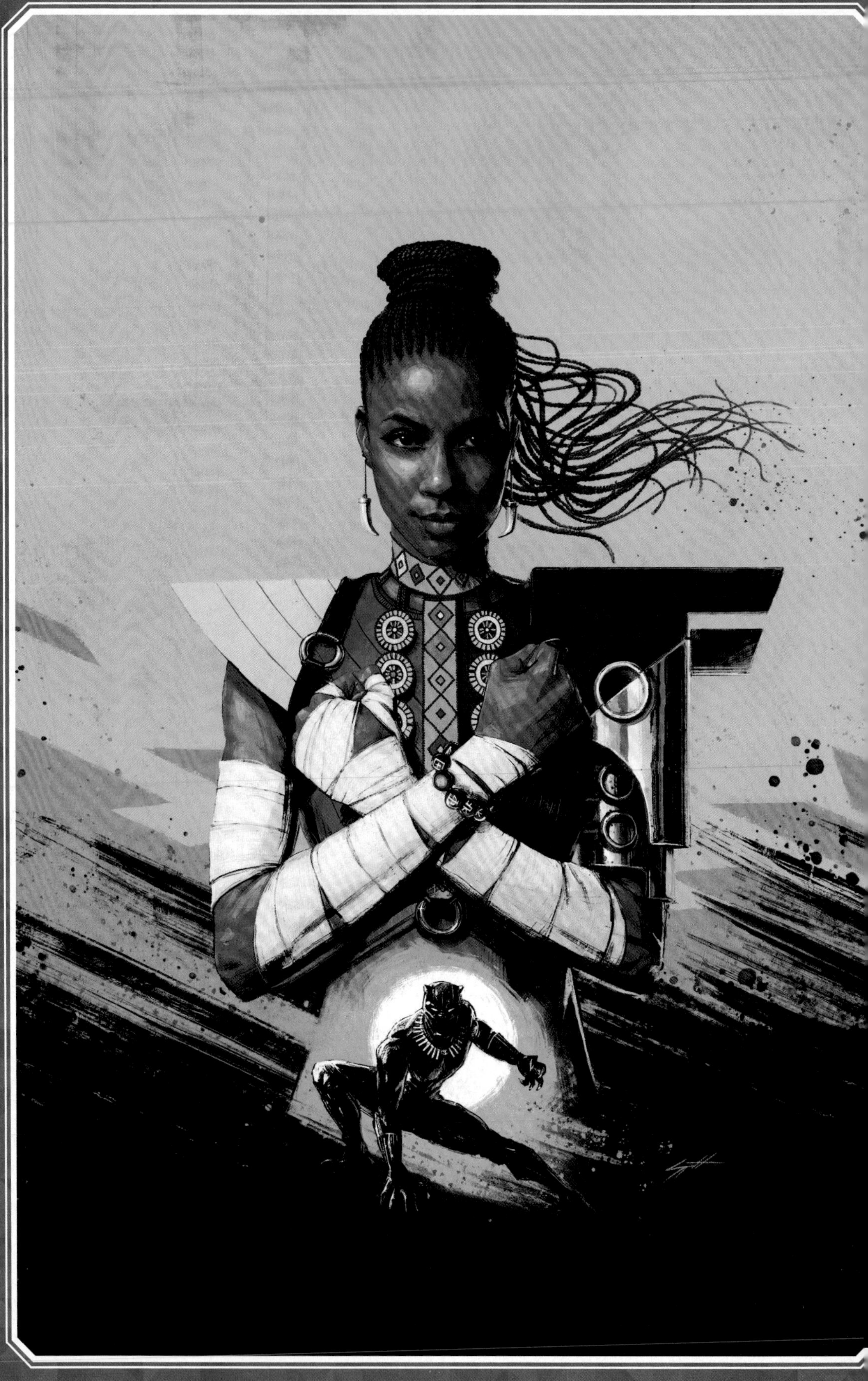

1 – GONE

FOR YEARS, SHURI WATCHED HER OLDER BROTHER T'CHALLA RULE WAKANDA AS THE BLACK PANTHER, WHILE SHE DEVELOPED SKILLS OF HER OWN, SUCH AS BUILDING VIBRANIUM-BASED DEFENSES AND WEAPONS.

BUT THERE CAME A TIME WHEN T'CHALLA WAS NEEDED ELSEWHERE AND THE BLACK PANTHER MANTLE FELL TO SHURI.

WHEN THANOS' BLACK ORDER INVADED WAKANDA, SHURI FOUGHT THEM OFF--BUT AT THE COST OF HER OWN LIFE.

HER SOUL JOURNEYED TO THE DJALIA, THE PLANE OF WAKANDAN MEMORY. THERE, THE SPIRITS OF HER ANCESTORS ENDOWED SHURI WITH THE POWERS OF WAKANDA'S LEGENDARY WARRIORS AND THE KNOWLEDGE OF WAKANDA'S LONG HISTORY BEFORE SHE RETURNED TO THE LAND OF THE LIVING.

WITH HER BROTHER AND THE DORA MILAJE AT HER SIDE, SHURI NOW USES HER ACCUMULATED SKILLS AND WISDOM TO HELP SAFEGUARD HER NATION. WAKANDA FOREVER.

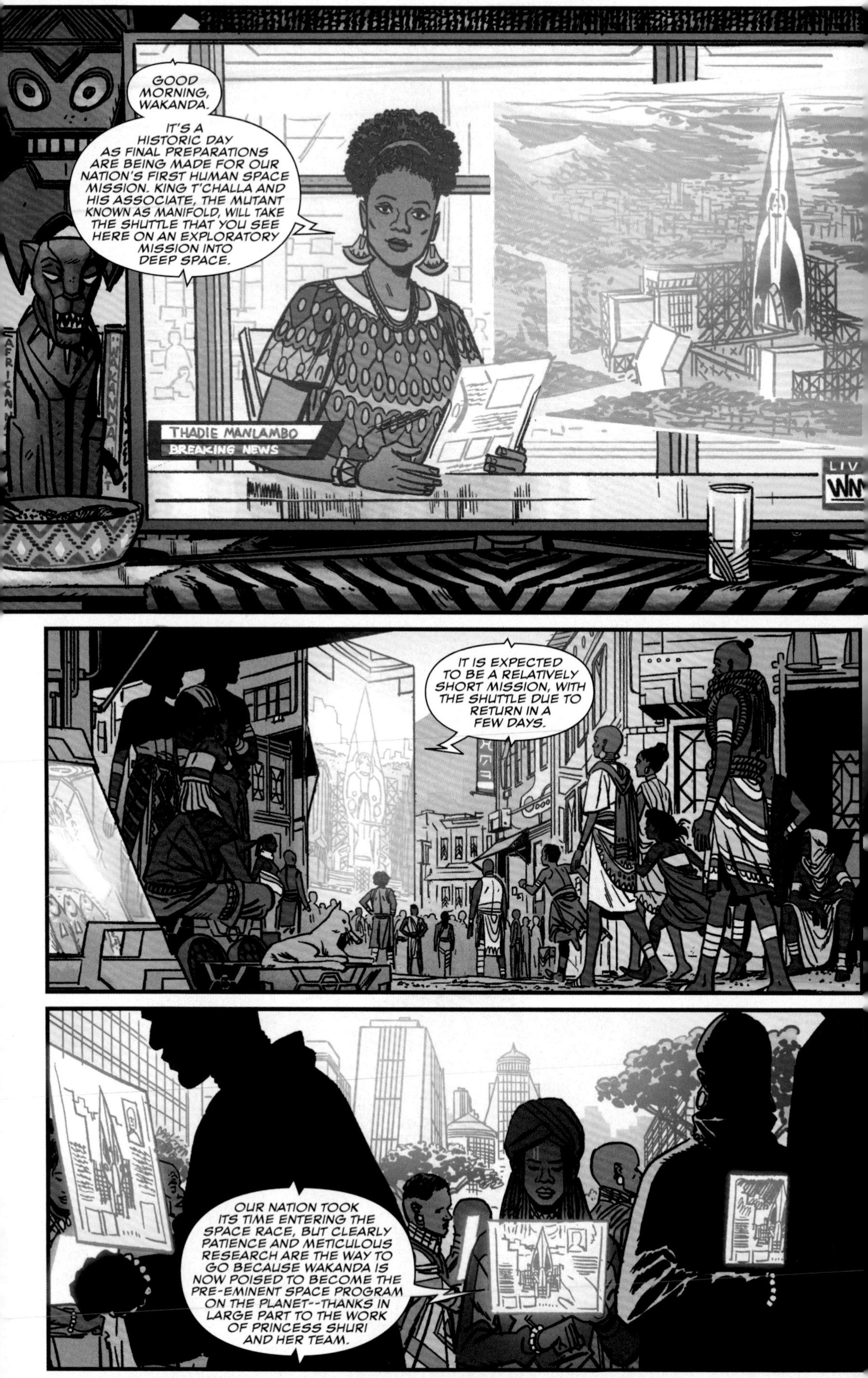
GOOD MORNING, WAKANDA.
IT'S A HISTORIC DAY AS FINAL PREPARATIONS ARE BEING MADE FOR OUR NATION'S FIRST HUMAN SPACE MISSION. KING T'CHALLA AND HIS ASSOCIATE, THE MUTANT KNOWN AS MANIFOLD, WILL TAKE THE SHUTTLE THAT YOU SEE HERE ON AN EXPLORATORY MISSION INTO DEEP SPACE.
THADIE MANLAMBO
BREAKING NEWS
IT IS EXPECTED TO BE A RELATIVELY SHORT MISSION, WITH THE SHUTTLE DUE TO RETURN IN A FEW DAYS.
OUR NATION TOOK ITS TIME ENTERING THE SPACE RACE, BUT CLEARLY PATIENCE AND METICULOUS RESEARCH ARE THE WAY TO GO BECAUSE WAKANDA IS NOW POISED TO BECOME THE PRE-EMINENT SPACE PROGRAM ON THE PLANET--THANKS IN LARGE PART TO THE WORK OF PRINCESS SHURI AND HER TEAM.

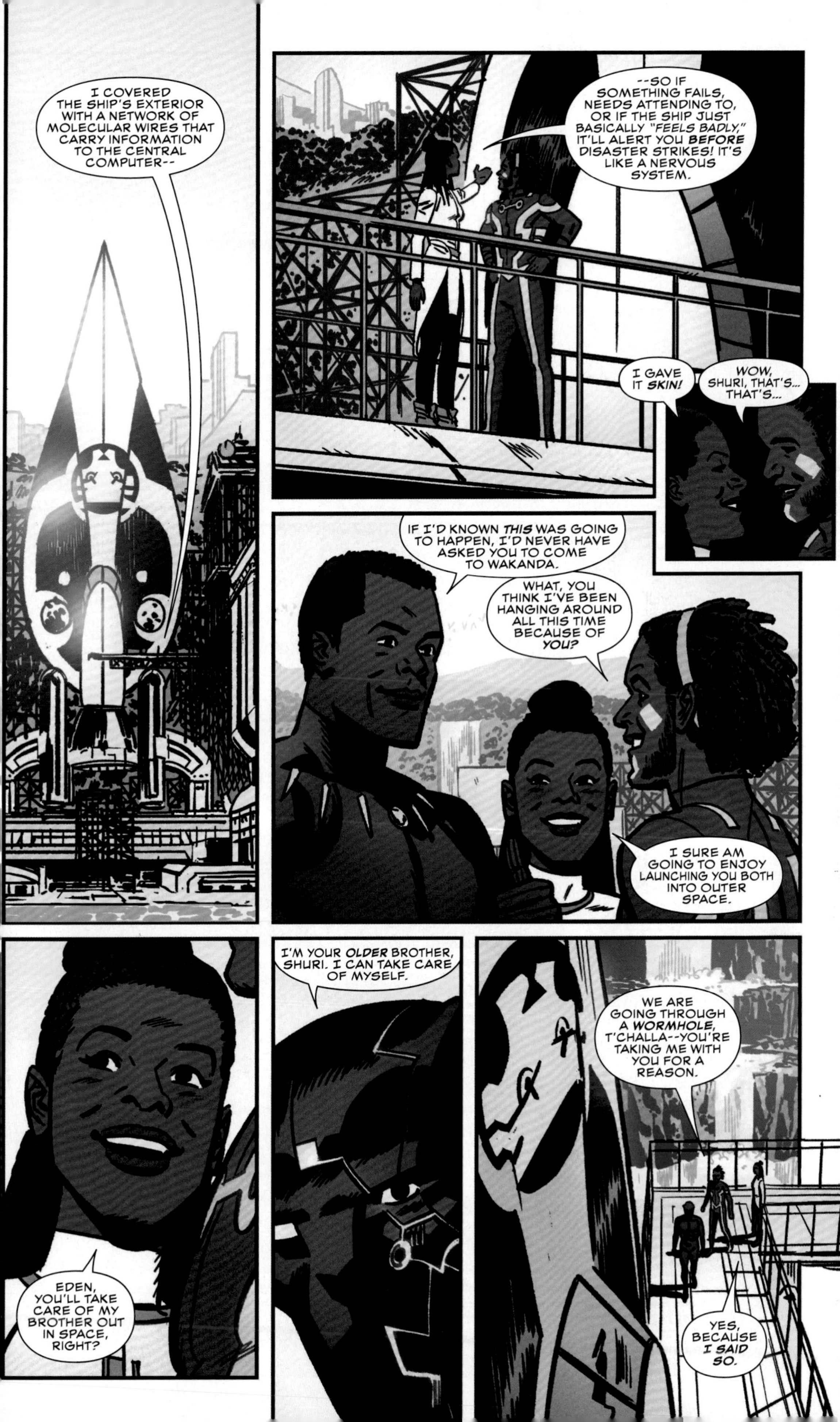
I COVERED THE SHIP'S EXTERIOR WITH A NETWORK OF MOLECULAR WIRES THAT CARRY INFORMATION TO THE CENTRAL COMPUTER--
--SO IF SOMETHING FAILS, NEEDS ATTENDING TO, OR IF THE SHIP JUST BASICALLY "FEELS BADLY," IT'LL ALERT YOU BEFORE DISASTER STRIKES! IT'S LIKE A NERVOUS SYSTEM.
I GAVE IT SKIN!
WOW, SHURI, THAT'S... THAT'S...
IF I'D KNOWN THIS WAS GOING TO HAPPEN, I'D NEVER HAVE ASKED YOU TO COME TO WAKANDA.
WHAT, YOU THINK I'VE BEEN HANGING AROUND ALL THIS TIME BECAUSE OF YOU?
I SURE AM GOING TO ENJOY LAUNCHING YOU BOTH INTO OUTER SPACE.
EDEN, YOU'LL TAKE CARE OF MY BROTHER OUT IN SPACE, RIGHT?
I'M YOUR OLDER BROTHER, SHURI. I CAN TAKE CARE OF MYSELF.
WE ARE GOING THROUGH A WORMHOLE, T'CHALLA--YOU'RE TAKING ME WITH YOU FOR A REASON.
YES, BECAUSE I SAID SO.

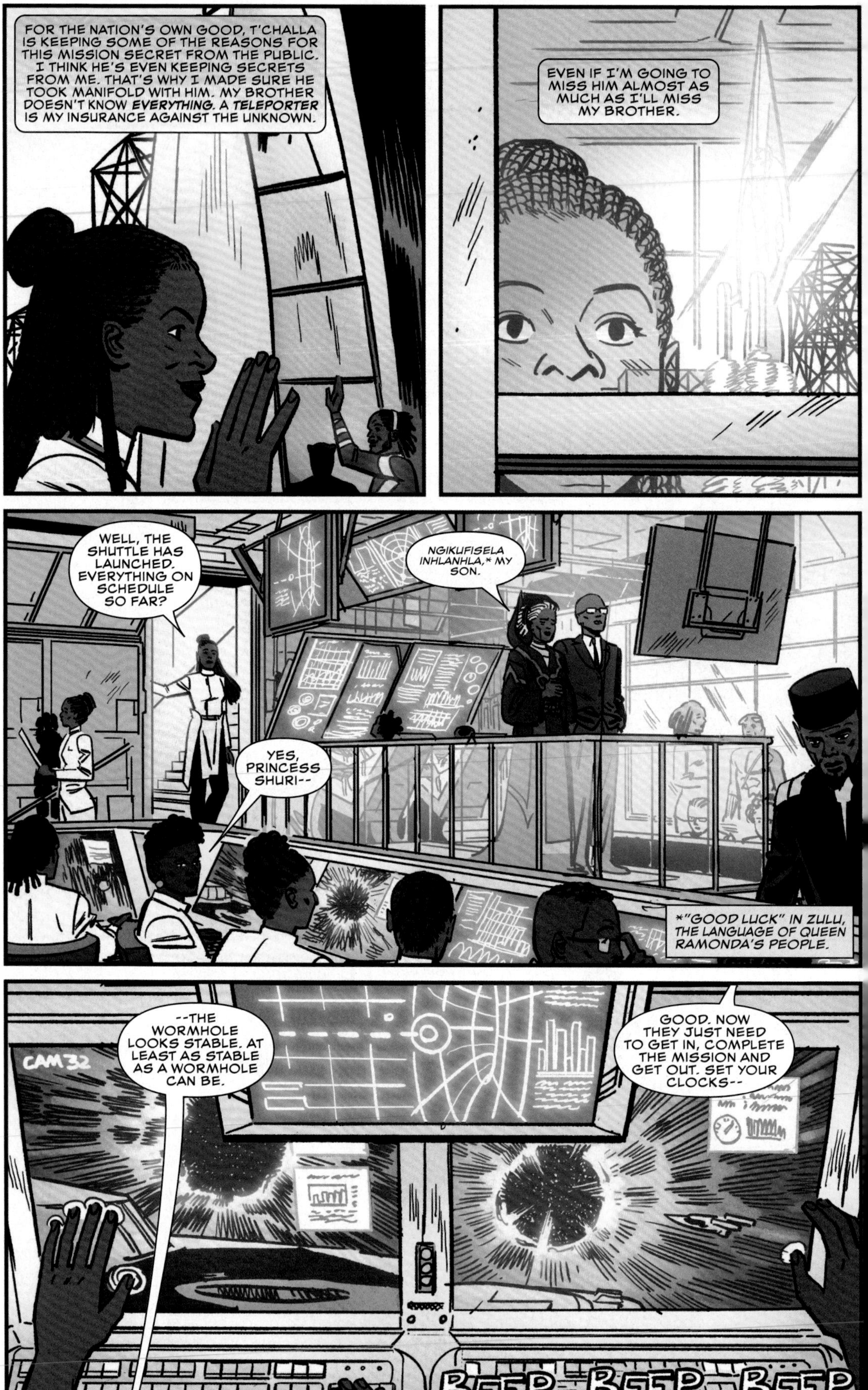
FOR THE NATION'S OWN GOOD, T'CHALLA IS KEEPING SOME OF THE REASONS FOR THIS MISSION SECRET FROM THE PUBLIC. I THINK HE'S EVEN KEEPING SECRETS FROM ME. THAT'S WHY I MADE SURE HE TOOK MANIFOLD WITH HIM. MY BROTHER DOESN'T KNOW EVERYTHING. A TELEPORTER IS MY INSURANCE AGAINST THE UNKNOWN.
EVEN IF I'M GOING TO MISS HIM ALMOST AS MUCH AS I'LL MISS MY BROTHER.
WELL, THE SHUTTLE HAS LAUNCHED. EVERYTHING ON SCHEDULE SO FAR?
NGIKUFISELA INHLANHLA,* MY SON.
YES, PRINCESS SHURI--
*"GOOD LUCK" IN ZULU, THE LANGUAGE OF QUEEN RAMONDA'S PEOPLE.
--THE WORMHOLE LOOKS STABLE. AT LEAST AS STABLE AS A WORMHOLE CAN BE.
GOOD. NOW THEY JUST NEED TO GET IN, COMPLETE THE MISSION AND GET OUT. SET YOUR CLOCKS--
CAM 32
BEEP-BEEP-BEEP-

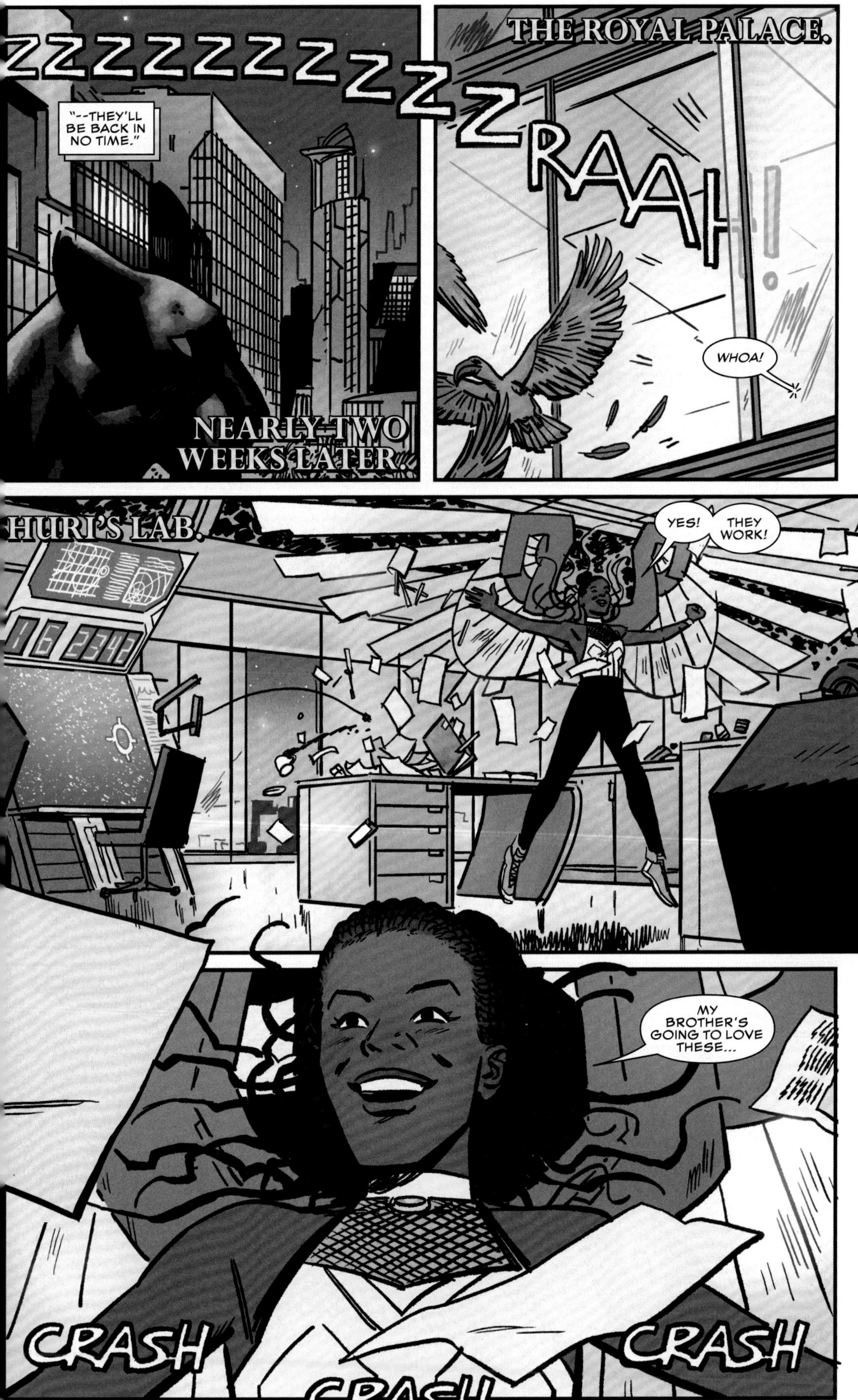
ZZZZZZZZZZZZ
"--THEY'LL BE BACK IN NO TIME."
NEARLY TWO WEEKS LATER.
THE ROYAL PALACE.
RAAH!
WHOA!
HURI'S LAB.
YES!
THEY WORK!
MY BROTHER'S GOING TO LOVE THESE...
CRASH
CRASH
CRASH

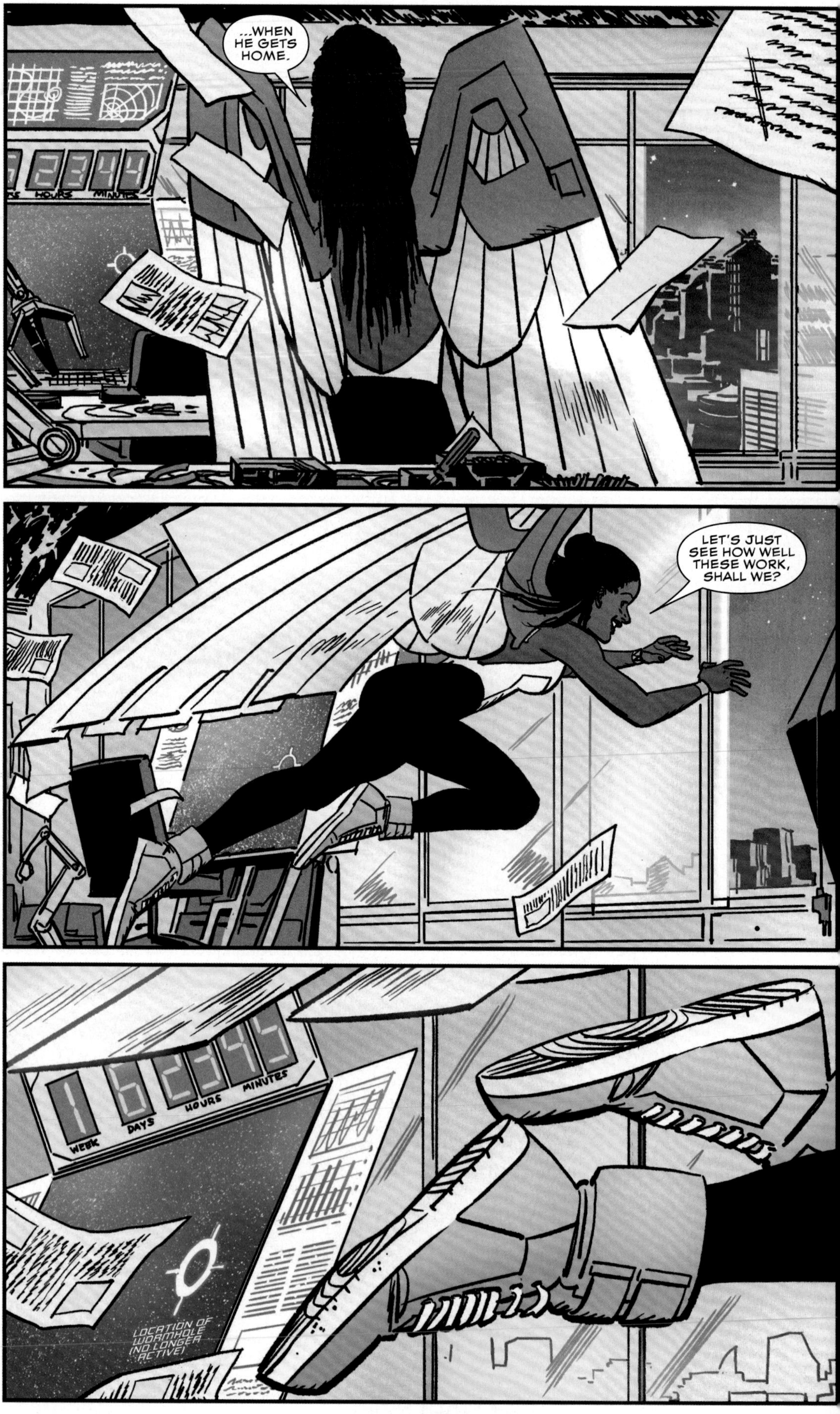
...WHEN HE GETS HOME.
HOURS
MINUTES
LET'S JUST SEE HOW WELL THESE WORK, SHALL WE?
WEEK
DAYS
HOURS
MINUTES
LOCATION OF WORMHOLE (NO LONGER ACTIVE)

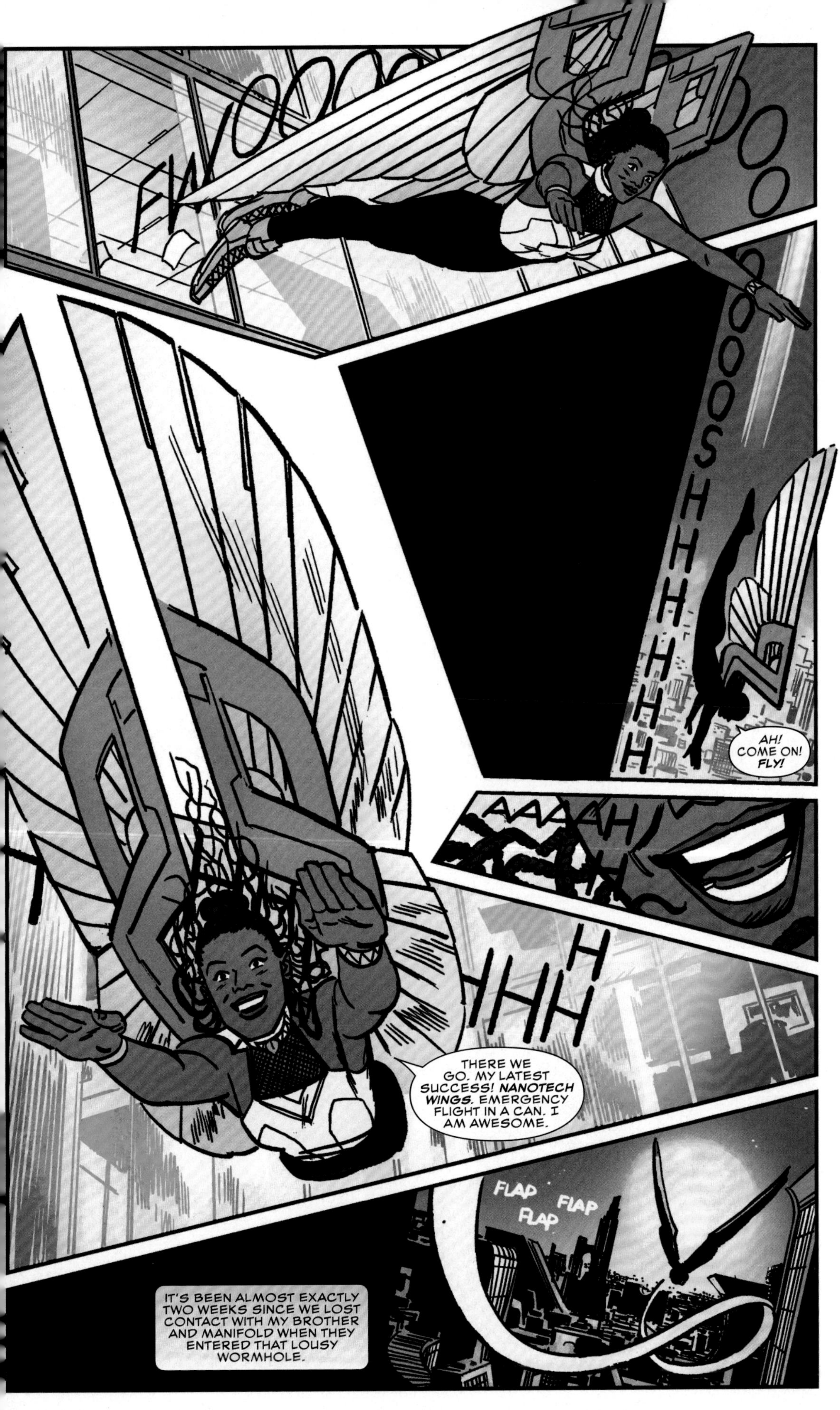
FWOOOOOOOOOOOOOOOSHHHHHHHHHHHH
AH! COME ON! FLY!
AAAAHHHHHHH
THERE WE GO. MY LATEST SUCCESS! NANOTECH WINGS. EMERGENCY FLIGHT IN A CAN. I AM AWESOME.
FLAP FLAP FLAP
IT'S BEEN ALMOST EXACTLY TWO WEEKS SINCE WE LOST CONTACT WITH MY BROTHER AND MANIFOLD WHEN THEY ENTERED THAT LOUSY WORMHOLE.

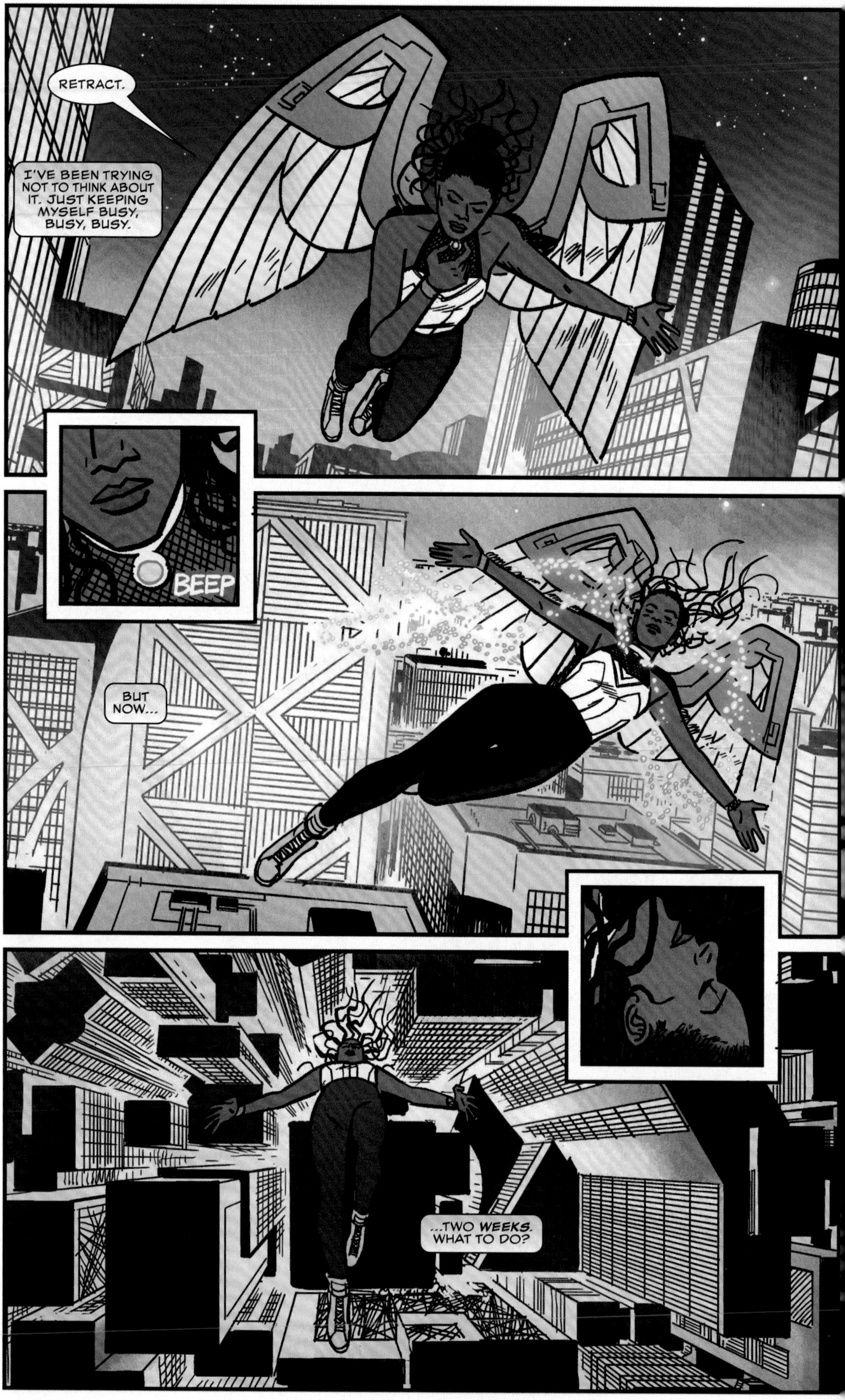
RETRACT.
I'VE BEEN TRYING NOT TO THINK ABOUT IT. JUST KEEPING MYSELF BUSY, BUSY, BUSY.
BEEP
BUT NOW...
...TWO WEEKS. WHAT TO DO?

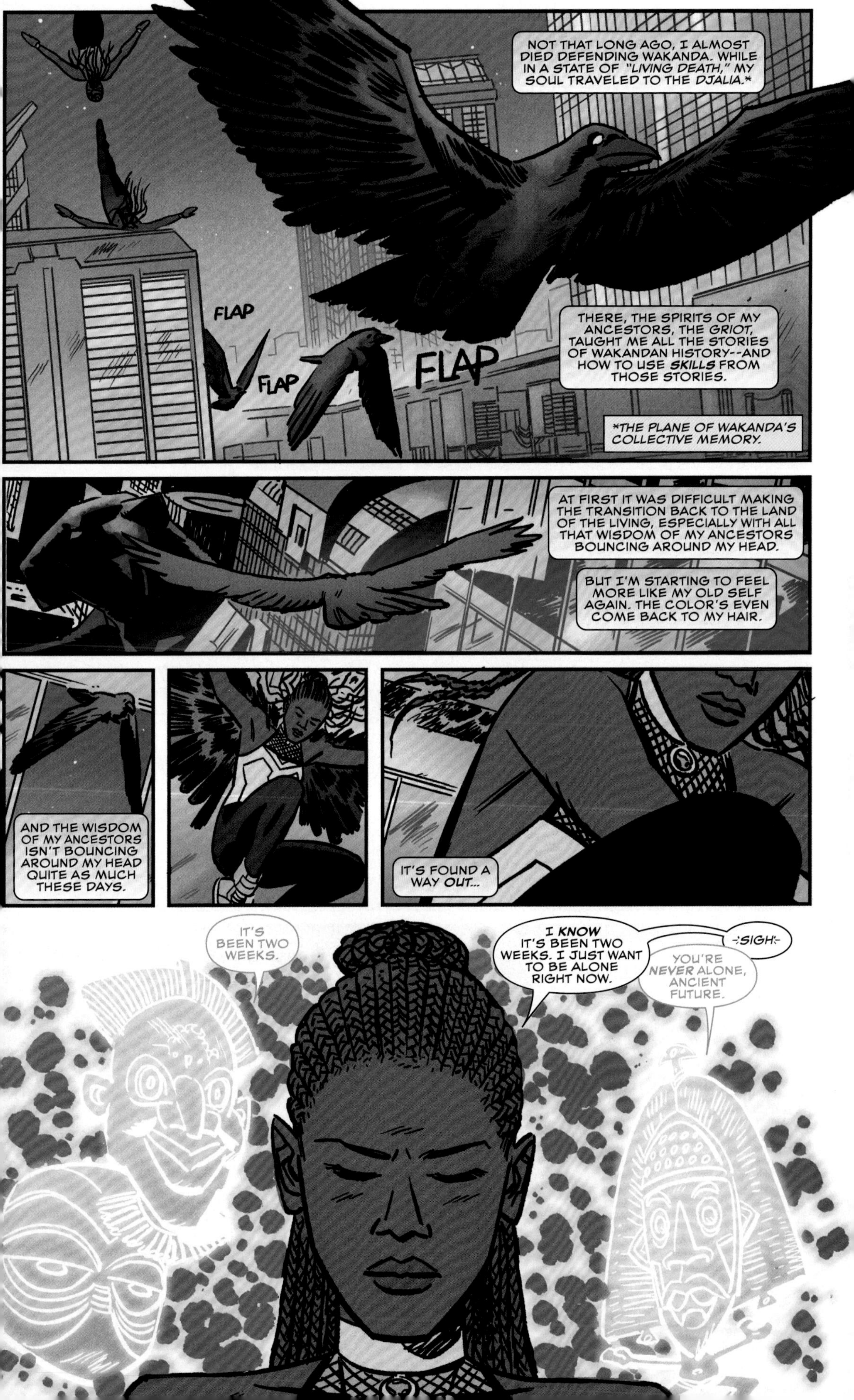
NOT THAT LONG AGO, I ALMOST DIED DEFENDING WAKANDA. WHILE IN A STATE OF "LIVING DEATH," MY SOUL TRAVELED TO THE DJALIA.*
FLAP
FLAP
FLAP
THERE, THE SPIRITS OF MY ANCESTORS, THE GRIOT, TAUGHT ME ALL THE STORIES OF WAKANDAN HISTORY--AND HOW TO USE SKILLS FROM THOSE STORIES.
*THE PLANE OF WAKANDA'S COLLECTIVE MEMORY.
AT FIRST IT WAS DIFFICULT MAKING THE TRANSITION BACK TO THE LAND OF THE LIVING, ESPECIALLY WITH ALL THAT WISDOM OF MY ANCESTORS BOUNCING AROUND MY HEAD.
BUT I'M STARTING TO FEEL MORE LIKE MY OLD SELF AGAIN. THE COLOR'S EVEN COME BACK TO MY HAIR.
AND THE WISDOM OF MY ANCESTORS ISN'T BOUNCING AROUND MY HEAD QUITE AS MUCH THESE DAYS.
IT'S FOUND A WAY OUT...
IT'S BEEN TWO WEEKS.
I KNOW IT'S BEEN TWO WEEKS. I JUST WANT TO BE ALONE RIGHT NOW.
-SIGH-
YOU'RE NEVER ALONE, ANCIENT FUTURE.

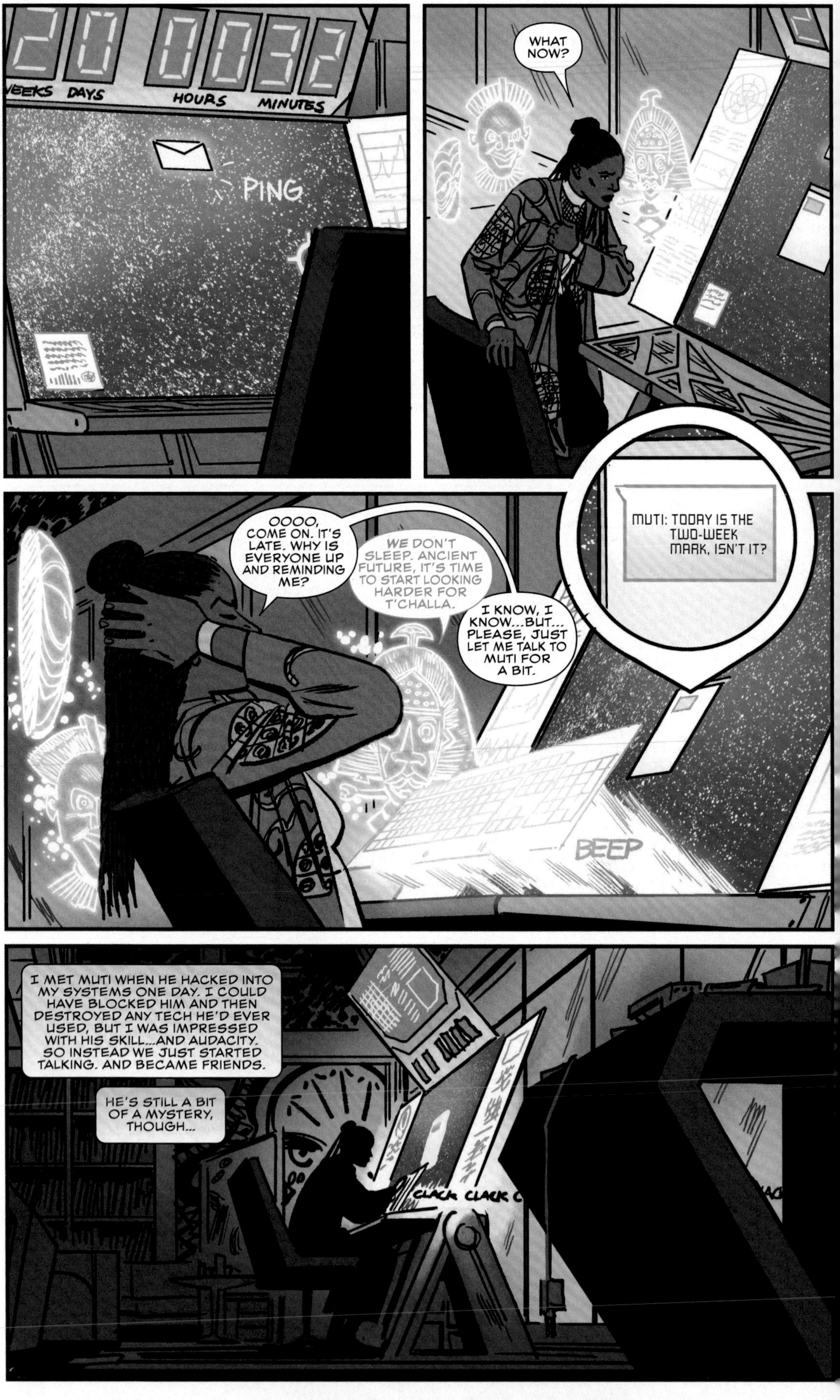

WEEKS DAYS HOURS MINUTES
PING
WHAT NOW?
MUTI: TODAY IS THE TWO-WEEK MARK, ISN'T IT?
OOOO, COME ON. IT'S LATE. WHY IS EVERYONE UP AND REMINDING ME?
WE DON'T SLEEP. ANCIENT FUTURE, IT'S TIME TO START LOOKING HARDER FOR T'CHALLA.
I KNOW, I KNOW...BUT... PLEASE, JUST LET ME TALK TO MUTI FOR A BIT.
BEEP
I MET MUTI WHEN HE HACKED INTO MY SYSTEMS ONE DAY. I COULD HAVE BLOCKED HIM AND THEN DESTROYED ANY TECH HE'D EVER USED, BUT I WAS IMPRESSED WITH HIS SKILL...AND AUDACITY. SO INSTEAD WE JUST STARTED TALKING. AND BECAME FRIENDS.
HE'S STILL A BIT OF A MYSTERY, THOUGH...
CLACK CLACK C

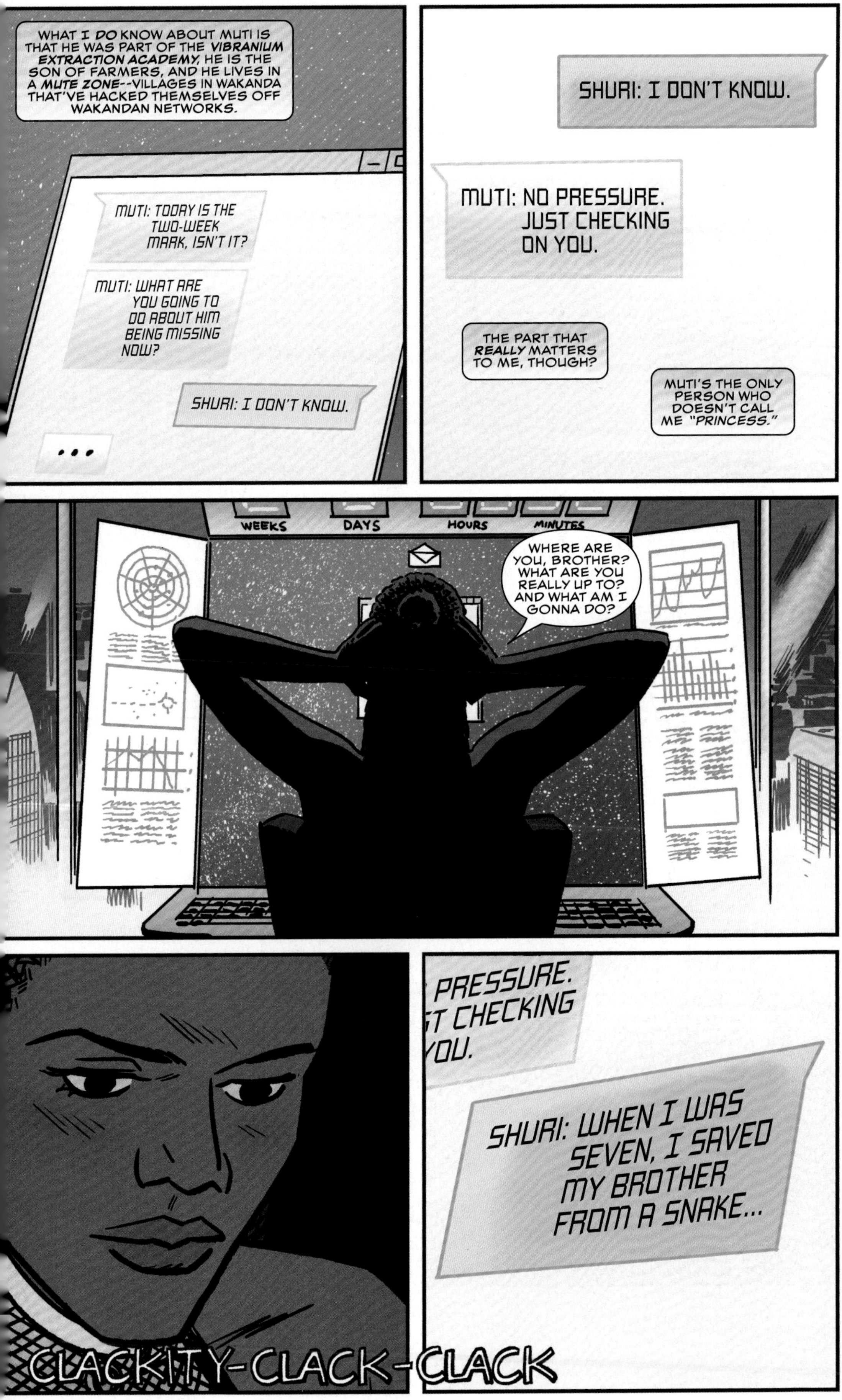
WHAT I *DO* KNOW ABOUT MUTI IS THAT HE WAS PART OF THE *VIBRANIUM EXTRACTION ACADEMY*, HE IS THE SON OF FARMERS, AND HE LIVES IN A *MUTE ZONE*--VILLAGES IN WAKANDA THAT'VE HACKED THEMSELVES OFF WAKANDAN NETWORKS.
MUTI: TODAY IS THE TWO-WEEK MARK, ISN'T IT?
MUTI: WHAT ARE YOU GOING TO DO ABOUT HIM BEING MISSING NOW?
SHURI: I DON'T KNOW.
...
SHURI: I DON'T KNOW.
MUTI: NO PRESSURE. JUST CHECKING ON YOU.
THE PART THAT *REALLY* MATTERS TO ME, THOUGH?
MUTI'S THE ONLY PERSON WHO DOESN'T CALL ME *"PRINCESS."*
WEEKS
DAYS
HOURS
MINUTES
WHERE ARE YOU, BROTHER? WHAT ARE YOU REALLY UP TO? AND WHAT AM I GONNA DO?
PRESSURE.
CHECKING
YOU.
SHURI: WHEN I WAS SEVEN, I SAVED MY BROTHER FROM A SNAKE...
CLACKITY-CLACK-CLACK

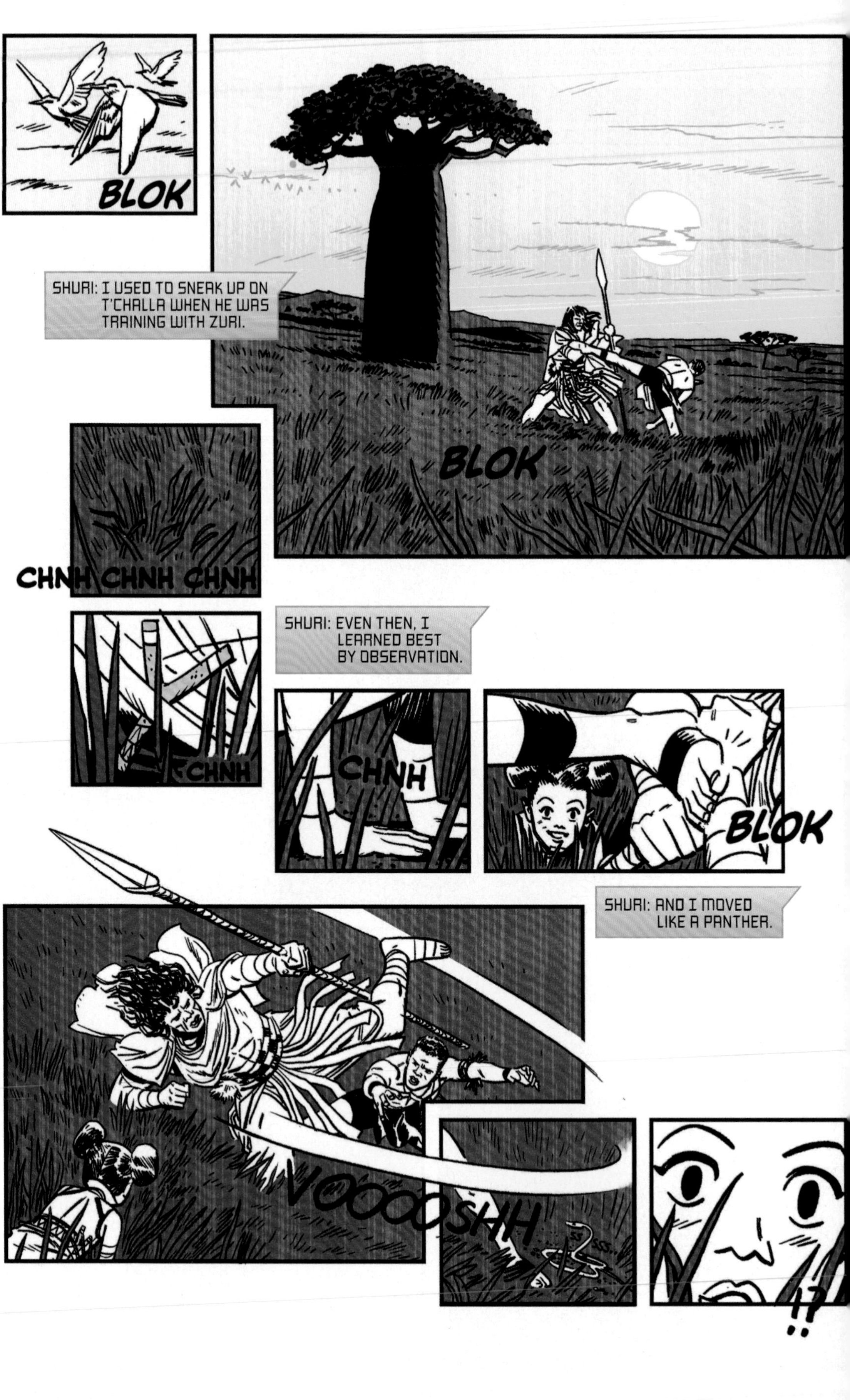
BLOK
SHURI: I USED TO SNEAK UP ON T'CHALLA WHEN HE WAS TRAINING WITH ZURI.
BLOK
CHNH CHNH CHNH
SHURI: EVEN THEN, I LEARNED BEST BY OBSERVATION.
CHNH
CHNH
BLOK
SHURI: AND I MOVED LIKE A PANTHER.
VOOOOOSHH
!!?

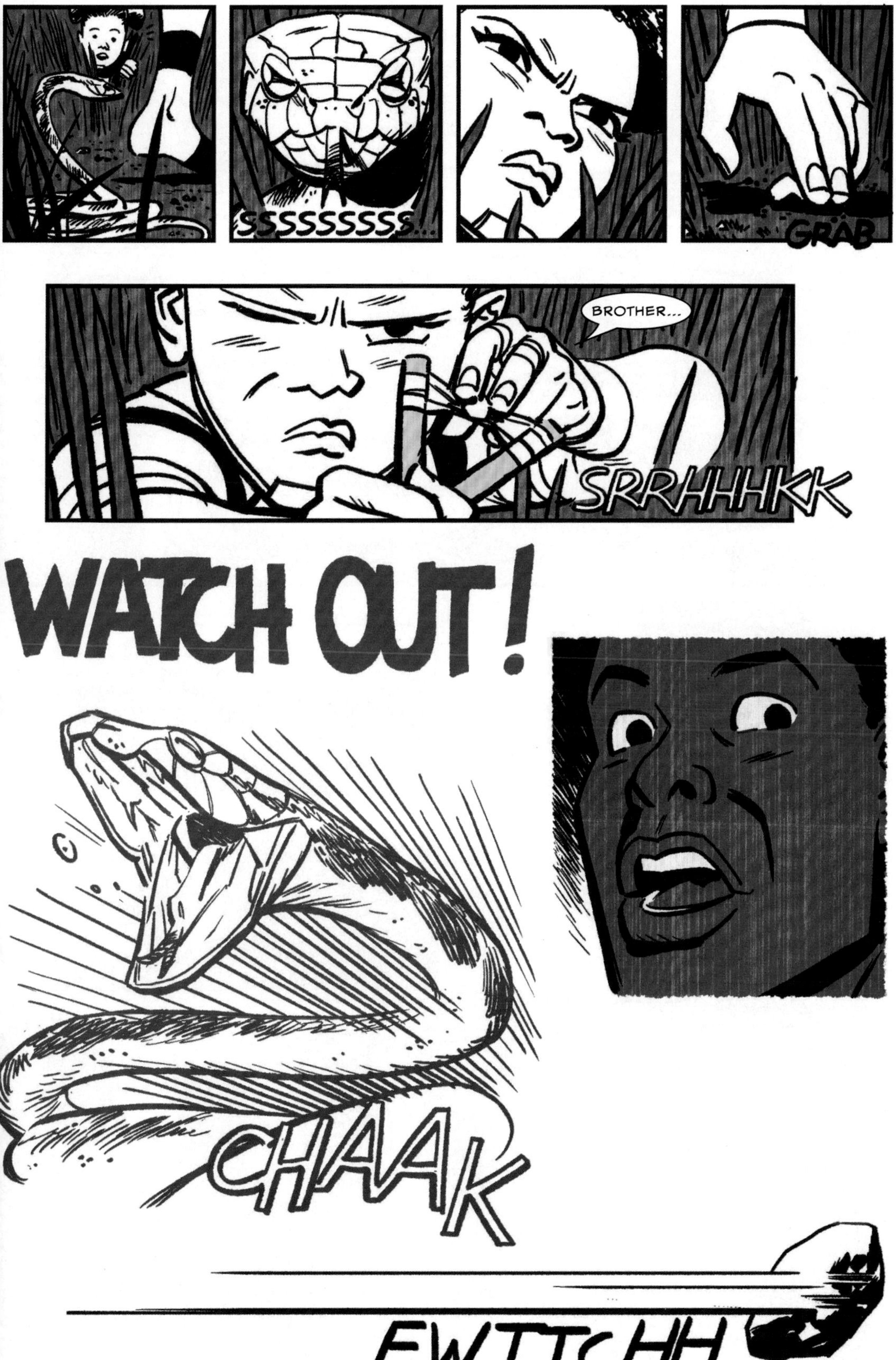

SSSSSSSSS...
GRAB
BROTHER...
SRRHHHKK
WATCH OUT!
CHAAK
FWTTCHH

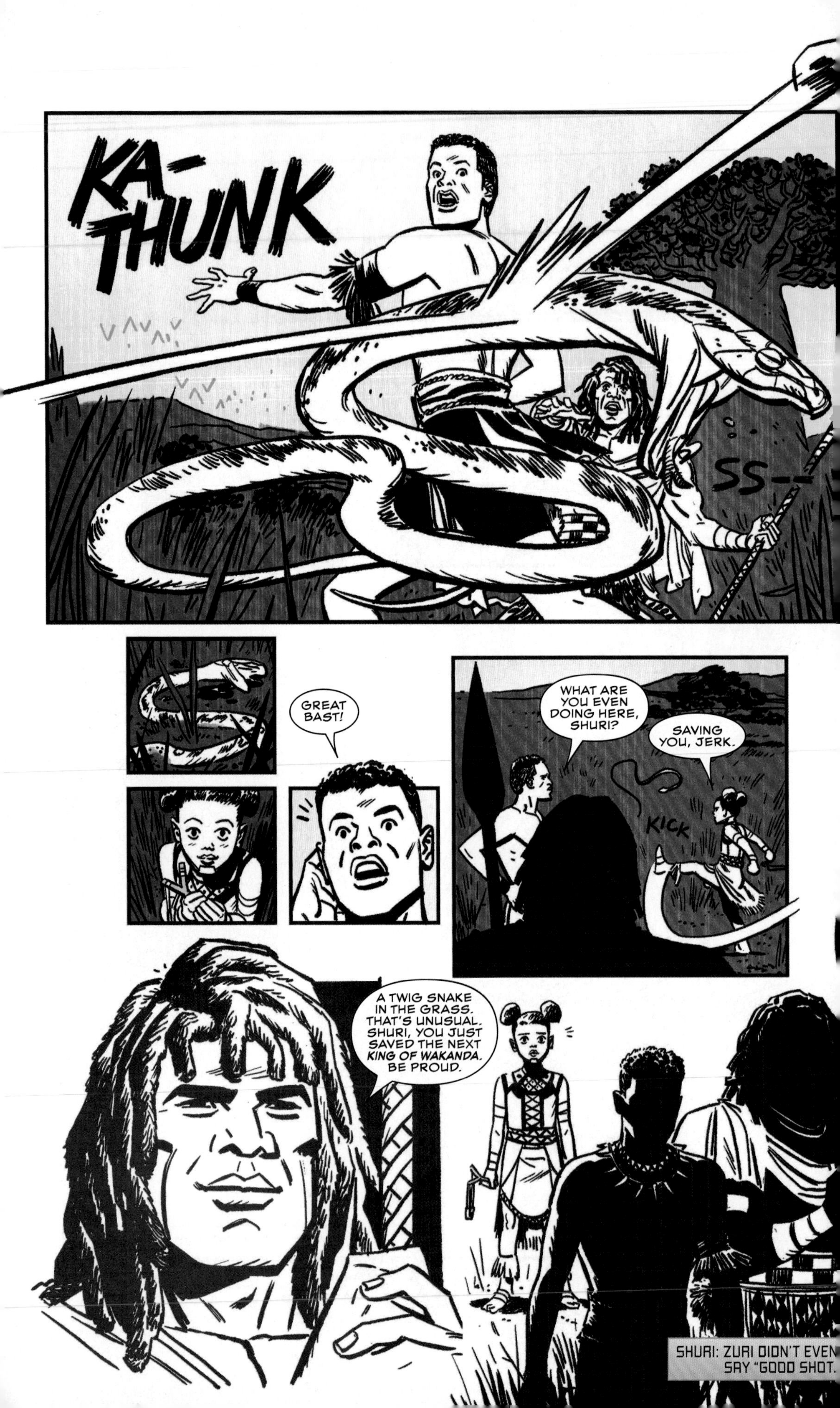
KA-THUNK
SS--
GREAT BAST!
WHAT ARE YOU EVEN DOING HERE, SHURI?
SAVING YOU, JERK.
KICK
A TWIG SNAKE IN THE GRASS. THAT'S UNUSUAL. SHURI, YOU JUST SAVED THE NEXT *KING OF WAKANDA*. BE PROUD.
SHURI: ZURI DIDN'T EVEN SAY "GOOD SHOT

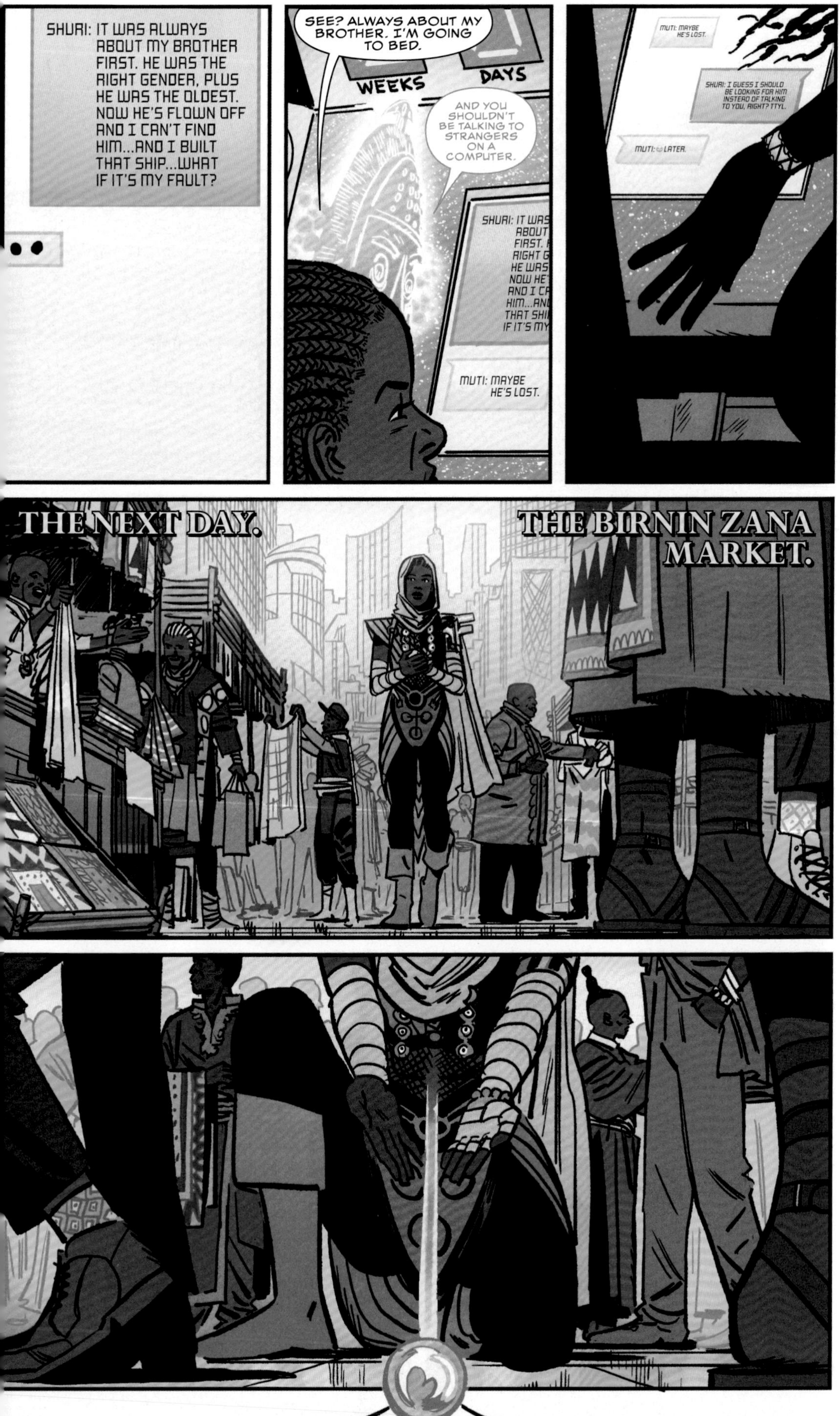
SHURI: IT WAS ALWAYS ABOUT MY BROTHER FIRST. HE WAS THE RIGHT GENDER, PLUS HE WAS THE OLDEST. NOW HE'S FLOWN OFF AND I CAN'T FIND HIM...AND I BUILT THAT SHIP...WHAT IF IT'S MY FAULT?
SEE? ALWAYS ABOUT MY BROTHER. I'M GOING TO BED.
WEEKS
DAYS
AND YOU SHOULDN'T BE TALKING TO STRANGERS ON A COMPUTER.
MUTI: MAYBE HE'S LOST.
MUTI: MAYBE HE'S LOST.
SHURI: I GUESS I SHOULD BE LOOKING FOR HIM INSTEAD OF TALKING TO YOU, RIGHT? TTYL.
MUTI: LATER.
THE NEXT DAY.
THE BIRNIN ZANA MARKET.

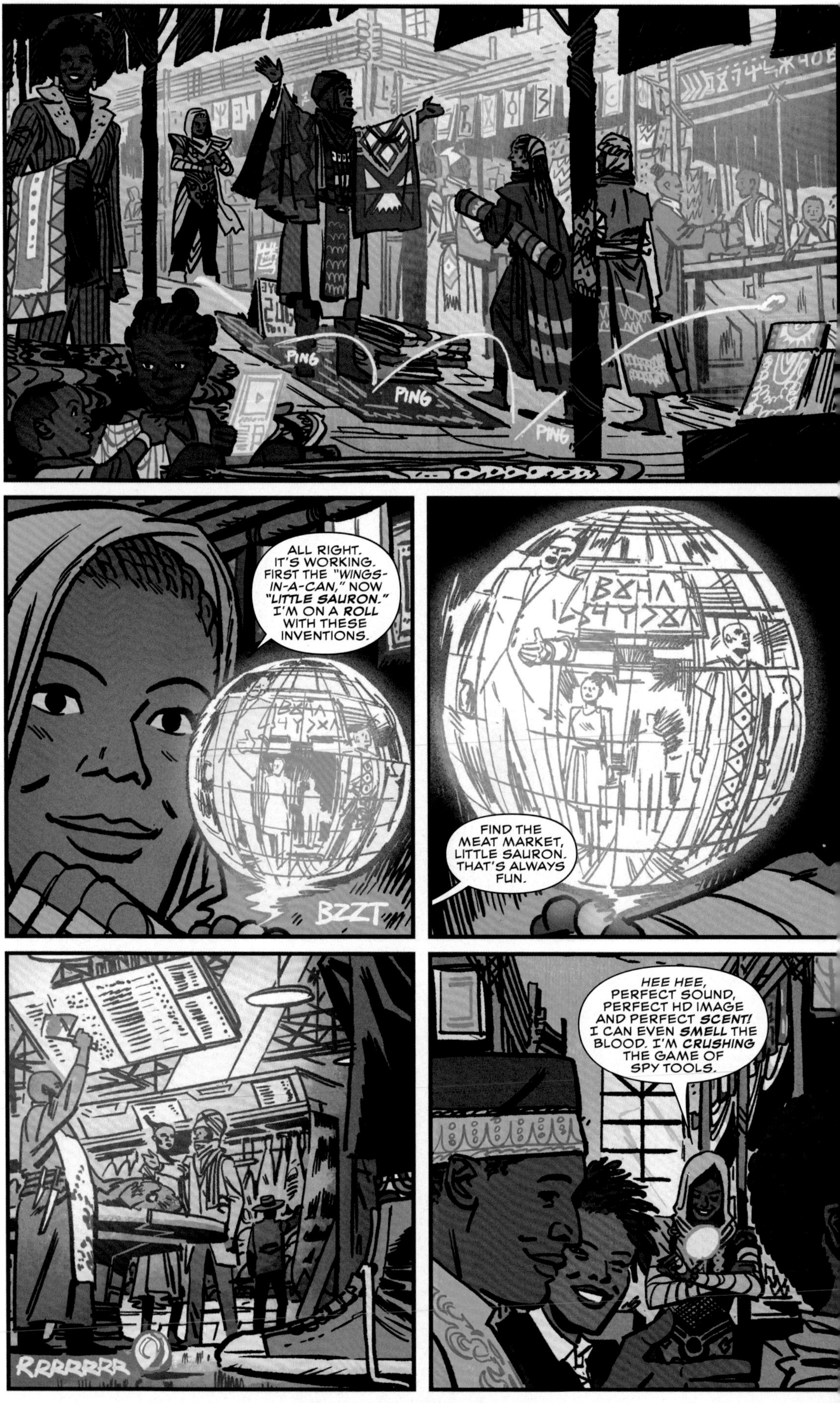
PING
PING
PING
ALL RIGHT. IT'S WORKING. FIRST THE "WINGS-IN-A-CAN," NOW "LITTLE SAURON." I'M ON A ROLL WITH THESE INVENTIONS.
BZZT
FIND THE MEAT MARKET, LITTLE SAURON. THAT'S ALWAYS FUN.
RRRRRRR
HEE HEE, PERFECT SOUND, PERFECT HD IMAGE AND PERFECT SCENT! I CAN EVEN SMELL THE BLOOD. I'M CRUSHING THE GAME OF SPY TOOLS.

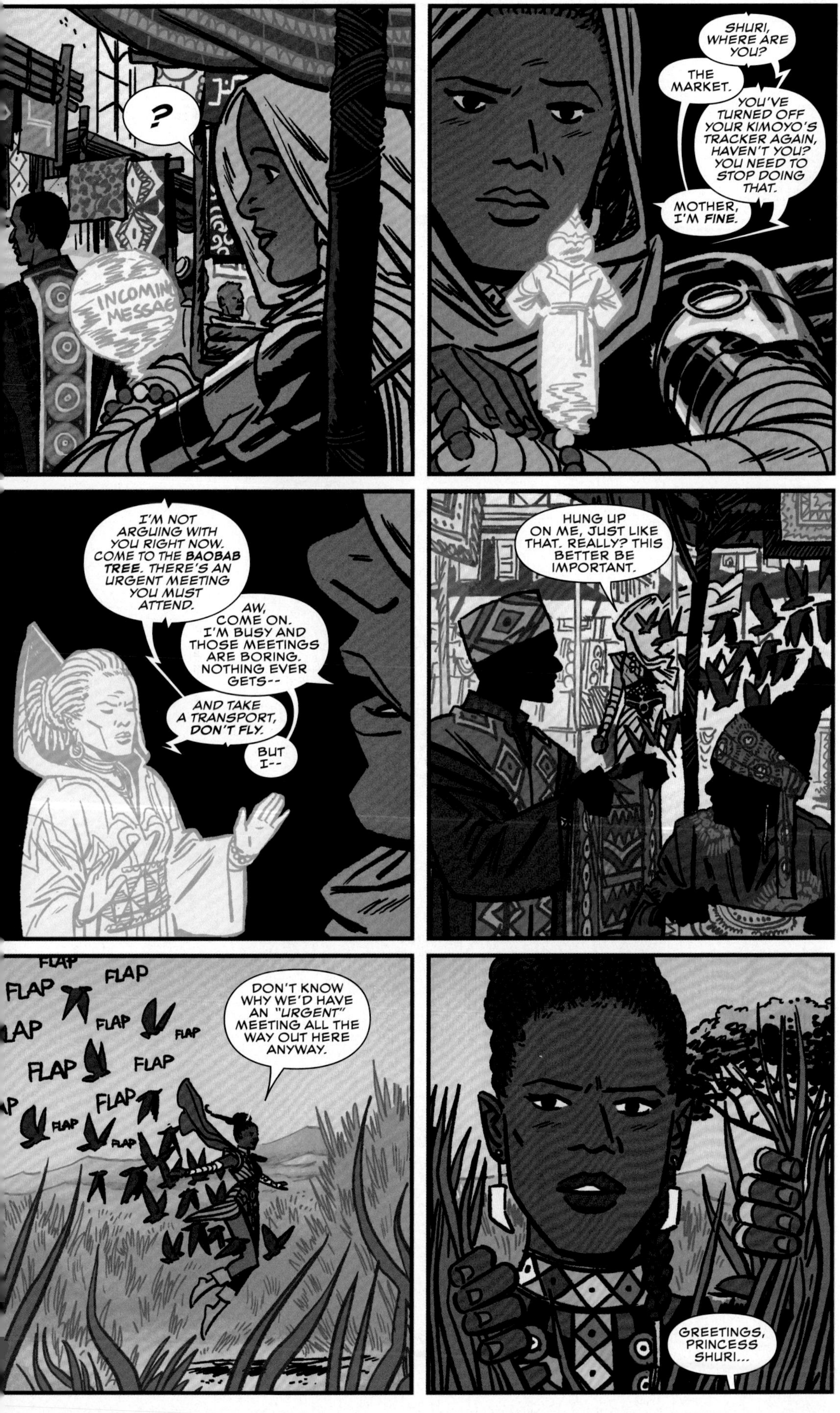
?
INCOMING MESSAGE
SHURI, WHERE ARE YOU?
THE MARKET.
YOU'VE TURNED OFF YOUR KIMOYO'S TRACKER AGAIN, HAVEN'T YOU? YOU NEED TO STOP DOING THAT.
MOTHER, I'M *FINE*.
I'M NOT ARGUING WITH YOU RIGHT NOW. COME TO THE **BAOBAB TREE**. THERE'S AN URGENT MEETING YOU MUST ATTEND.
AW, COME ON. I'M BUSY AND THOSE MEETINGS ARE BORING. NOTHING EVER GETS--
AND TAKE A TRANSPORT, *DON'T FLY*.
BUT I--
HUNG UP ON ME, JUST LIKE THAT. REALLY? THIS BETTER BE IMPORTANT.
FLAP FLAP FLAP FLAP FLAP FLAP FLAP FLAP FLAP FLAP FLAP FLAP
DON'T KNOW WHY WE'D HAVE AN *"URGENT"* MEETING ALL THE WAY OUT HERE ANYWAY.
GREETINGS, PRINCESS SHURI...

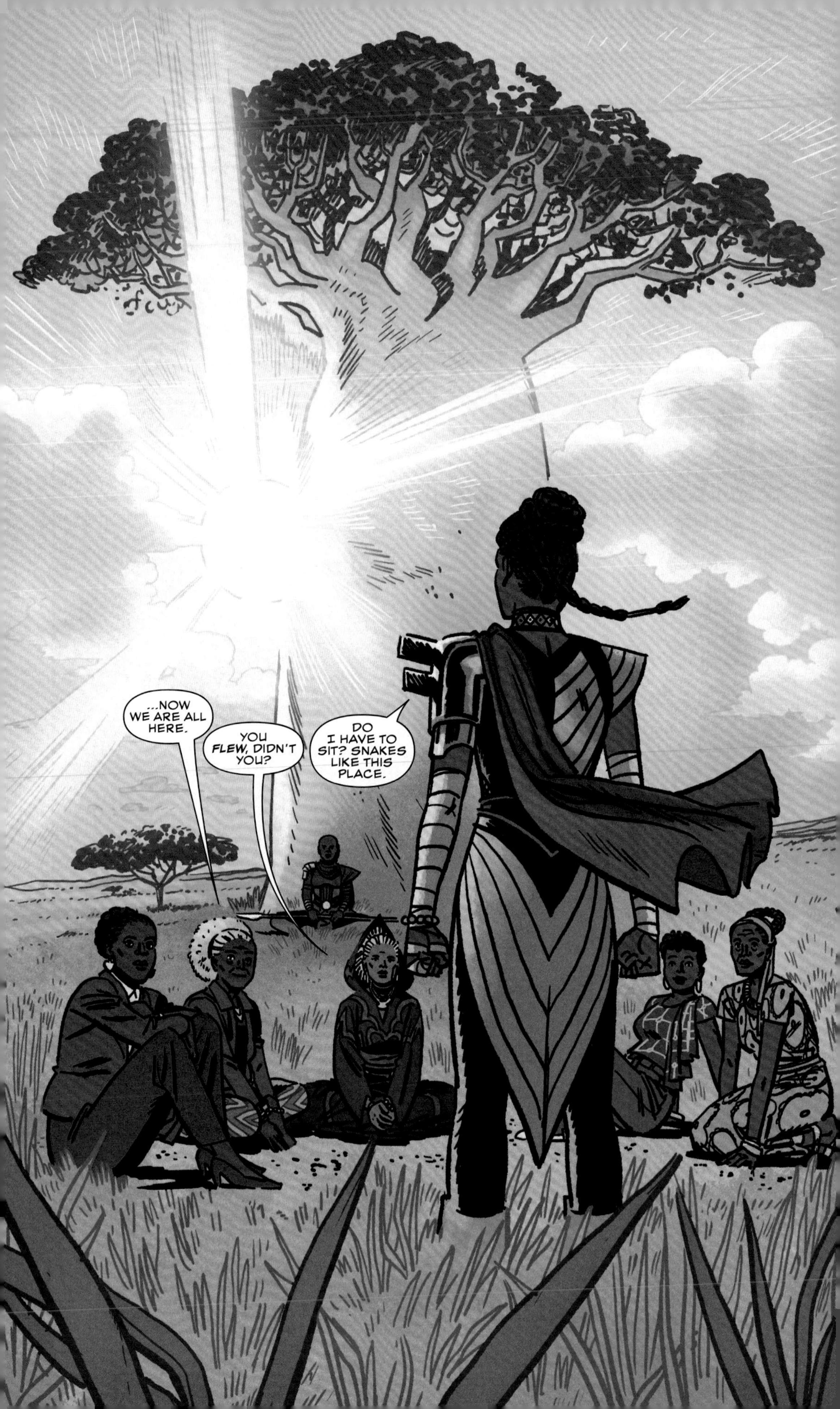
...NOW WE ARE ALL HERE.
YOU FLEW, DIDN'T YOU?
DO I HAVE TO SIT? SNAKES LIKE THIS PLACE.

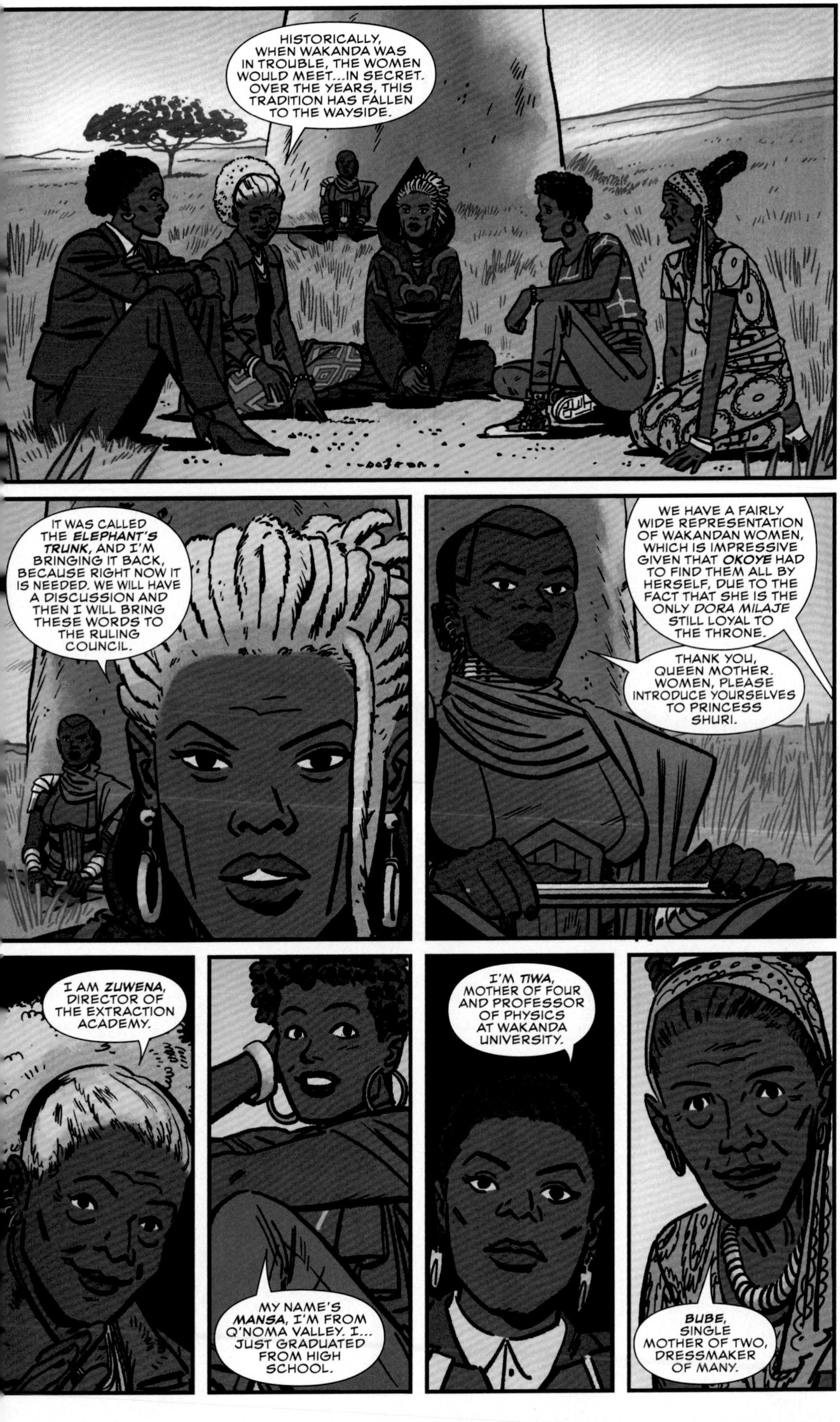
HISTORICALLY, WHEN WAKANDA WAS IN TROUBLE, THE WOMEN WOULD MEET...IN SECRET. OVER THE YEARS, THIS TRADITION HAS FALLEN TO THE WAYSIDE.
IT WAS CALLED THE ELEPHANT'S TRUNK, AND I'M BRINGING IT BACK, BECAUSE RIGHT NOW IT IS NEEDED. WE WILL HAVE A DISCUSSION AND THEN I WILL BRING THESE WORDS TO THE RULING COUNCIL.
WE HAVE A FAIRLY WIDE REPRESENTATION OF WAKANDAN WOMEN, WHICH IS IMPRESSIVE GIVEN THAT OKOYE HAD TO FIND THEM ALL BY HERSELF, DUE TO THE FACT THAT SHE IS THE ONLY DORA MILAJE STILL LOYAL TO THE THRONE.
THANK YOU, QUEEN MOTHER. WOMEN, PLEASE INTRODUCE YOURSELVES TO PRINCESS SHURI.
I AM ZUWENA, DIRECTOR OF THE EXTRACTION ACADEMY.
MY NAME'S MANSA, I'M FROM Q'NOMA VALLEY. I... JUST GRADUATED FROM HIGH SCHOOL.
I'M TIWA, MOTHER OF FOUR AND PROFESSOR OF PHYSICS AT WAKANDA UNIVERSITY.
BUBE, SINGLE MOTHER OF TWO, DRESSMAKER OF MANY.

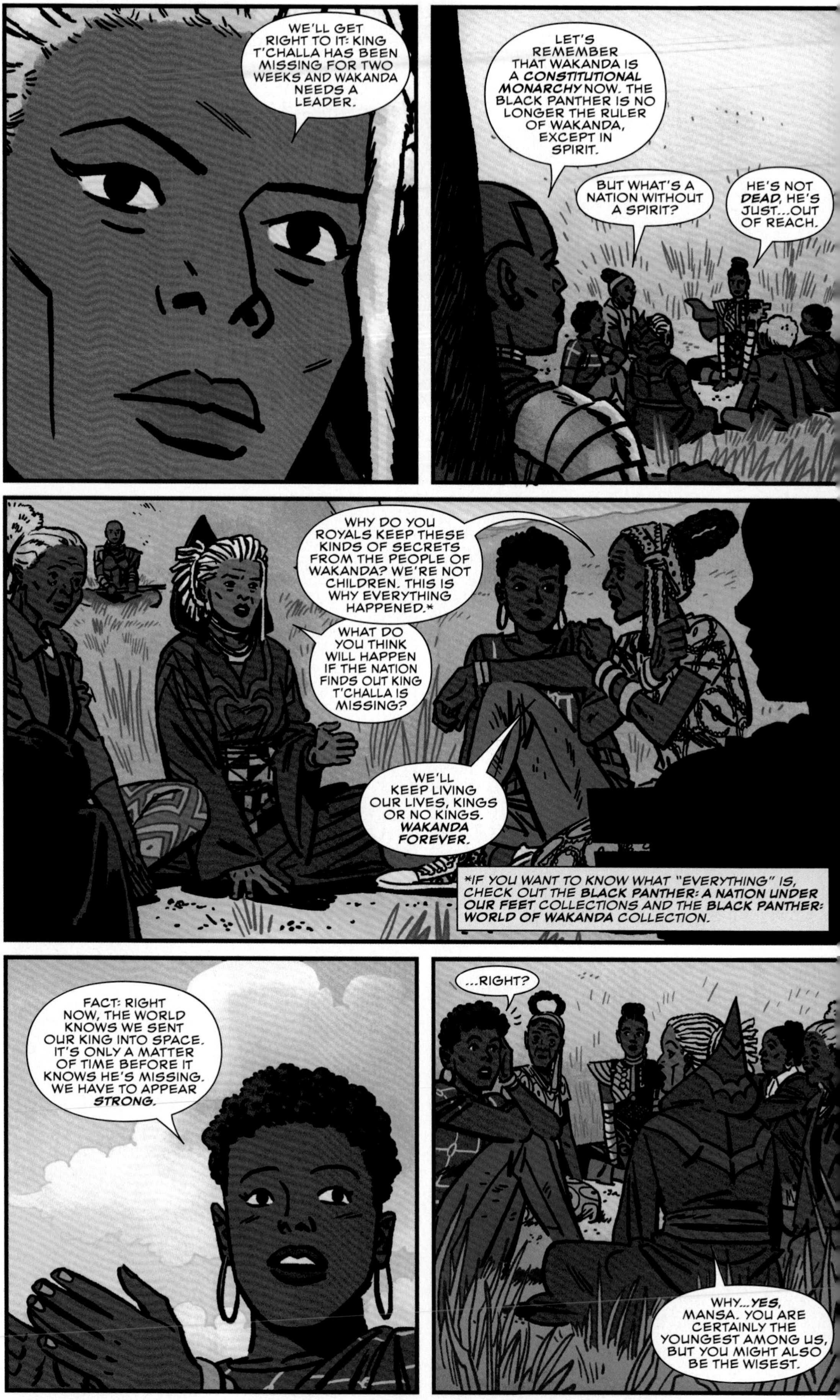
WE'LL GET RIGHT TO IT: KING T'CHALLA HAS BEEN MISSING FOR TWO WEEKS AND WAKANDA NEEDS A LEADER.
LET'S REMEMBER THAT WAKANDA IS A *CONSTITUTIONAL MONARCHY* NOW. THE BLACK PANTHER IS NO LONGER THE RULER OF WAKANDA, EXCEPT IN SPIRIT.
BUT WHAT'S A NATION WITHOUT A SPIRIT?
HE'S NOT *DEAD*, HE'S JUST...OUT OF REACH.
WHY DO YOU ROYALS KEEP THESE KINDS OF SECRETS FROM THE PEOPLE OF WAKANDA? WE'RE NOT CHILDREN. THIS IS WHY EVERYTHING HAPPENED.*
WHAT DO YOU THINK WILL HAPPEN IF THE NATION FINDS OUT KING T'CHALLA IS MISSING?
WE'LL KEEP LIVING OUR LIVES, KINGS OR NO KINGS. ***WAKANDA FOREVER.***
*IF YOU WANT TO KNOW WHAT "EVERYTHING" IS, CHECK OUT THE **BLACK PANTHER: A NATION UNDER OUR FEET** COLLECTIONS AND THE **BLACK PANTHER: WORLD OF WAKANDA** COLLECTION.
FACT: RIGHT NOW, THE WORLD KNOWS WE SENT OUR KING INTO SPACE. IT'S ONLY A MATTER OF TIME BEFORE IT KNOWS HE'S MISSING. WE HAVE TO APPEAR ***STRONG.***
...RIGHT?
WHY...***YES,*** MANSA. YOU ARE CERTAINLY THE YOUNGEST AMONG US, BUT YOU MIGHT ALSO BE THE WISEST.

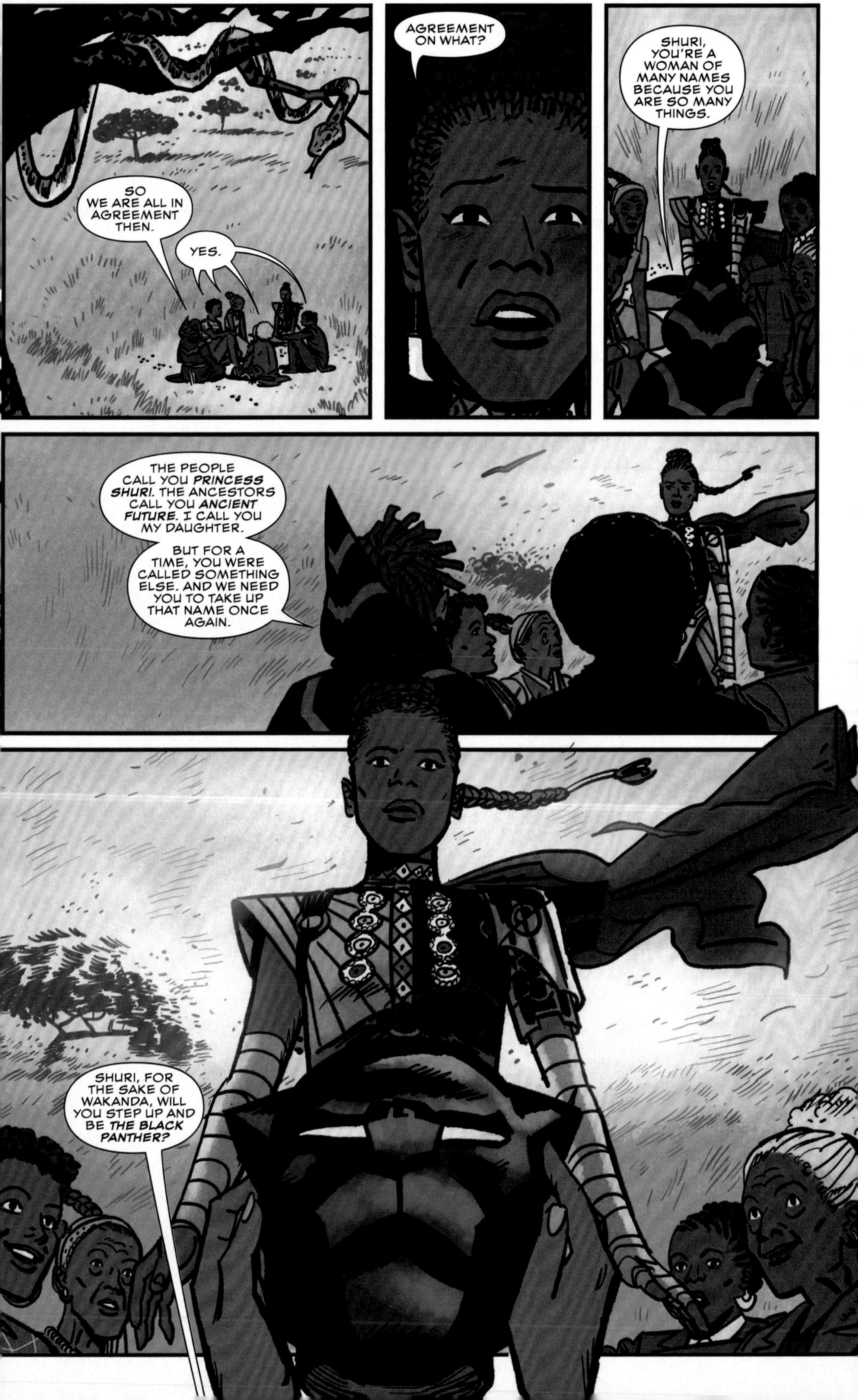
SO WE ARE ALL IN AGREEMENT THEN.
YES.
AGREEMENT ON WHAT?
SHURI, YOU'RE A WOMAN OF MANY NAMES BECAUSE YOU ARE SO MANY THINGS.
THE PEOPLE CALL YOU PRINCESS SHURI. THE ANCESTORS CALL YOU ANCIENT FUTURE. I CALL YOU MY DAUGHTER.
BUT FOR A TIME, YOU WERE CALLED SOMETHING ELSE. AND WE NEED YOU TO TAKE UP THAT NAME ONCE AGAIN.
SHURI, FOR THE SAKE OF WAKANDA, WILL YOU STEP UP AND BE THE BLACK PANTHER?

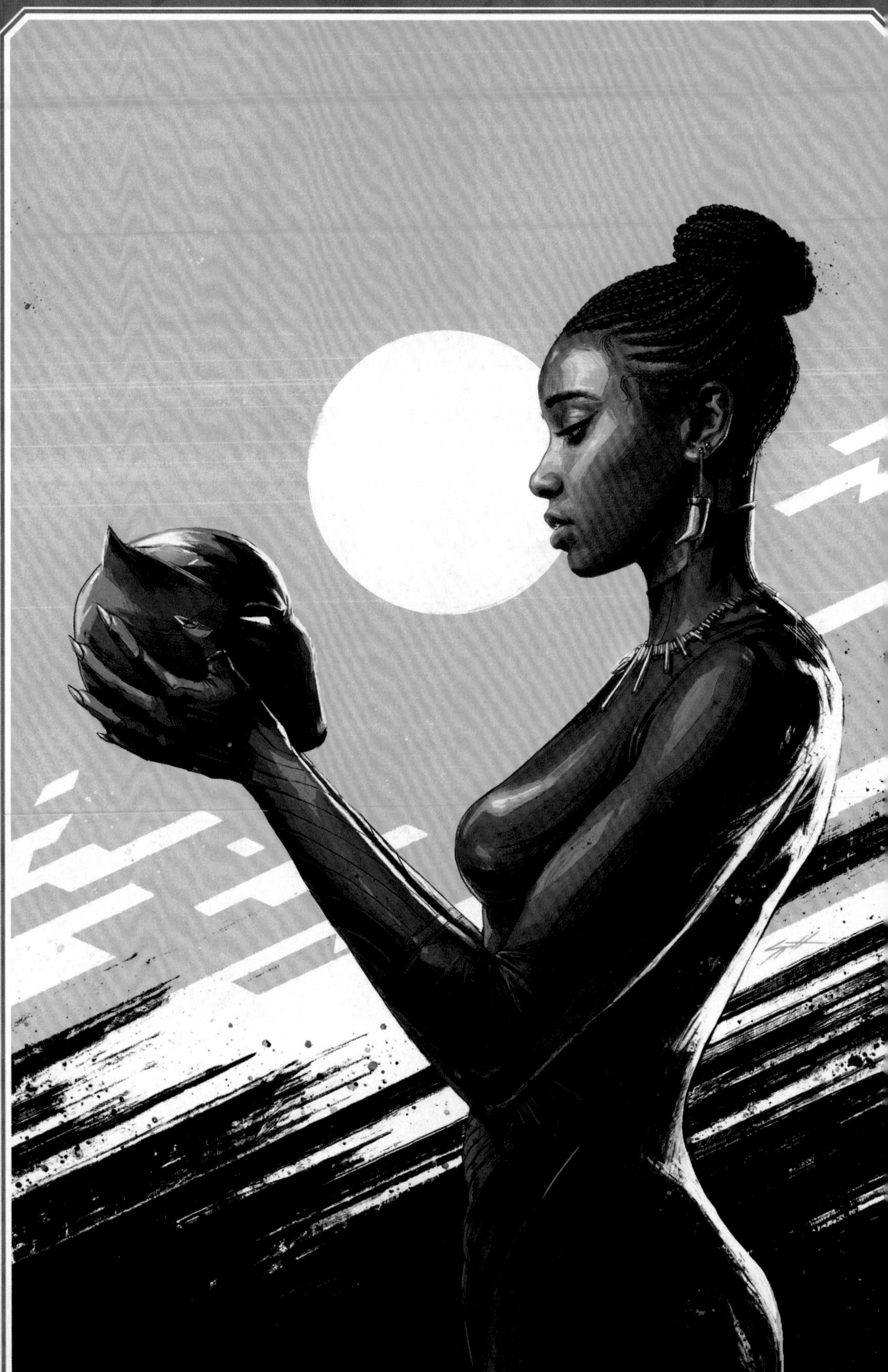

2 – THE BAOBAB TREE

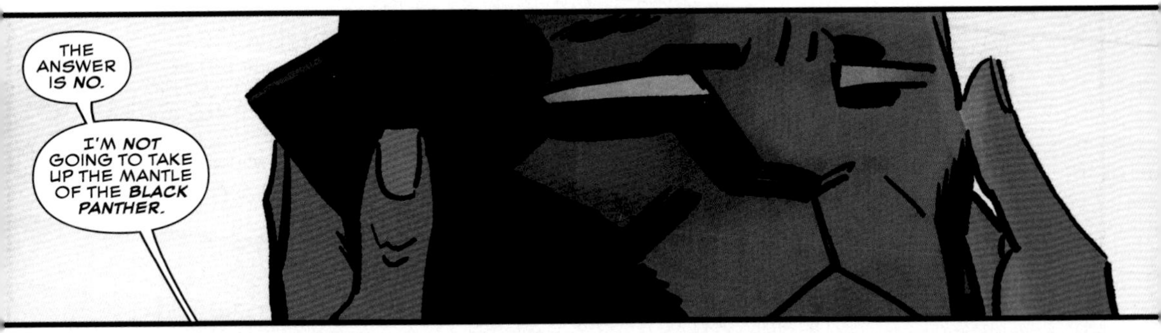
THE ANSWER IS *NO.*
I'M *NOT* GOING TO TAKE UP THE MANTLE OF THE *BLACK PANTHER.*

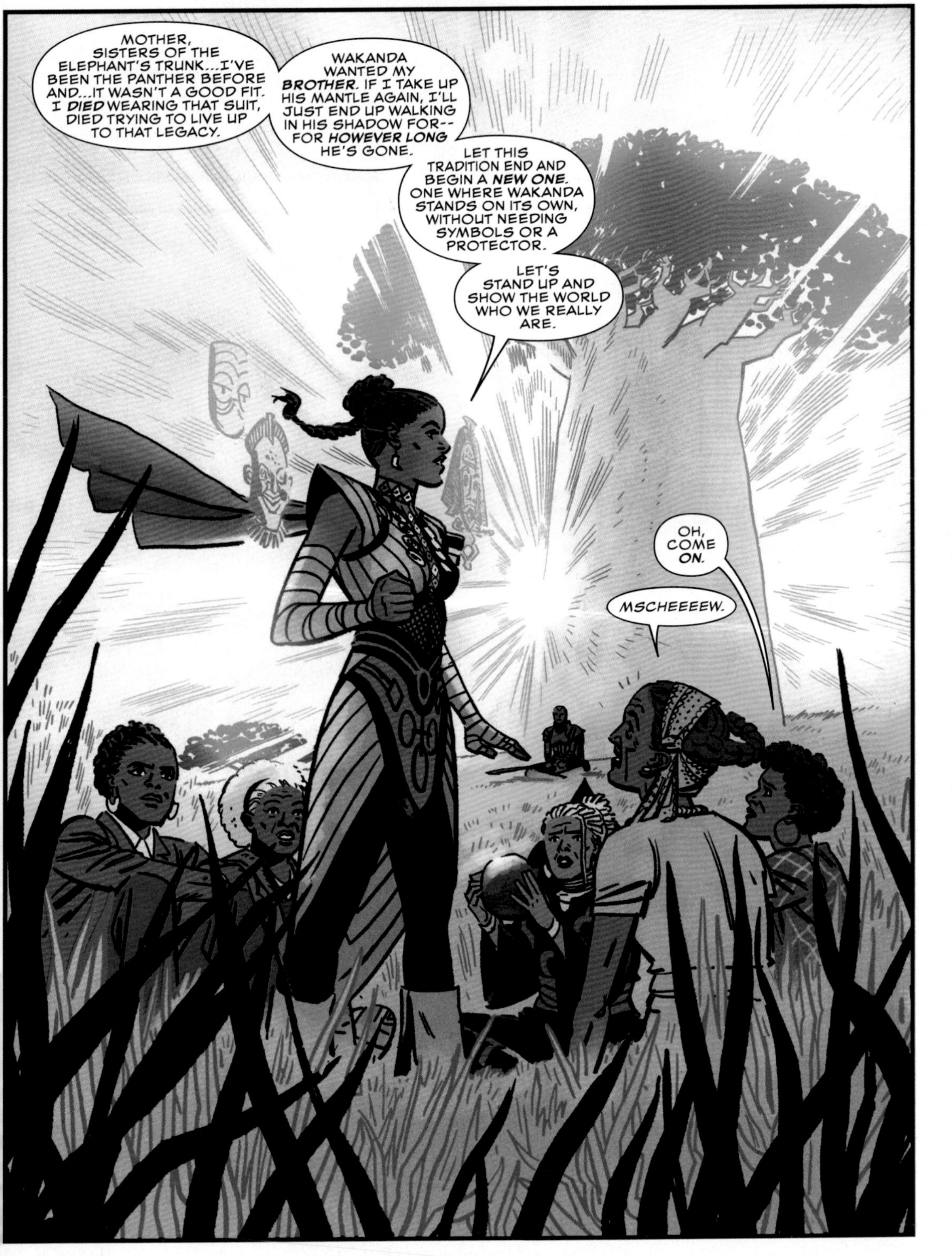
MOTHER, SISTERS OF THE ELEPHANT'S TRUNK...I'VE BEEN THE PANTHER BEFORE AND...IT WASN'T A GOOD FIT. I *DIED* WEARING THAT SUIT, DIED TRYING TO LIVE UP TO THAT LEGACY.
WAKANDA WANTED MY *BROTHER.* IF I TAKE UP HIS MANTLE AGAIN, I'LL JUST END UP WALKING IN HIS SHADOW FOR-- FOR *HOWEVER LONG* HE'S GONE.
LET THIS TRADITION END AND BEGIN A *NEW ONE.* ONE WHERE WAKANDA STANDS ON ITS OWN, WITHOUT NEEDING SYMBOLS OR A PROTECTOR.
LET'S STAND UP AND SHOW THE WORLD WHO WE REALLY ARE.
OH, COME *ON.*
MSCHEEEEW.

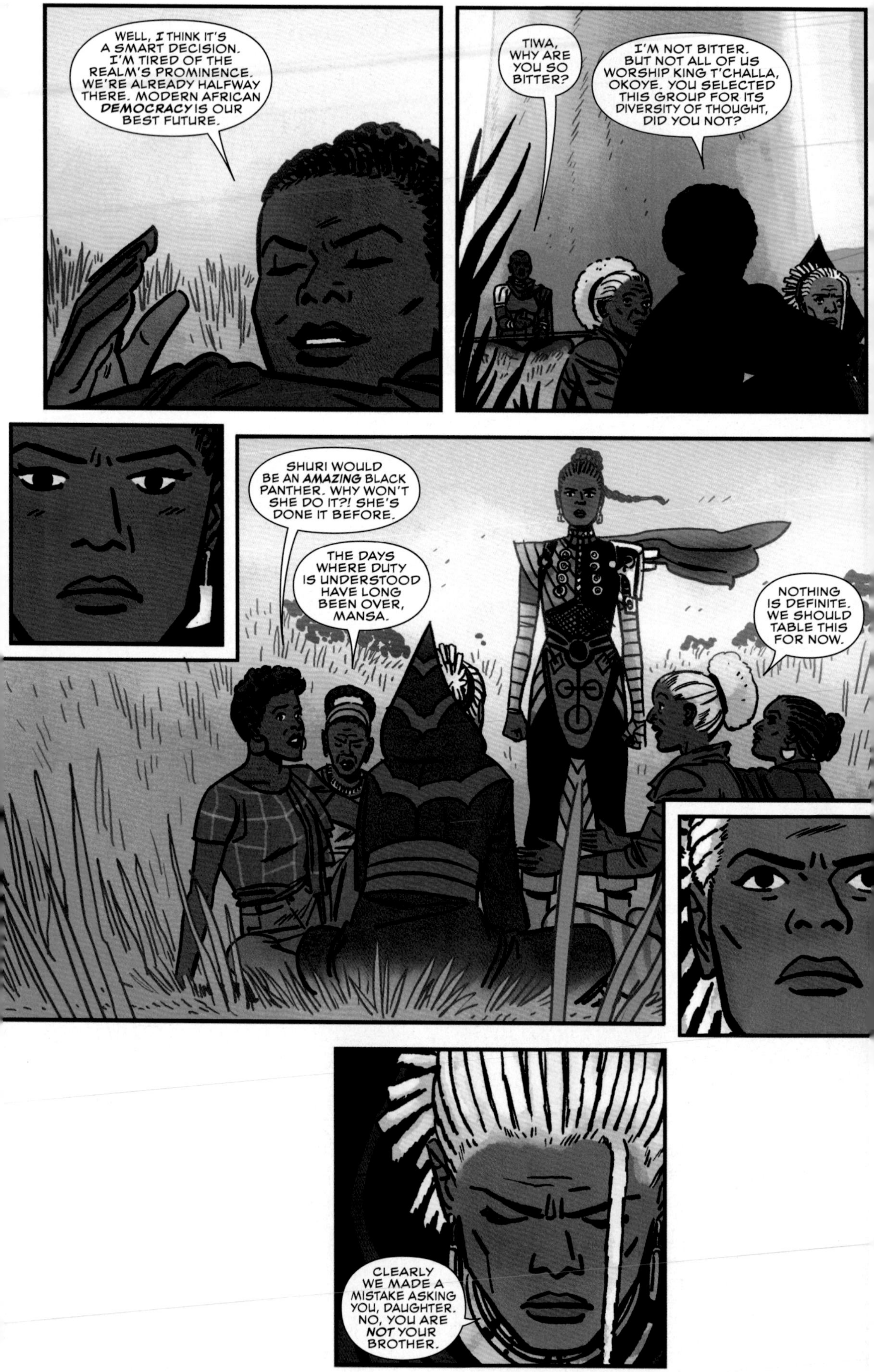
WELL, *I* THINK IT'S A SMART DECISION. I'M TIRED OF THE REALM'S PROMINENCE. WE'RE ALREADY HALFWAY THERE. MODERN AFRICAN *DEMOCRACY* IS OUR BEST FUTURE.
TIWA, WHY ARE YOU SO BITTER?
I'M NOT BITTER. BUT NOT ALL OF US WORSHIP KING T'CHALLA, OKOYE. YOU SELECTED THIS GROUP FOR ITS DIVERSITY OF THOUGHT, DID YOU NOT?
SHURI WOULD BE AN *AMAZING* BLACK PANTHER. WHY WON'T SHE DO IT?! SHE'S DONE IT BEFORE.
THE DAYS WHERE DUTY IS UNDERSTOOD HAVE LONG BEEN OVER, MANSA.
NOTHING IS DEFINITE. WE SHOULD TABLE THIS FOR NOW.
CLEARLY WE MADE A MISTAKE ASKING YOU, DAUGHTER. NO, YOU ARE *NOT* YOUR BROTHER.

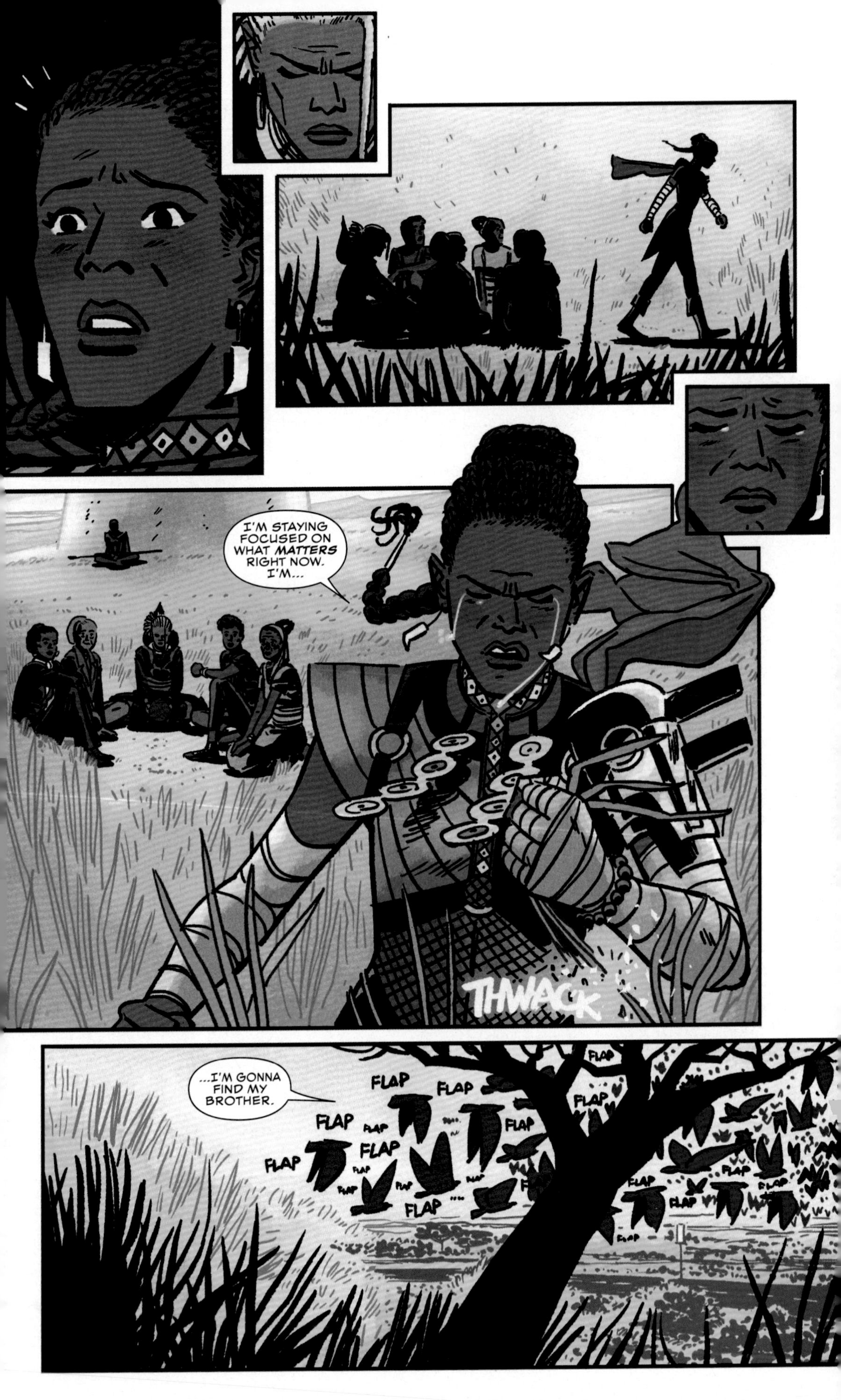
I'M STAYING FOCUSED ON WHAT MATTERS RIGHT NOW. I'M...
THWACK
...I'M GONNA FIND MY BROTHER.
FLAP
FLAP
FLAP
FLAP
FLAP
FLAP
FLAP
FLAP
FLAP
FLAP

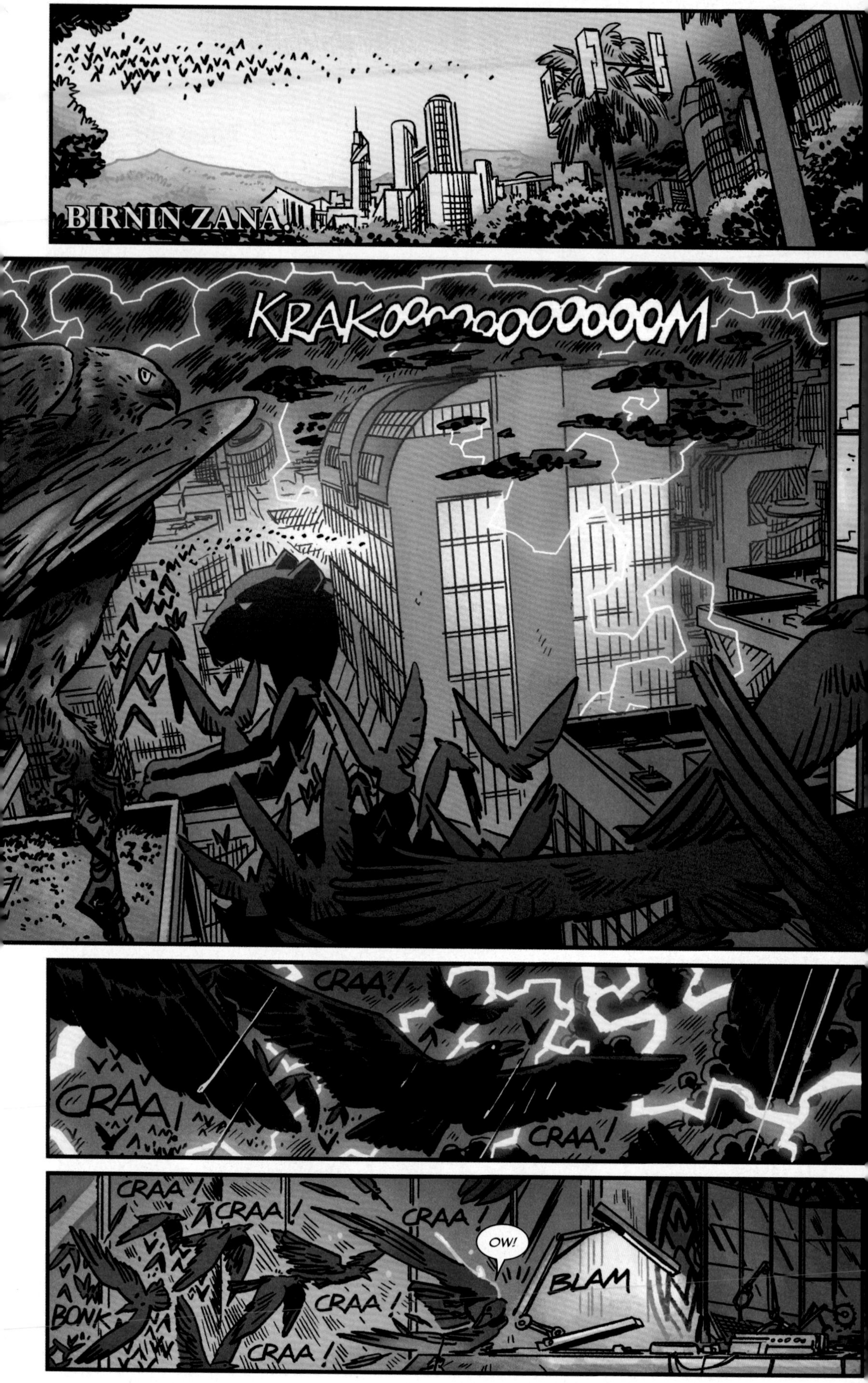
BIRNIN ZANA.
KRAKOOOOOOOOOOOOM
CRAA!
CRAA!
CRAA!
CRAA!
CRAA!
CRAA!
OW!
BLAM
BONK
CRAA!
CRAA!

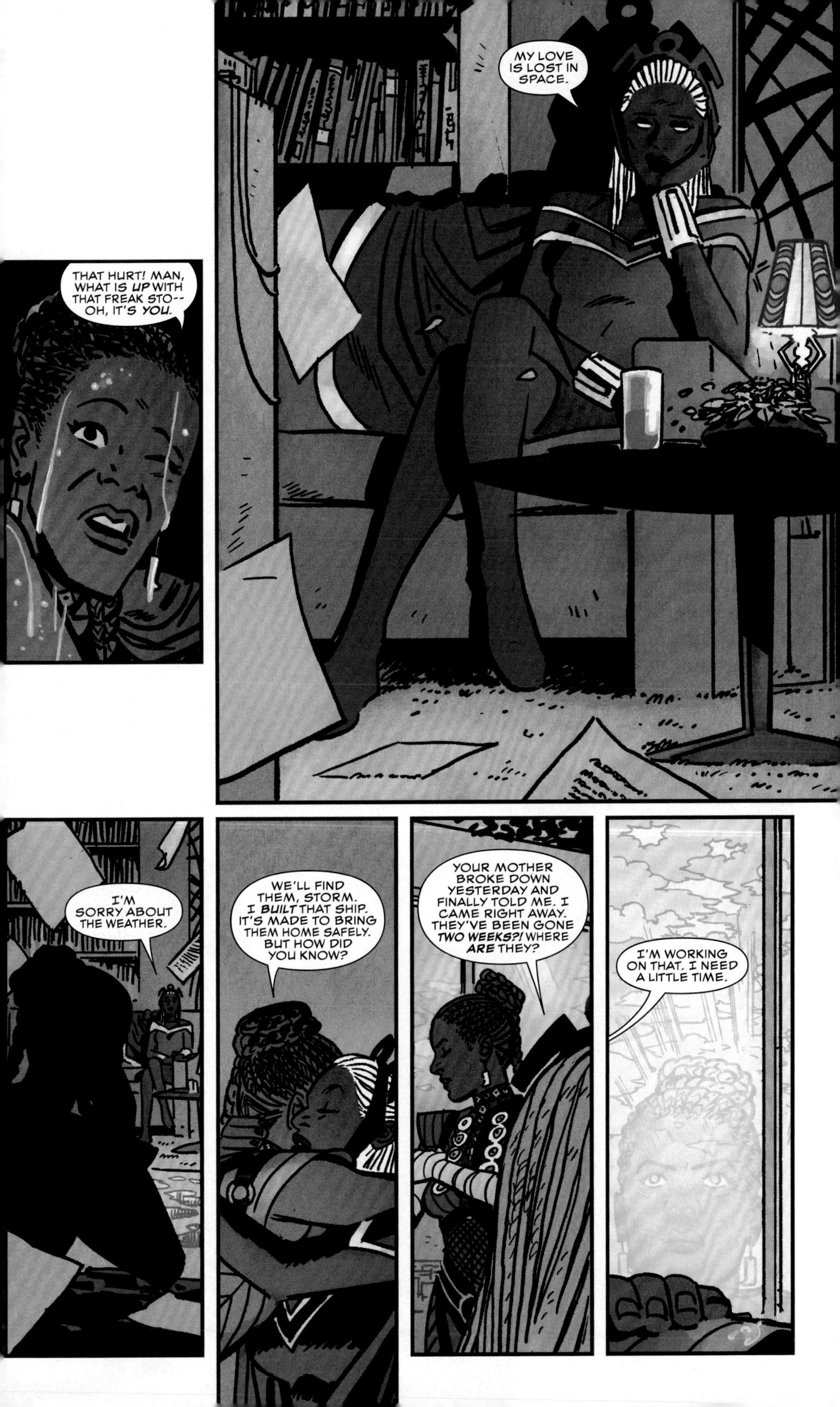

THAT HURT! MAN, WHAT IS UP WITH THAT FREAK STO-- OH, IT'S YOU.
MY LOVE IS LOST IN SPACE.
I'M SORRY ABOUT THE WEATHER.
WE'LL FIND THEM, STORM. I BUILT THAT SHIP. IT'S MADE TO BRING THEM HOME SAFELY. BUT HOW DID YOU KNOW?
YOUR MOTHER BROKE DOWN YESTERDAY AND FINALLY TOLD ME. I CAME RIGHT AWAY. THEY'VE BEEN GONE TWO WEEKS?! WHERE ARE THEY?
I'M WORKING ON THAT. I NEED A LITTLE TIME.

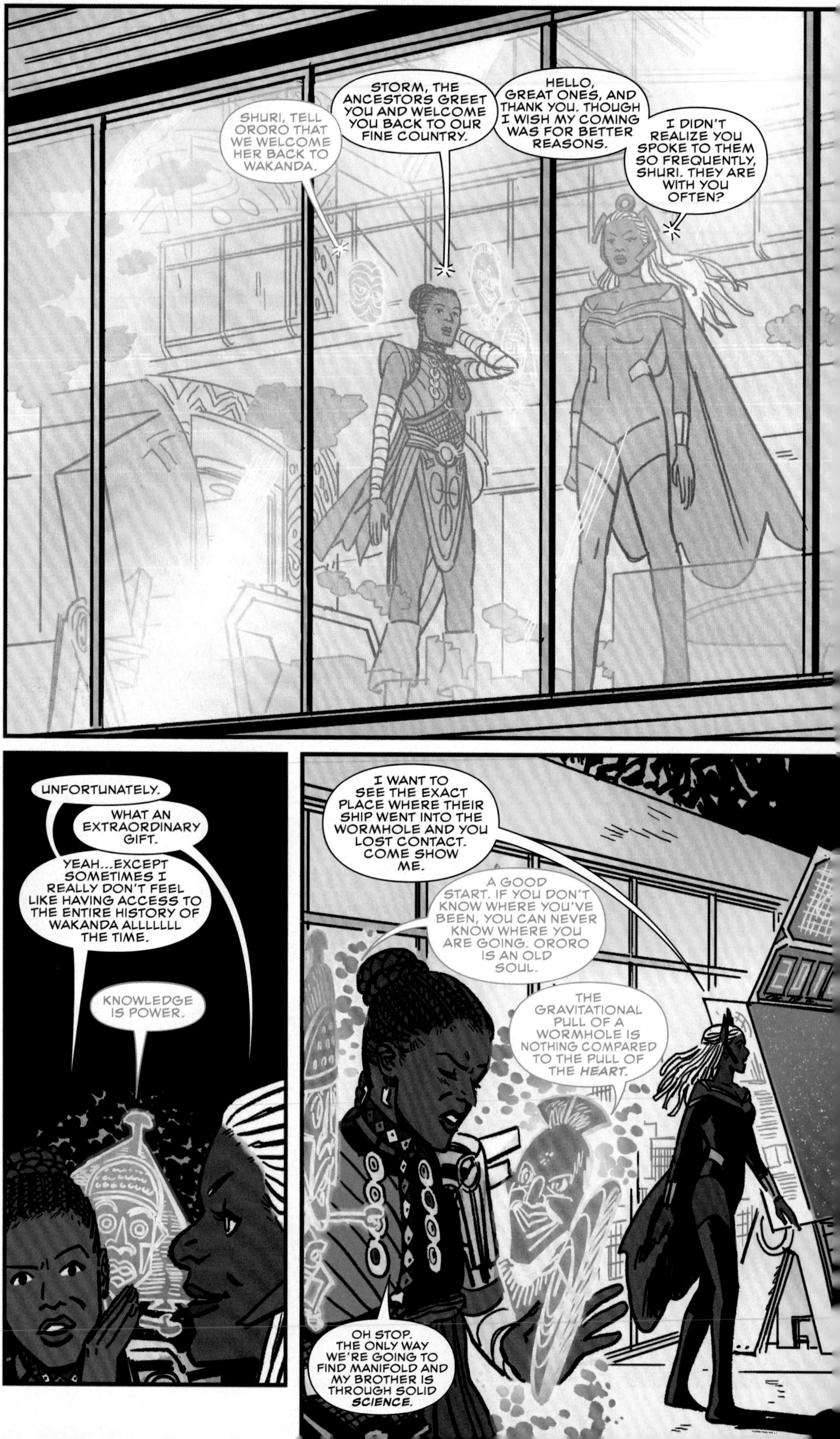
SHURI, TELL ORORO THAT WE WELCOME HER BACK TO WAKANDA.
STORM, THE ANCESTORS GREET YOU AND WELCOME YOU BACK TO OUR FINE COUNTRY.
HELLO, GREAT ONES, AND THANK YOU. THOUGH I WISH MY COMING WAS FOR BETTER REASONS.
I DIDN'T REALIZE YOU SPOKE TO THEM SO FREQUENTLY, SHURI. THEY ARE WITH YOU OFTEN?
UNFORTUNATELY.
WHAT AN EXTRAORDINARY GIFT.
YEAH...EXCEPT SOMETIMES I REALLY DON'T FEEL LIKE HAVING ACCESS TO THE ENTIRE HISTORY OF WAKANDA ALLLLLLL THE TIME.
KNOWLEDGE IS POWER.
I WANT TO SEE THE EXACT PLACE WHERE THEIR SHIP WENT INTO THE WORMHOLE AND YOU LOST CONTACT. COME SHOW ME.
A GOOD START. IF YOU DON'T KNOW WHERE YOU'VE BEEN, YOU CAN NEVER KNOW WHERE YOU ARE GOING. ORORO IS AN OLD SOUL.
THE GRAVITATIONAL PULL OF A WORMHOLE IS NOTHING COMPARED TO THE PULL OF THE HEART.
OH STOP. THE ONLY WAY WE'RE GOING TO FIND MANIFOLD AND MY BROTHER IS THROUGH SOLID SCIENCE.

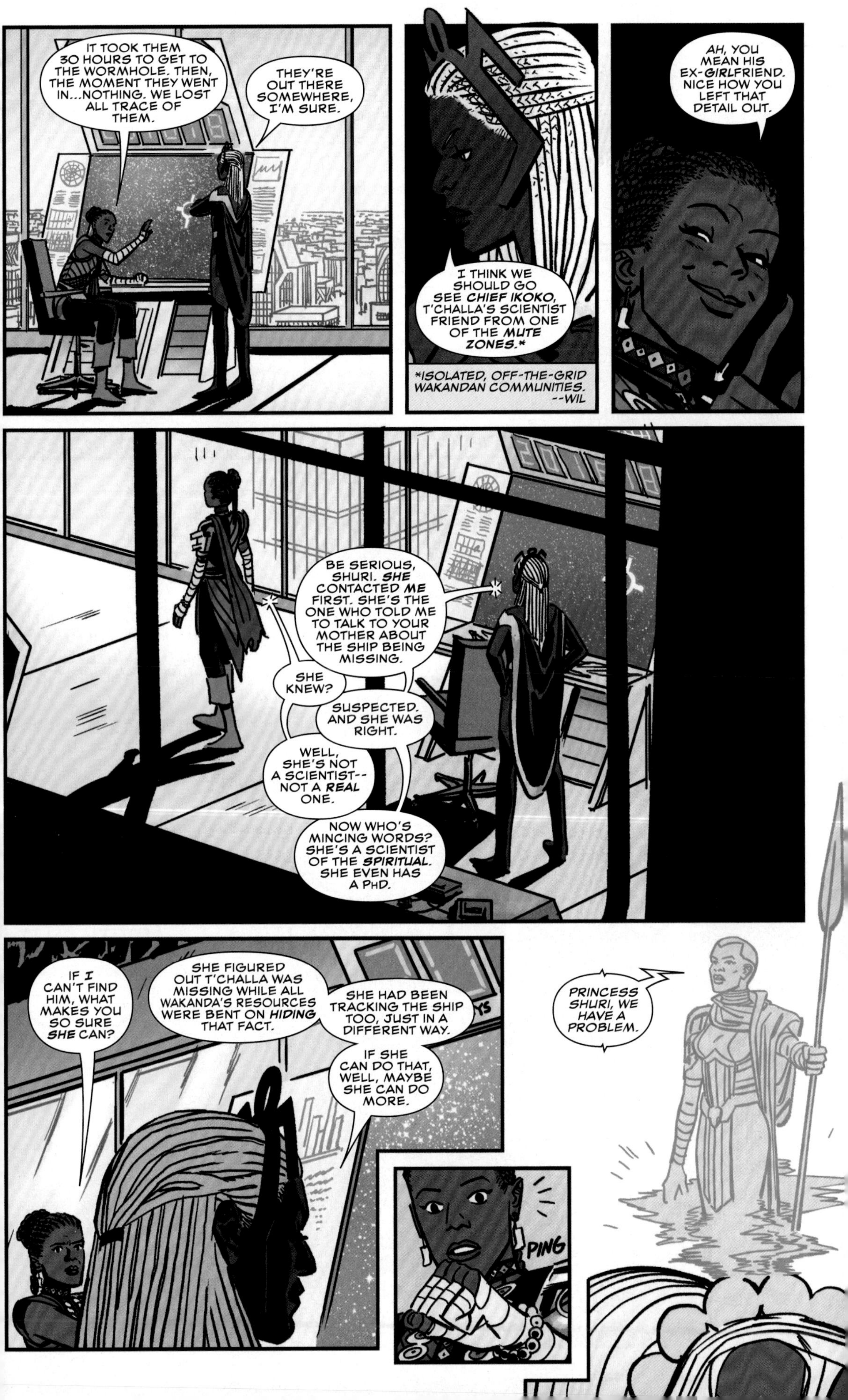

IT TOOK THEM 30 HOURS TO GET TO THE WORMHOLE. THEN, THE MOMENT THEY WENT IN...NOTHING. WE LOST ALL TRACE OF THEM.
THEY'RE OUT THERE SOMEWHERE, I'M SURE.
I THINK WE SHOULD GO SEE CHIEF IKOKO, T'CHALLA'S SCIENTIST FRIEND FROM ONE OF THE MUTE ZONES.*
*ISOLATED, OFF-THE-GRID WAKANDAN COMMUNITIES. --WIL
AH, YOU MEAN HIS EX-GIRLFRIEND. NICE HOW YOU LEFT THAT DETAIL OUT.
BE SERIOUS, SHURI. SHE CONTACTED ME FIRST. SHE'S THE ONE WHO TOLD ME TO TALK TO YOUR MOTHER ABOUT THE SHIP BEING MISSING.
SHE KNEW?
SUSPECTED. AND SHE WAS RIGHT.
WELL, SHE'S NOT A SCIENTIST-- NOT A REAL ONE.
NOW WHO'S MINCING WORDS? SHE'S A SCIENTIST OF THE SPIRITUAL. SHE EVEN HAS A PhD.
IF I CAN'T FIND HIM, WHAT MAKES YOU SO SURE SHE CAN?
SHE FIGURED OUT T'CHALLA WAS MISSING WHILE ALL WAKANDA'S RESOURCES WERE BENT ON HIDING THAT FACT.
SHE HAD BEEN TRACKING THE SHIP TOO, JUST IN A DIFFERENT WAY.
IF SHE CAN DO THAT, WELL, MAYBE SHE CAN DO MORE.
PING
PRINCESS SHURI, WE HAVE A PROBLEM.

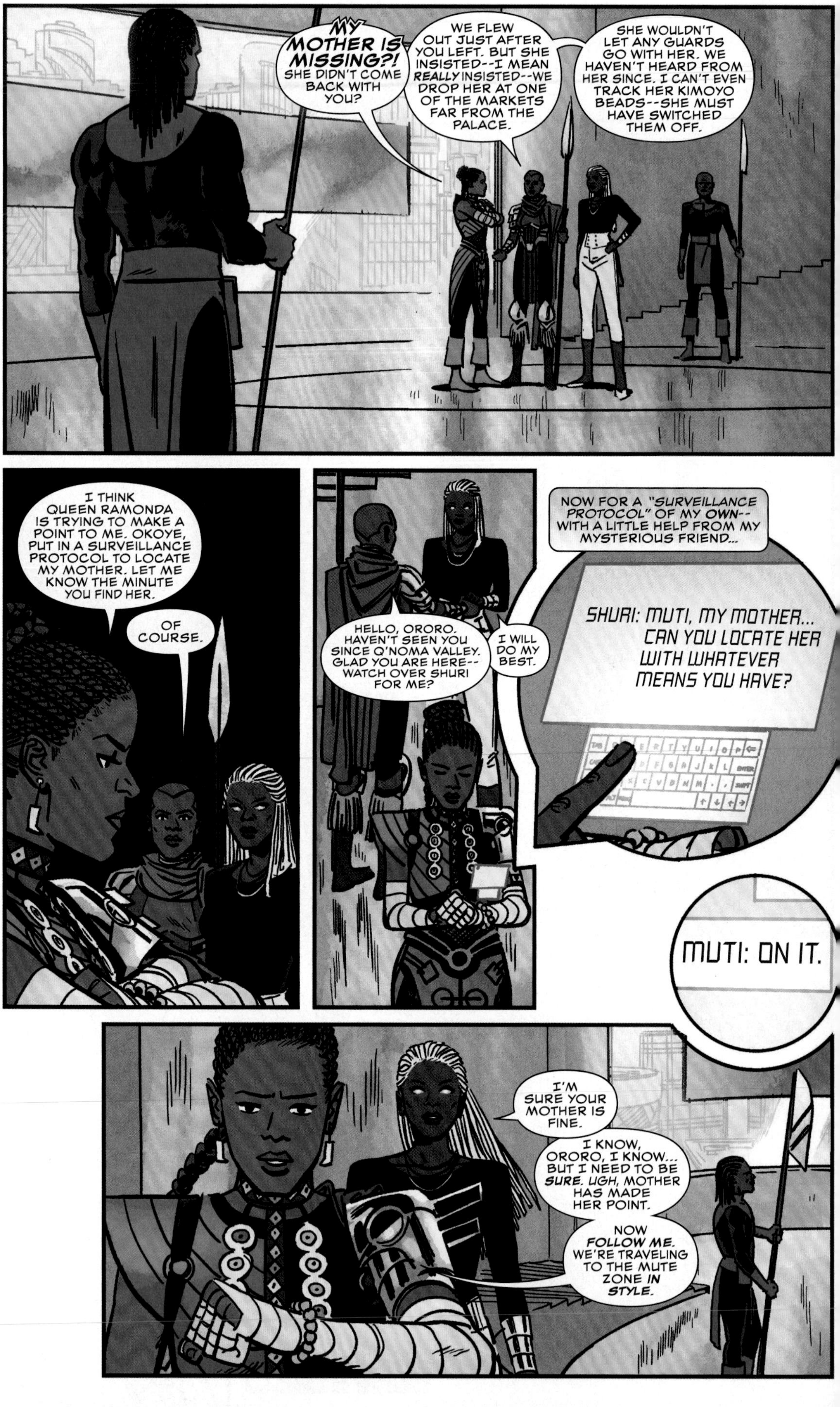
MY MOTHER IS MISSING?! SHE DIDN'T COME BACK WITH YOU?
WE FLEW OUT JUST AFTER YOU LEFT. BUT SHE INSISTED--I MEAN REALLY INSISTED--WE DROP HER AT ONE OF THE MARKETS FAR FROM THE PALACE.
SHE WOULDN'T LET ANY GUARDS GO WITH HER. WE HAVEN'T HEARD FROM HER SINCE. I CAN'T EVEN TRACK HER KIMOYO BEADS--SHE MUST HAVE SWITCHED THEM OFF.
I THINK QUEEN RAMONDA IS TRYING TO MAKE A POINT TO ME. OKOYE, PUT IN A SURVEILLANCE PROTOCOL TO LOCATE MY MOTHER. LET ME KNOW THE MINUTE YOU FIND HER.
OF COURSE.
HELLO, ORORO. HAVEN'T SEEN YOU SINCE Q'NOMA VALLEY. GLAD YOU ARE HERE--WATCH OVER SHURI FOR ME?
I WILL DO MY BEST.
NOW FOR A "SURVEILLANCE PROTOCOL" OF MY OWN--WITH A LITTLE HELP FROM MY MYSTERIOUS FRIEND...
SHURI: MUTI, MY MOTHER... CAN YOU LOCATE HER WITH WHATEVER MEANS YOU HAVE?
MUTI: ON IT.
I'M SURE YOUR MOTHER IS FINE.
I KNOW, ORORO, I KNOW... BUT I NEED TO BE SURE. UGH, MOTHER HAS MADE HER POINT.
NOW FOLLOW ME. WE'RE TRAVELING TO THE MUTE ZONE IN STYLE.

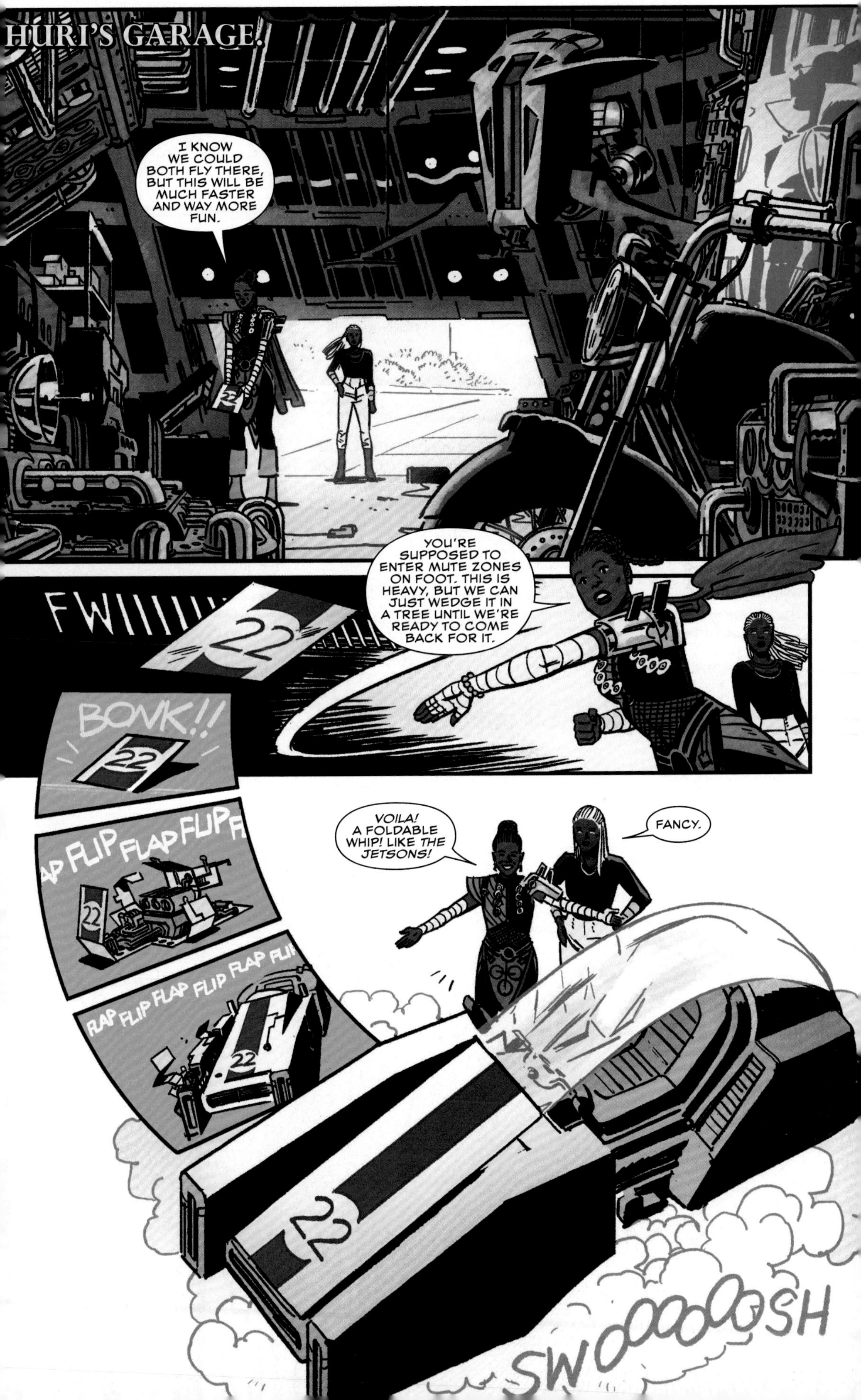

SHURI'S GARAGE.
I KNOW WE COULD BOTH FLY THERE, BUT THIS WILL BE MUCH FASTER AND WAY MORE FUN.
FWIIIII
YOU'RE SUPPOSED TO ENTER MUTE ZONES ON FOOT. THIS IS HEAVY, BUT WE CAN JUST WEDGE IT IN A TREE UNTIL WE'RE READY TO COME BACK FOR IT.
BONK!!
FLAP FLIP FLAP FLIP
FLAP FLIP FLAP FLIP FLAP FLIP
VOILA! A FOLDABLE WHIP! LIKE THE JETSONS!
FANCY.
SWOOOOOOSH

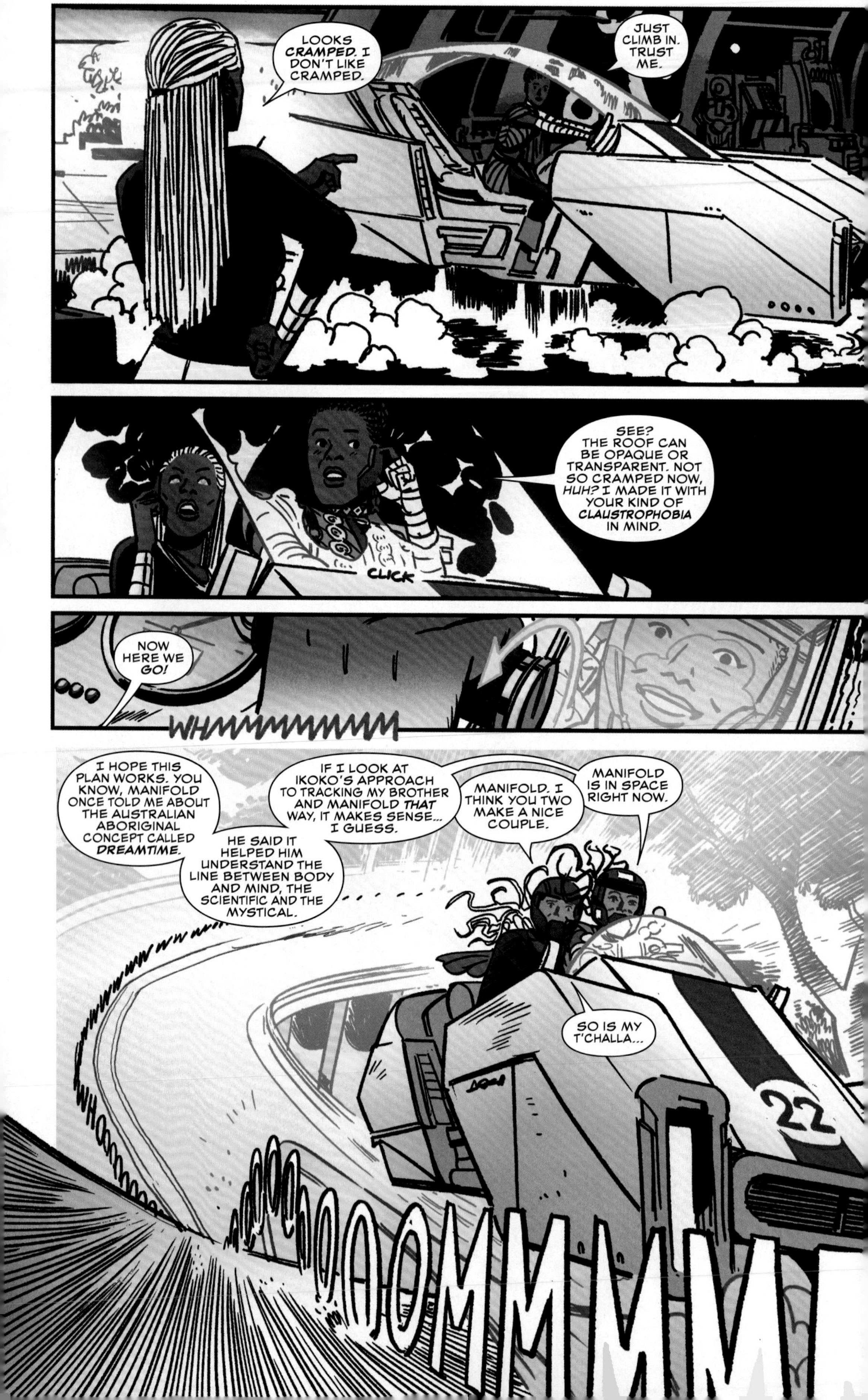
LOOKS *CRAMPED*. I DON'T LIKE CRAMPED.
JUST CLIMB IN. TRUST ME.
SEE? THE ROOF CAN BE OPAQUE OR TRANSPARENT. NOT SO CRAMPED NOW, *HUH?* I MADE IT WITH YOUR KIND OF *CLAUSTROPHOBIA* IN MIND.
CLICK
NOW HERE WE *GO!*
WHMMMMMMM
I HOPE THIS PLAN WORKS. YOU KNOW, MANIFOLD ONCE TOLD ME ABOUT THE AUSTRALIAN ABORIGINAL CONCEPT CALLED *DREAMTIME*.
HE SAID IT HELPED HIM UNDERSTAND THE LINE BETWEEN BODY AND MIND, THE SCIENTIFIC AND THE MYSTICAL.
IF I LOOK AT IKOKO'S APPROACH TO TRACKING MY BROTHER AND MANIFOLD *THAT* WAY, IT MAKES SENSE... I GUESS.
MANIFOLD. I THINK YOU TWO MAKE A NICE COUPLE.
MANIFOLD IS IN SPACE RIGHT NOW.
SO IS MY T'CHALLA...
22
WHOOOOOMMMM

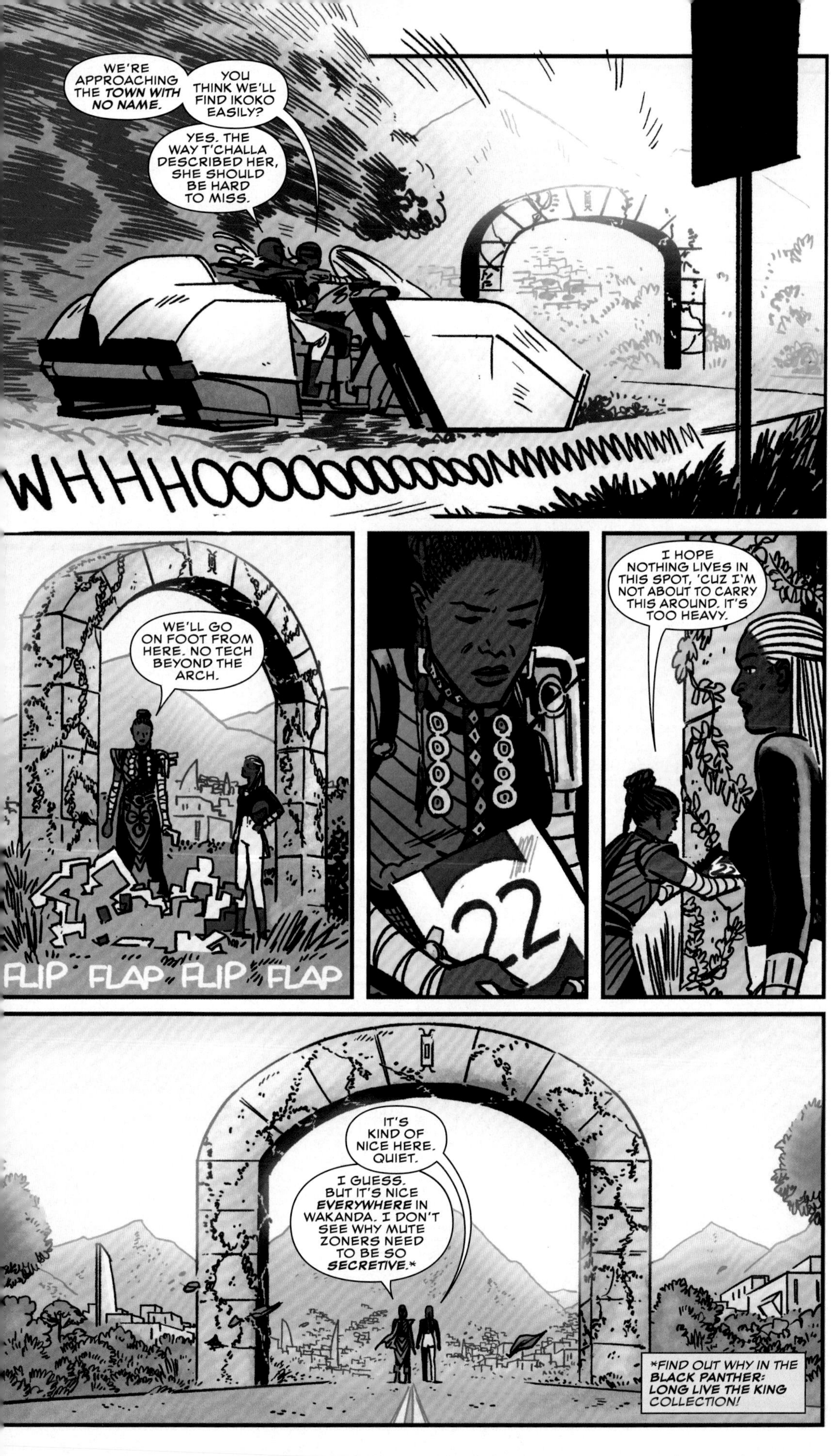
WE'RE APPROACHING THE *TOWN WITH NO NAME.*
YOU THINK WE'LL FIND IKOKO EASILY?
YES. THE WAY T'CHALLA DESCRIBED HER, SHE SHOULD BE HARD TO MISS.
WHHHOOOOOOOOOOOOMMMMMMMMMMM
WE'LL GO ON FOOT FROM HERE. NO TECH BEYOND THE ARCH.
FLIP FLAP FLIP FLAP
22
I HOPE NOTHING LIVES IN THIS SPOT, 'CUZ I'M NOT ABOUT TO CARRY THIS AROUND. IT'S TOO HEAVY.
IT'S KIND OF NICE HERE. QUIET.
I GUESS. BUT IT'S NICE *EVERYWHERE* IN WAKANDA. I DON'T SEE WHY MUTE ZONERS NEED TO BE SO *SECRETIVE.**
*FIND OUT WHY IN THE *BLACK PANTHER: LONG LIVE THE KING* COLLECTION!

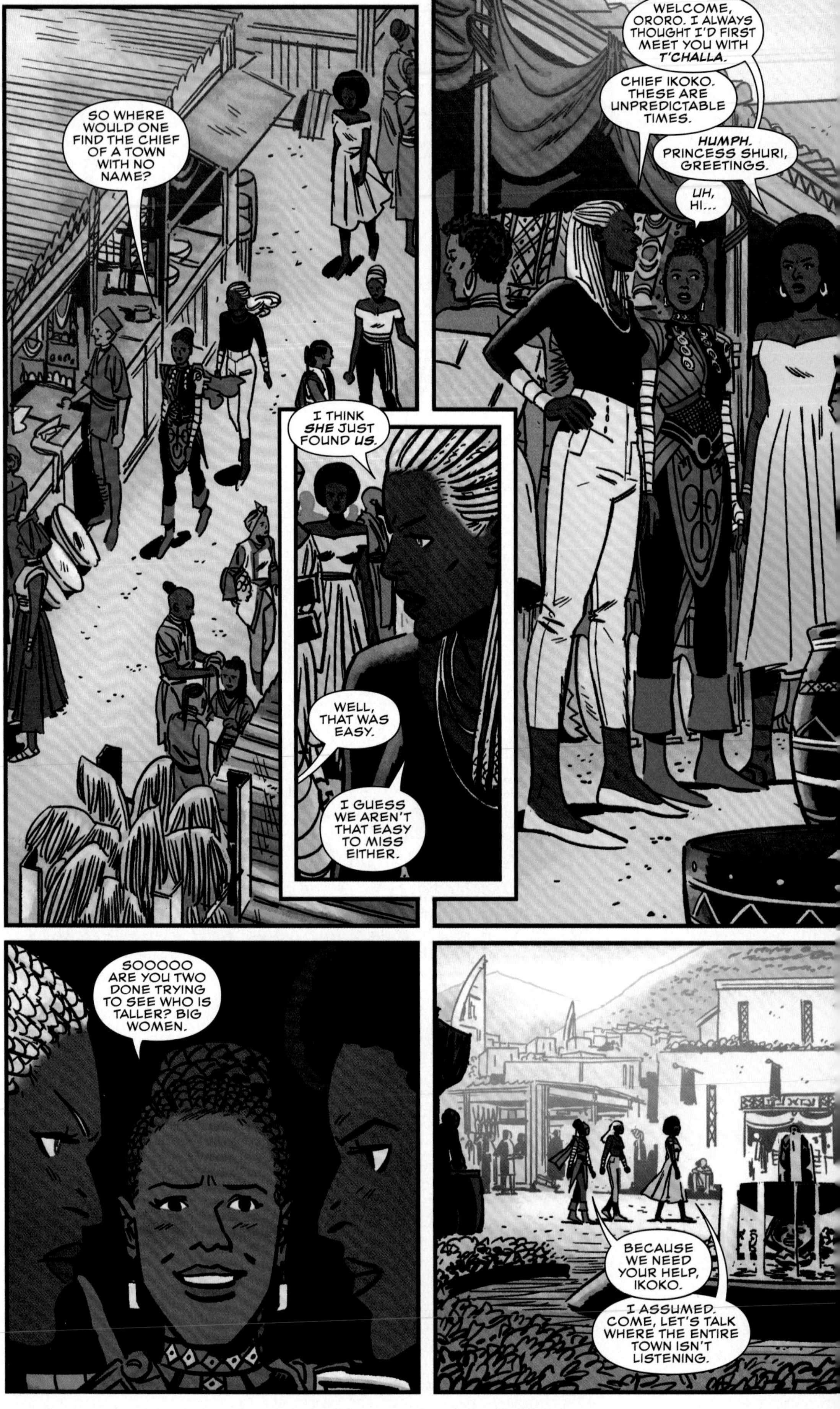
SO WHERE WOULD ONE FIND THE CHIEF OF A TOWN WITH NO NAME?
I THINK SHE JUST FOUND US.
WELL, THAT WAS EASY.
I GUESS WE AREN'T THAT EASY TO MISS EITHER.
WELCOME, ORORO. I ALWAYS THOUGHT I'D FIRST MEET YOU WITH T'CHALLA.
CHIEF IKOKO. THESE ARE UNPREDICTABLE TIMES.
HUMPH. PRINCESS SHURI, GREETINGS.
UH, HI...
SOOOOO ARE YOU TWO DONE TRYING TO SEE WHO IS TALLER? BIG WOMEN.
BECAUSE WE NEED YOUR HELP, IKOKO.
I ASSUMED. COME, LET'S TALK WHERE THE ENTIRE TOWN ISN'T LISTENING.

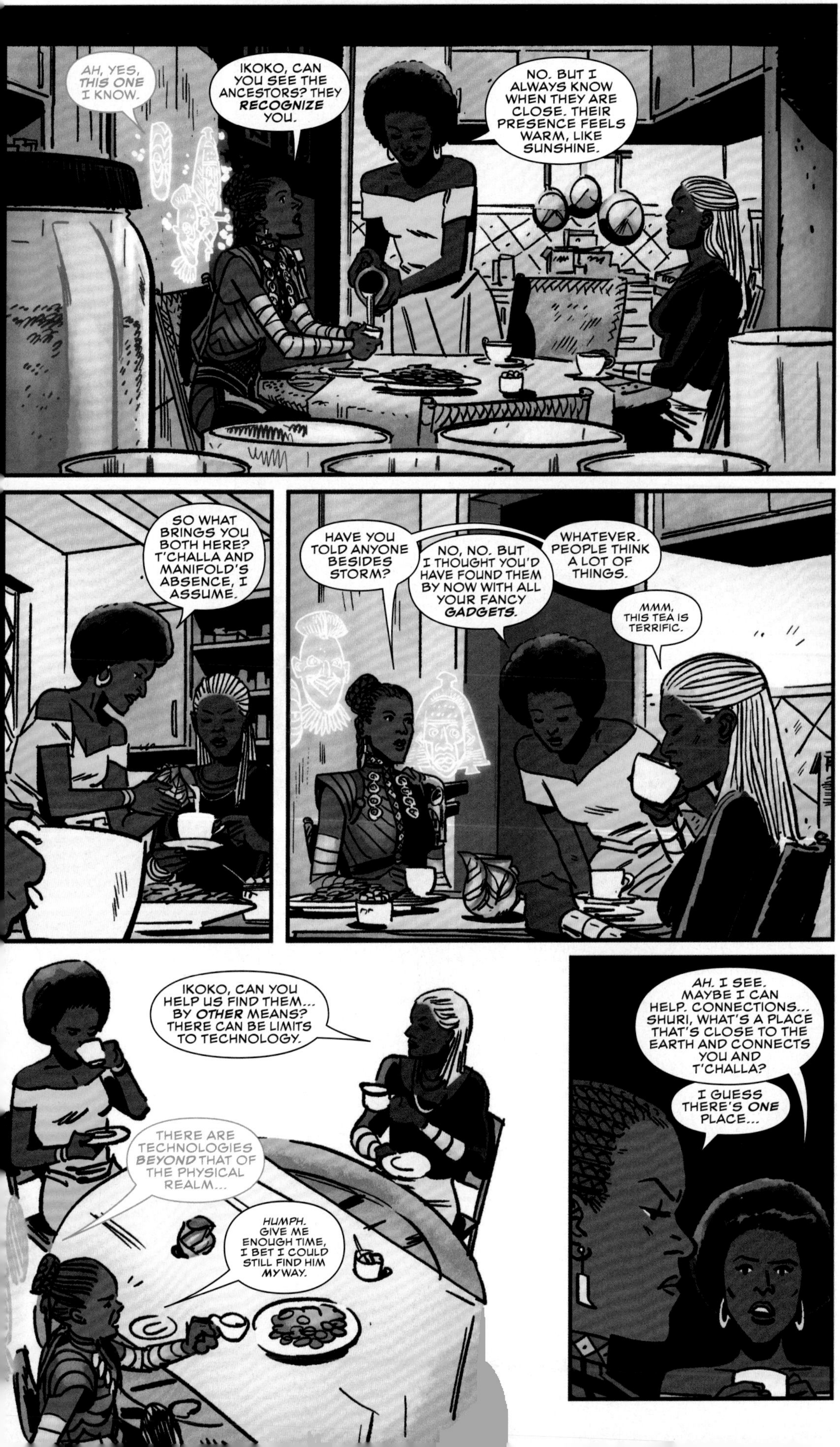
AH, YES, THIS ONE I KNOW.
IKOKO, CAN YOU SEE THE ANCESTORS? THEY RECOGNIZE YOU.
NO. BUT I ALWAYS KNOW WHEN THEY ARE CLOSE. THEIR PRESENCE FEELS WARM, LIKE SUNSHINE.
SO WHAT BRINGS YOU BOTH HERE? T'CHALLA AND MANIFOLD'S ABSENCE, I ASSUME.
HAVE YOU TOLD ANYONE BESIDES STORM?
NO, NO. BUT I THOUGHT YOU'D HAVE FOUND THEM BY NOW WITH ALL YOUR FANCY GADGETS.
WHATEVER. PEOPLE THINK A LOT OF THINGS.
MMM, THIS TEA IS TERRIFIC.
IKOKO, CAN YOU HELP US FIND THEM... BY OTHER MEANS? THERE CAN BE LIMITS TO TECHNOLOGY.
THERE ARE TECHNOLOGIES BEYOND THAT OF THE PHYSICAL REALM...
HUMPH. GIVE ME ENOUGH TIME, I BET I COULD STILL FIND HIM MY WAY.
AH. I SEE. MAYBE I CAN HELP. CONNECTIONS... SHURI, WHAT'S A PLACE THAT'S CLOSE TO THE EARTH AND CONNECTS YOU AND T'CHALLA?
I GUESS THERE'S ONE PLACE...

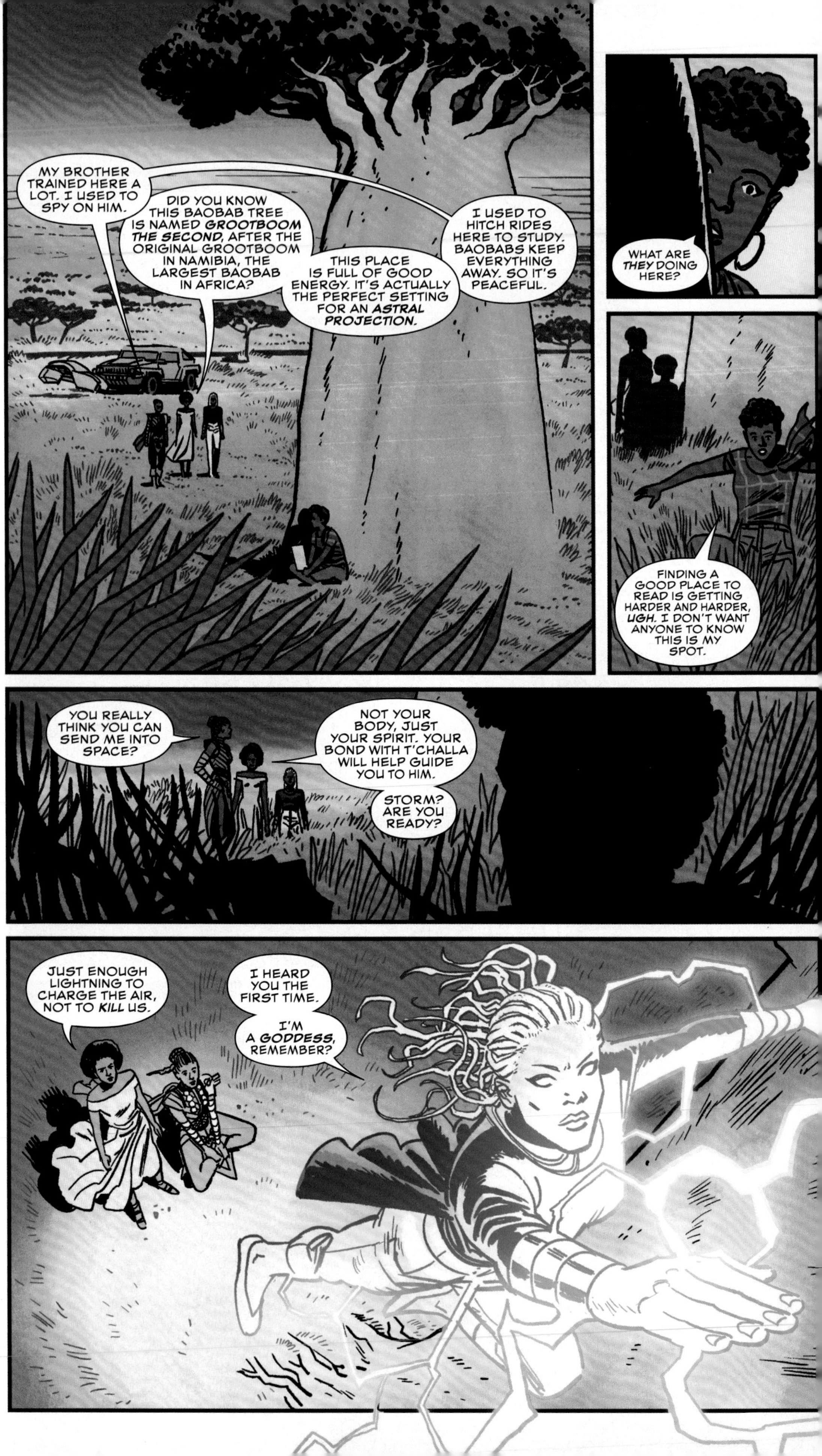

MY BROTHER TRAINED HERE A LOT. I USED TO SPY ON HIM.
DID YOU KNOW THIS BAOBAB TREE IS NAMED GROOTBOOM THE SECOND, AFTER THE ORIGINAL GROOTBOOM IN NAMIBIA, THE LARGEST BAOBAB IN AFRICA?
THIS PLACE IS FULL OF GOOD ENERGY. IT'S ACTUALLY THE PERFECT SETTING FOR AN ASTRAL PROJECTION.
I USED TO HITCH RIDES HERE TO STUDY. BAOBABS KEEP EVERYTHING AWAY. SO IT'S PEACEFUL.
WHAT ARE THEY DOING HERE?
FINDING A GOOD PLACE TO READ IS GETTING HARDER AND HARDER, UGH. I DON'T WANT ANYONE TO KNOW THIS IS MY SPOT.
YOU REALLY THINK YOU CAN SEND ME INTO SPACE?
NOT YOUR BODY, JUST YOUR SPIRIT. YOUR BOND WITH T'CHALLA WILL HELP GUIDE YOU TO HIM.
STORM? ARE YOU READY?
JUST ENOUGH LIGHTNING TO CHARGE THE AIR, NOT TO KILL US.
I HEARD YOU THE FIRST TIME.
I'M A GODDESS, REMEMBER?

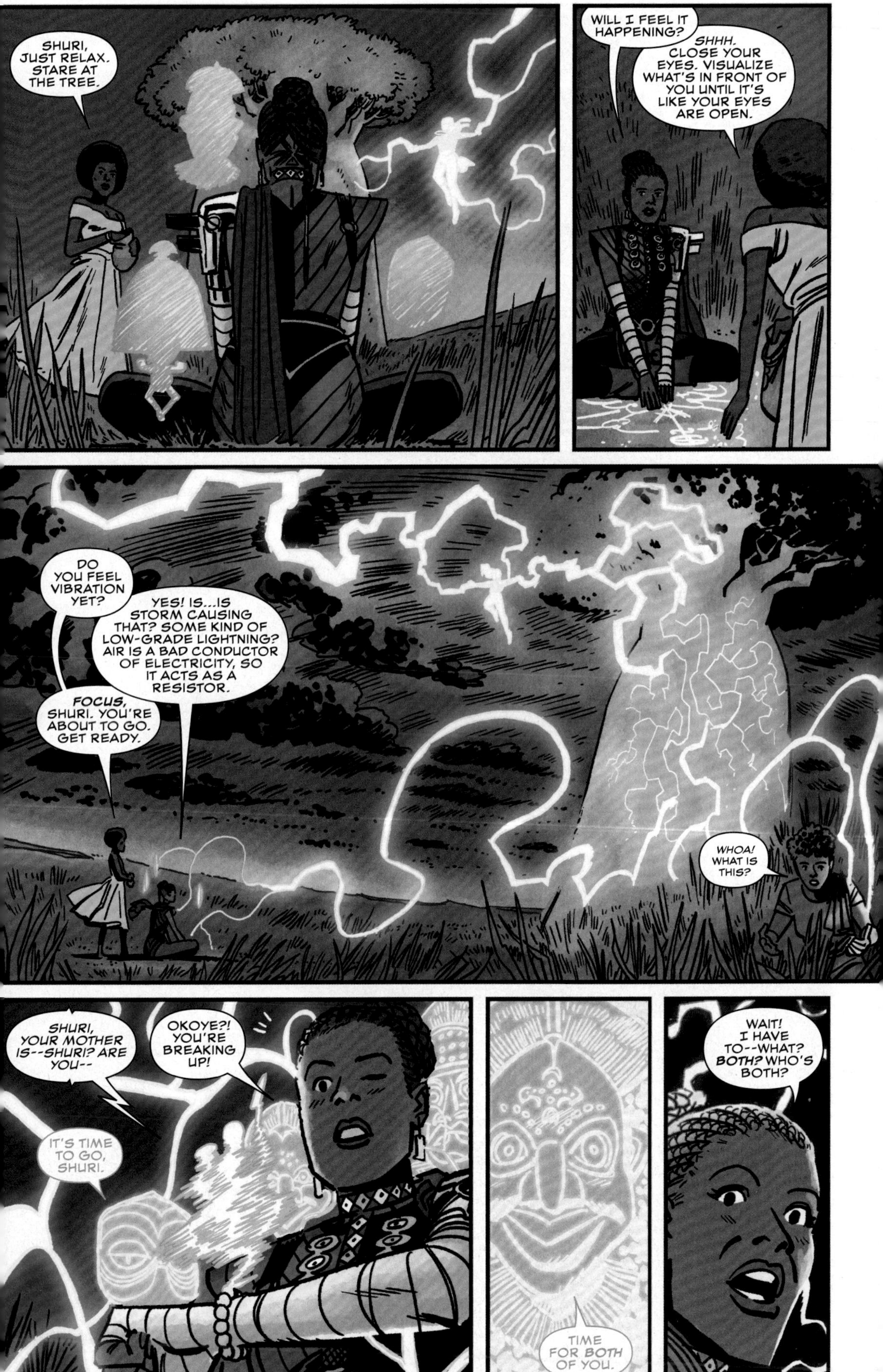
SHURI, JUST RELAX. STARE AT THE TREE.
WILL I FEEL IT HAPPENING?
SHHH. CLOSE YOUR EYES. VISUALIZE WHAT'S IN FRONT OF YOU UNTIL IT'S LIKE YOUR EYES ARE OPEN.
DO YOU FEEL VIBRATION YET?
YES! IS...IS STORM CAUSING THAT? SOME KIND OF LOW-GRADE LIGHTNING? AIR IS A BAD CONDUCTOR OF ELECTRICITY, SO IT ACTS AS A RESISTOR.
FOCUS, SHURI. YOU'RE ABOUT TO GO. GET READY.
WHOA! WHAT IS THIS?
SHURI, YOUR MOTHER IS--SHURI? ARE YOU--
OKOYE?! YOU'RE BREAKING UP!
IT'S TIME TO GO, SHURI.
TIME FOR BOTH OF YOU.
WAIT! I HAVE TO--WHAT? BOTH? WHO'S BOTH?

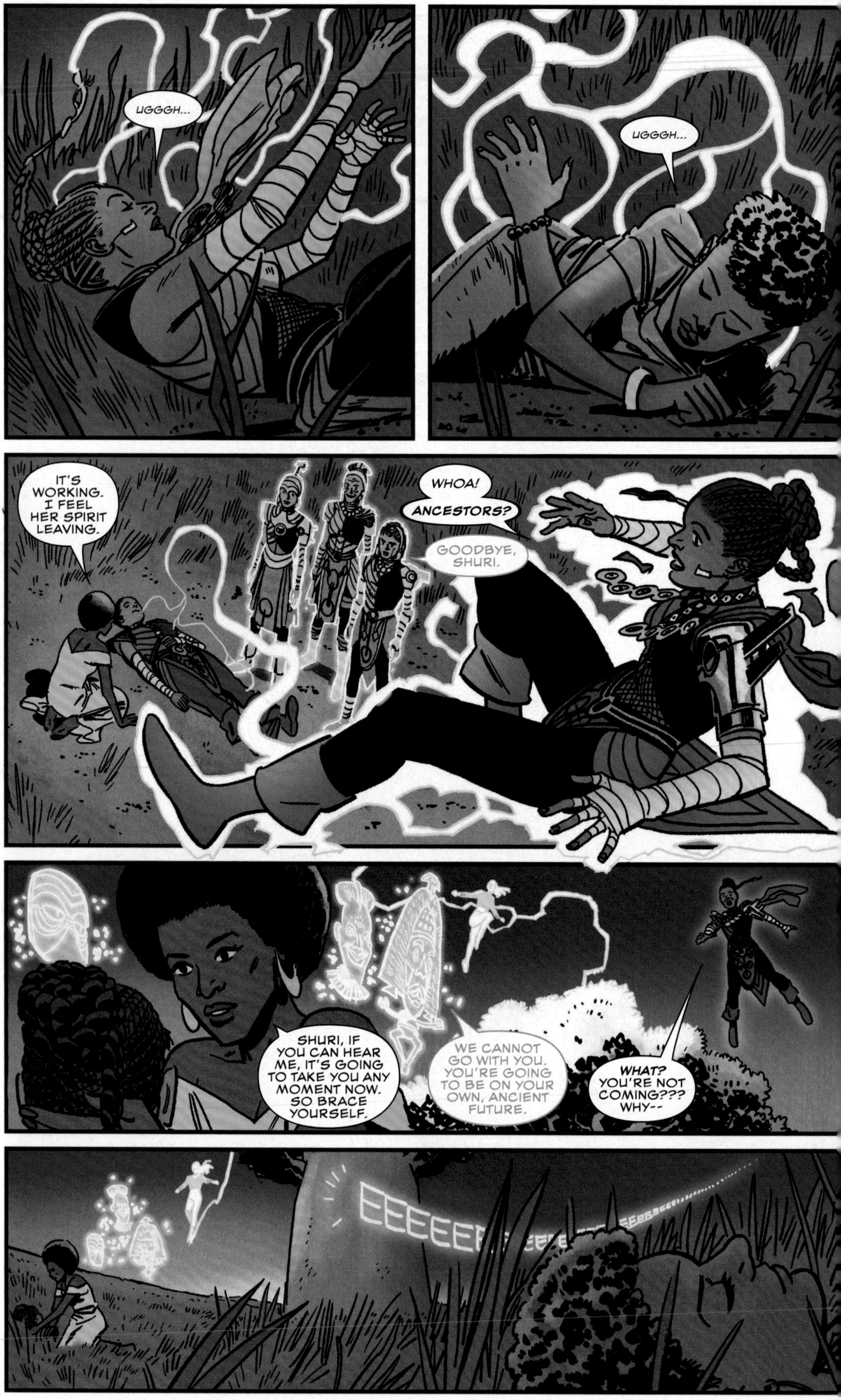
UGGGH...
UGGGH...
IT'S WORKING. I FEEL HER SPIRIT LEAVING.
WHOA!
ANCESTORS?
GOODBYE, SHURI.
SHURI, IF YOU CAN HEAR ME, IT'S GOING TO TAKE YOU ANY MOMENT NOW. SO BRACE YOURSELF.
WE CANNOT GO WITH YOU. YOU'RE GOING TO BE ON YOUR OWN, ANCIENT FUTURE.
WHAT? YOU'RE NOT COMING??? WHY--
EEEEEEE

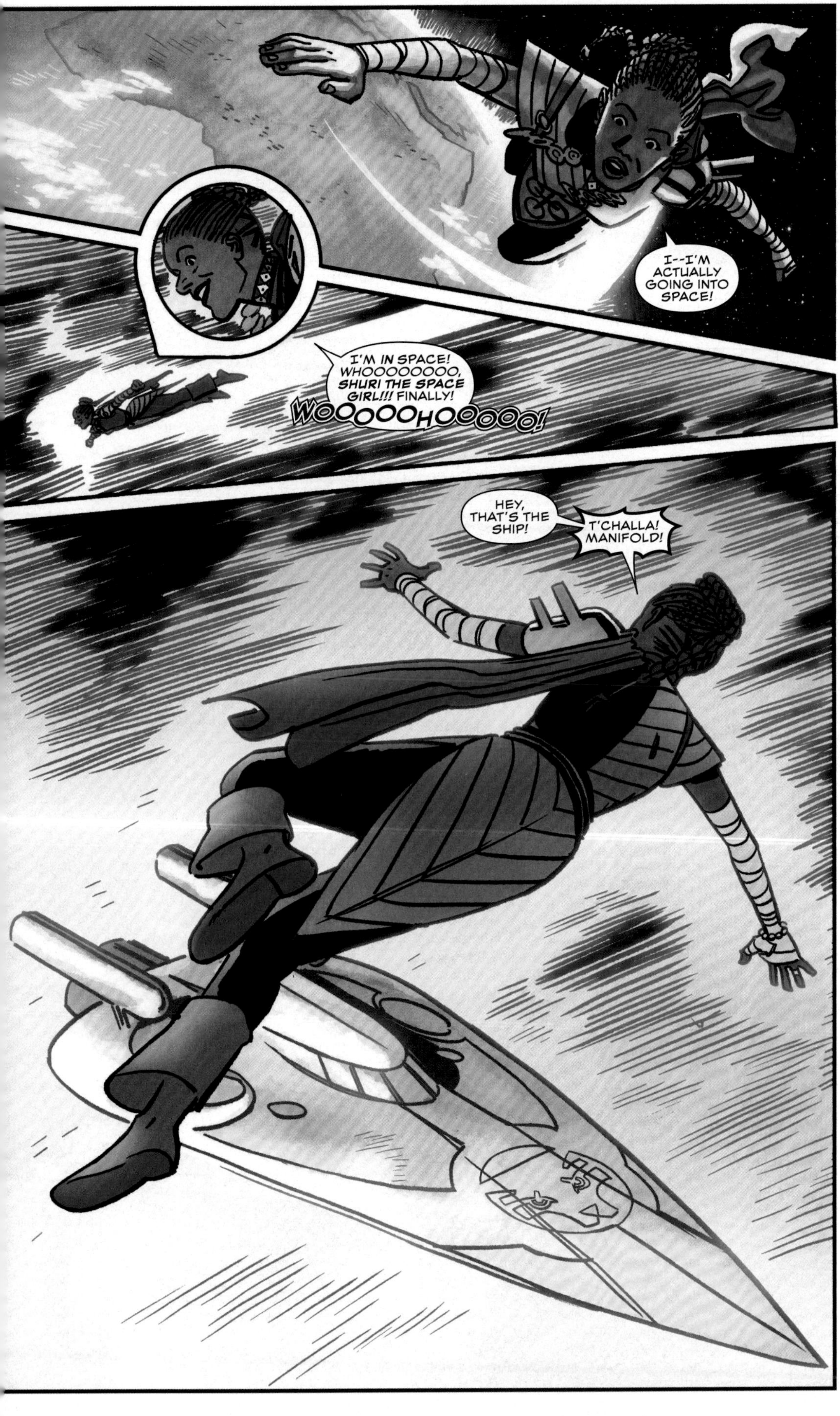
I--I'M ACTUALLY GOING INTO SPACE!
I'M IN SPACE! WHOOOOOOOOO, SHURI THE SPACE GIRL!!! FINALLY!
WOOOOOHOOOOO!
HEY, THAT'S THE SHIP!
T'CHALLA! MANIFOLD!

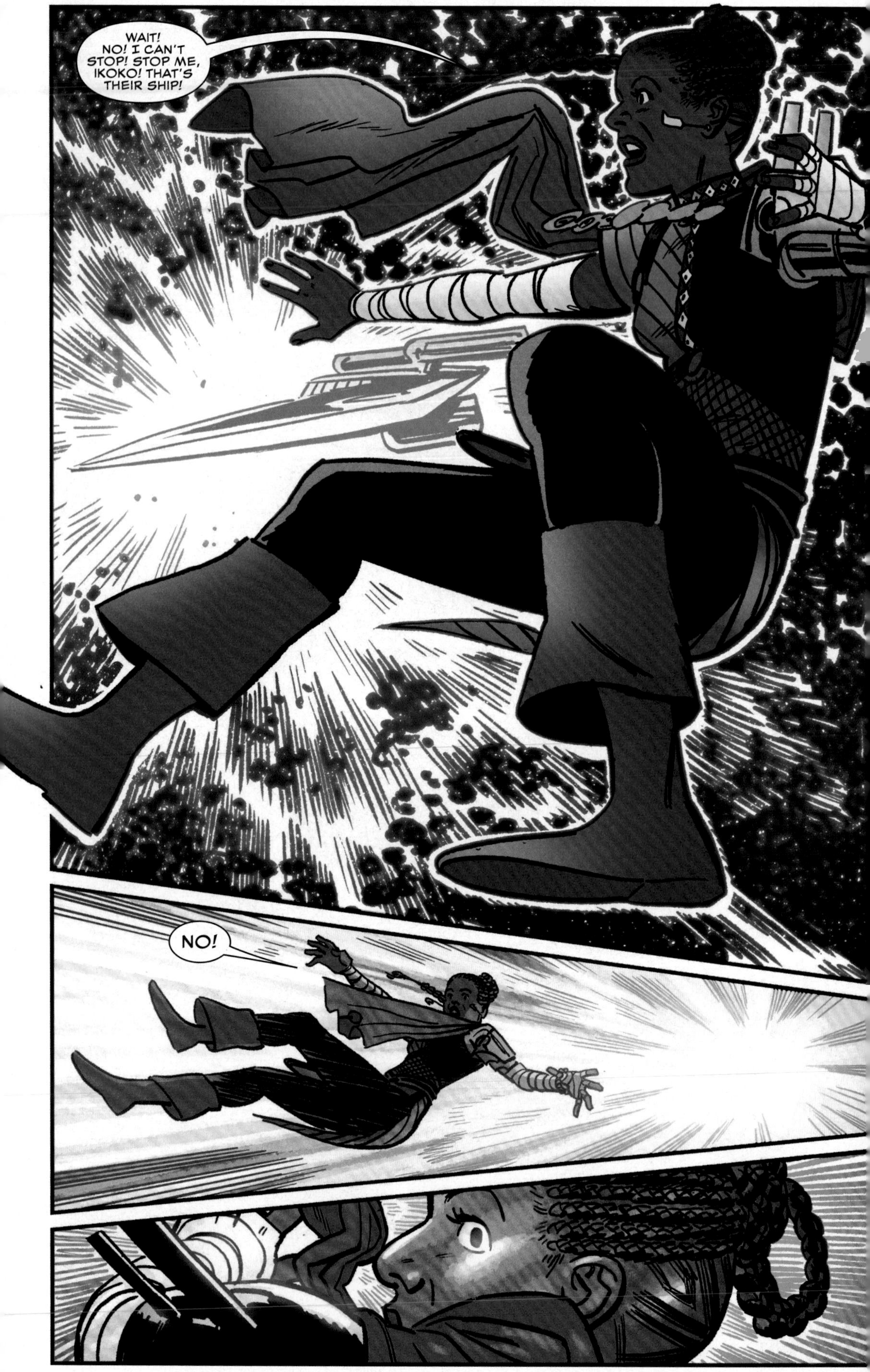

WAIT! NO! I CAN'T STOP! STOP ME, IKOKO! THAT'S THEIR SHIP!
NO!

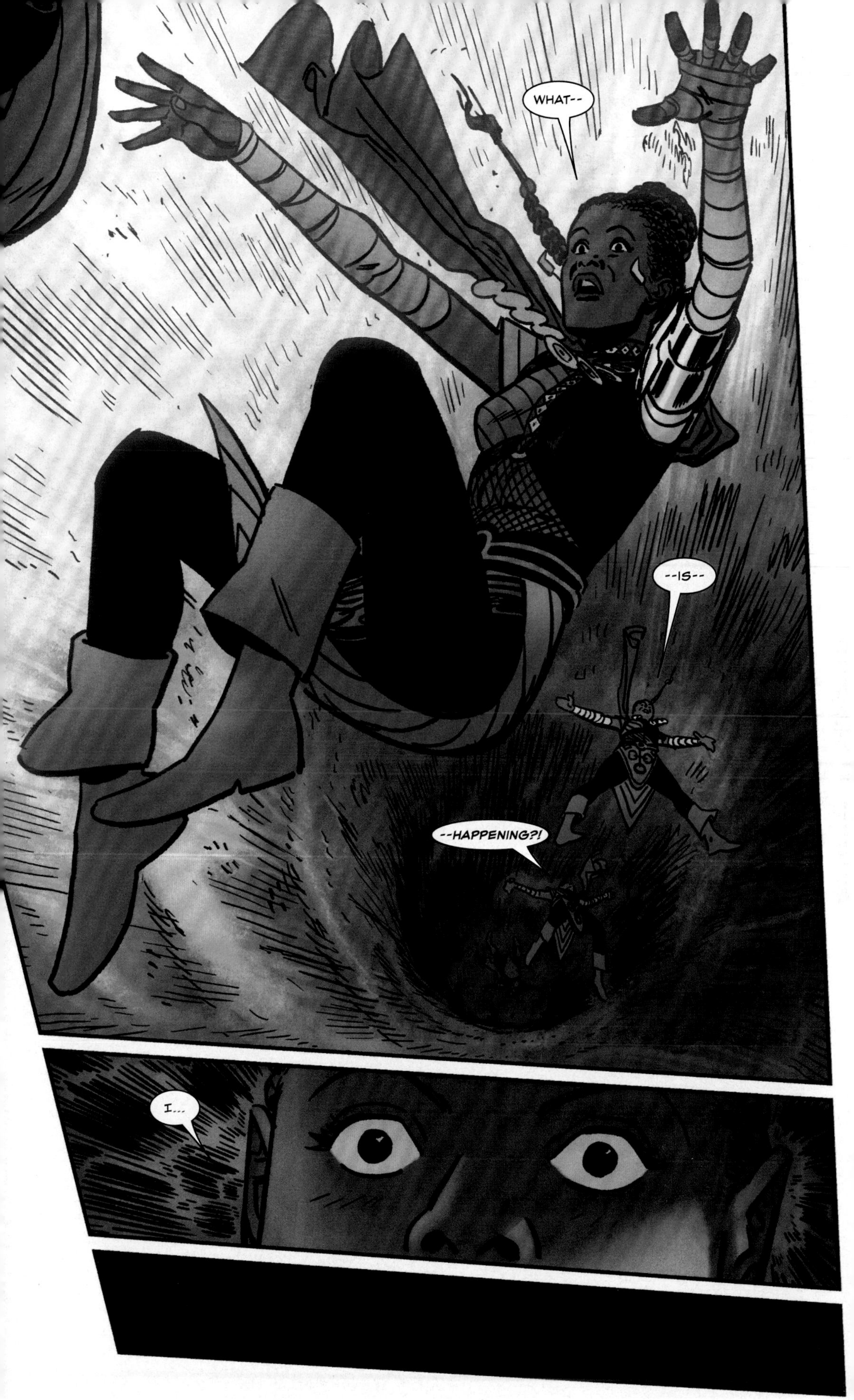
WHAT--
--IS--
--HAPPENING?!
I...

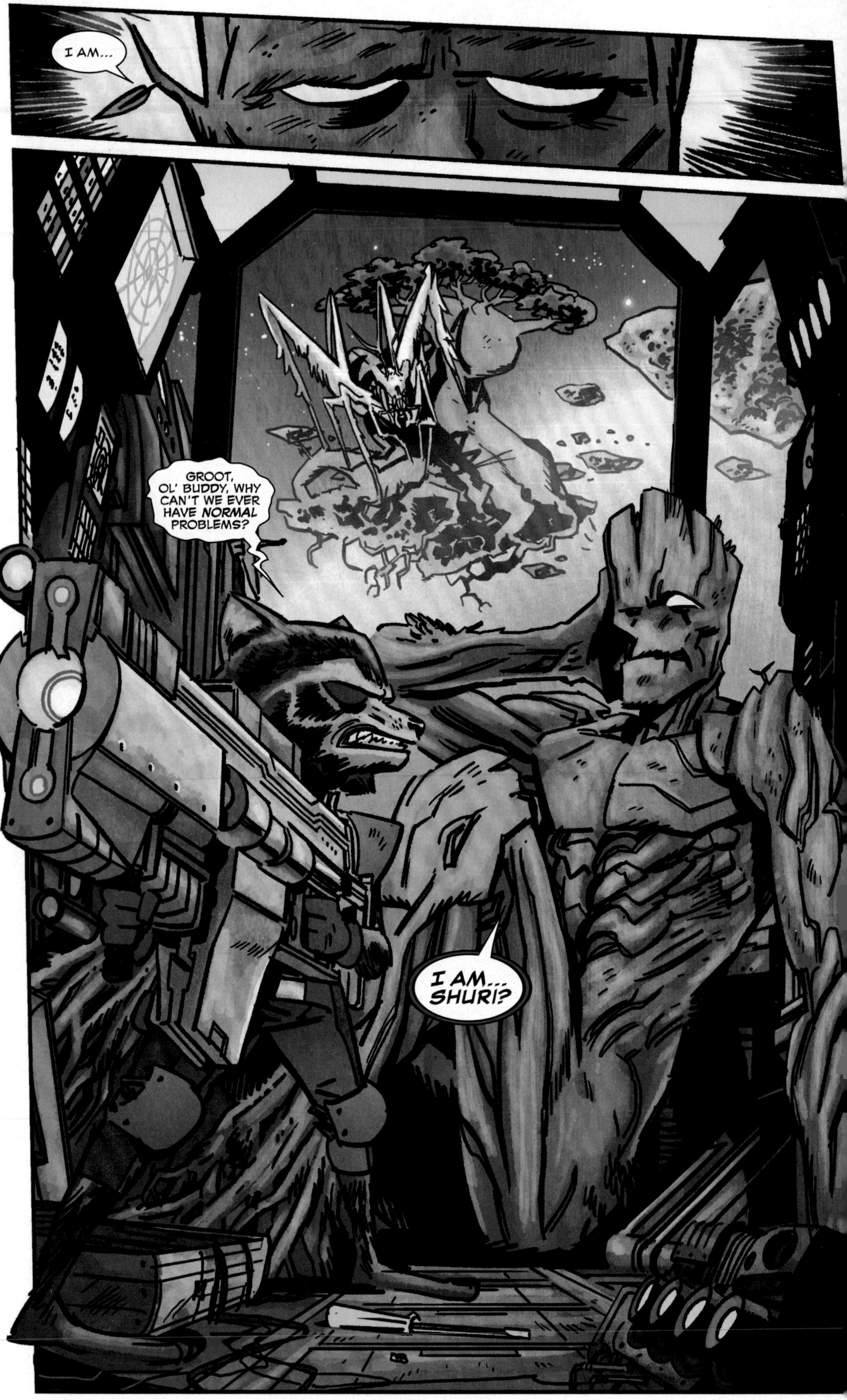
I AM...
GROOT, OL' BUDDY, WHY CAN'T WE EVER HAVE *NORMAL* PROBLEMS?
I AM... SHURI?

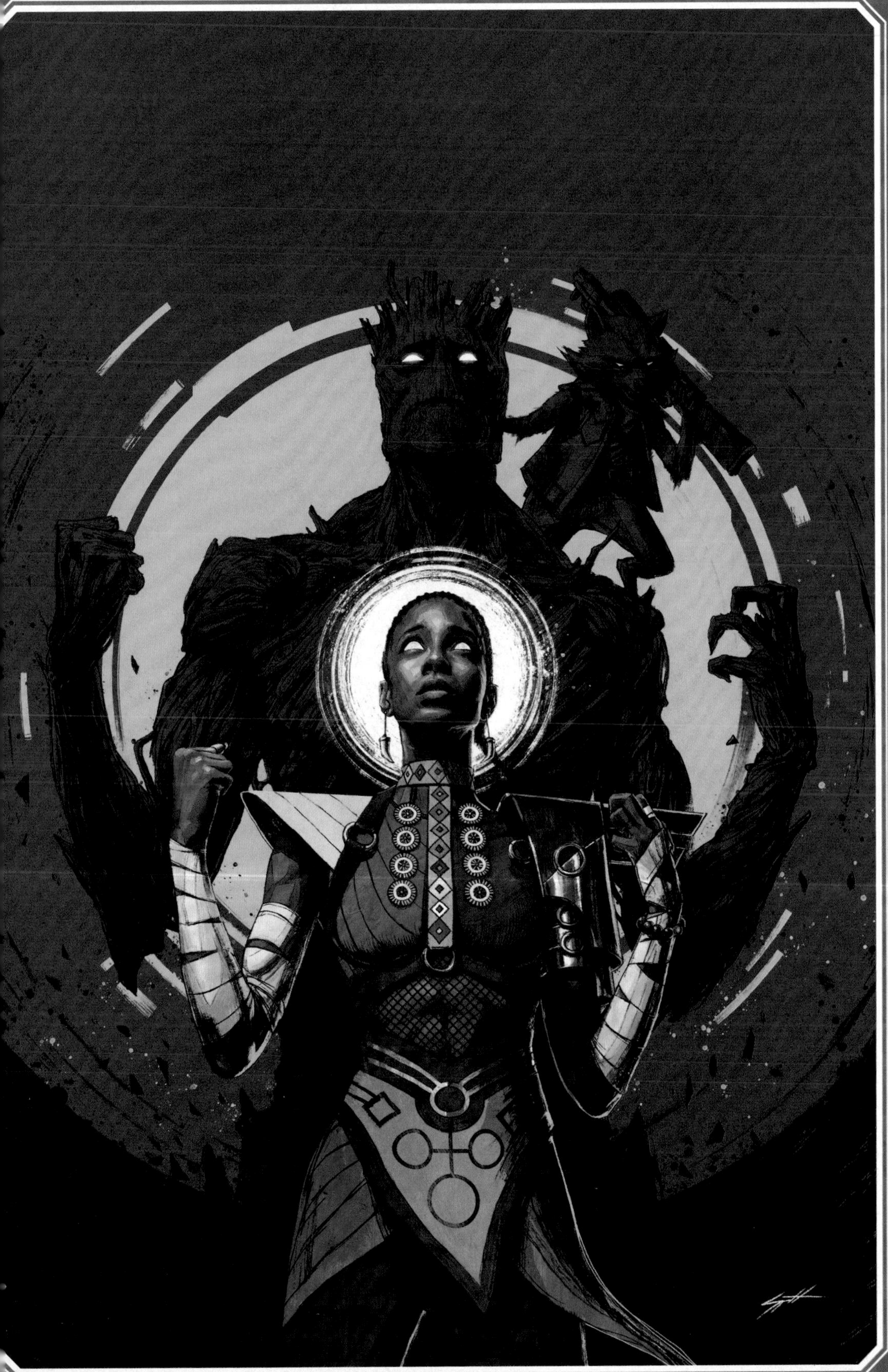

3 – GROOT BOOM

DEDICATED TO THE LATE, GREAT ARETHA FRANKLIN, THE QUEEN OF SOUL

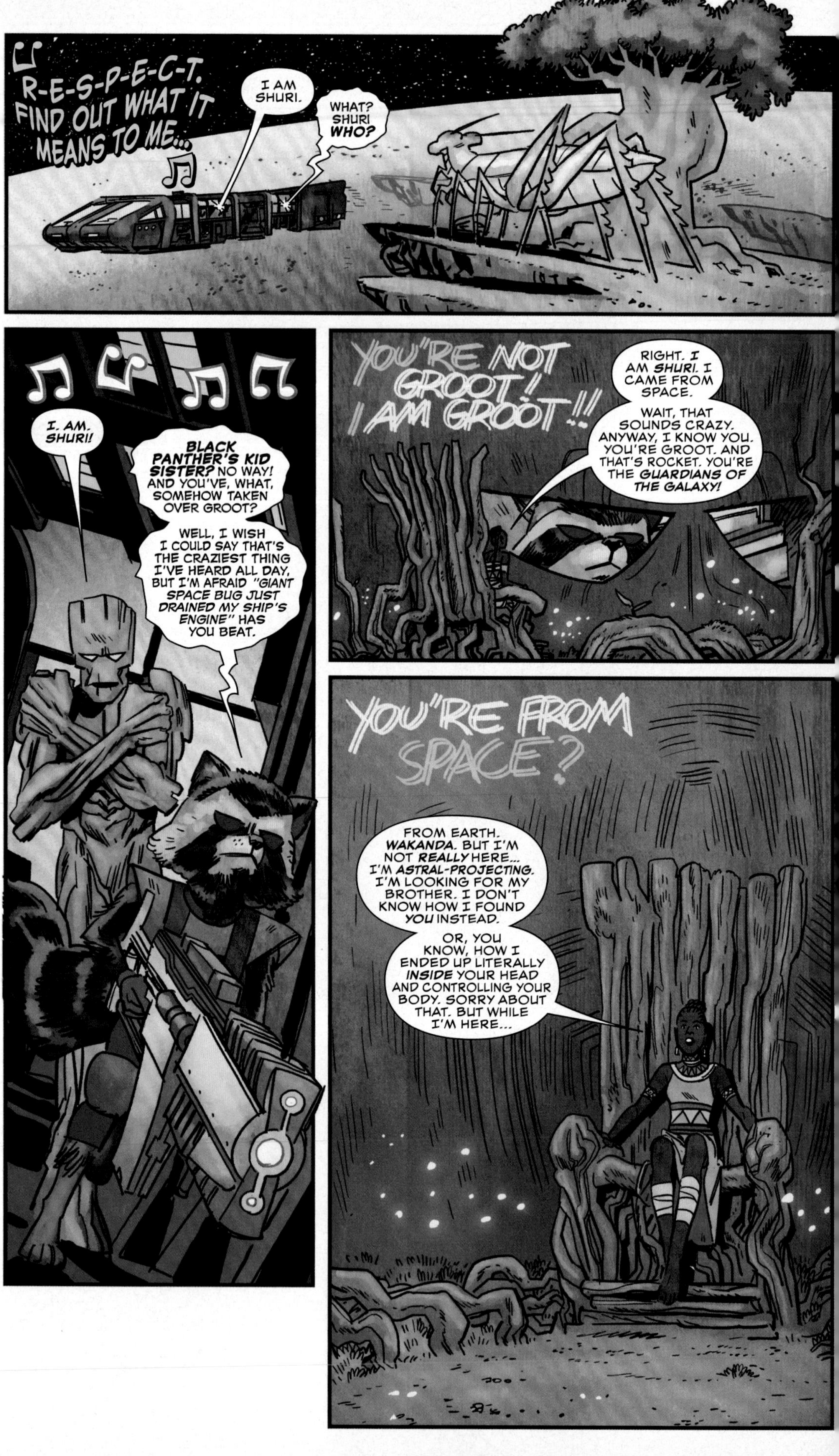
R-E-S-P-E-C-T. FIND OUT WHAT IT MEANS TO ME...
I AM SHURI.
WHAT? SHURI WHO?
I. AM. SHURI!
BLACK PANTHER'S KID SISTER? NO WAY! AND YOU'VE, WHAT, SOMEHOW TAKEN OVER GROOT?
WELL, I WISH I COULD SAY THAT'S THE CRAZIEST THING I'VE HEARD ALL DAY, BUT I'M AFRAID "GIANT SPACE BUG JUST DRAINED MY SHIP'S ENGINE" HAS YOU BEAT.
YOU'RE NOT GROOT! I AM GROOT!!
RIGHT. I AM SHURI. I CAME FROM SPACE.
WAIT, THAT SOUNDS CRAZY. ANYWAY, I KNOW YOU. YOU'RE GROOT. AND THAT'S ROCKET. YOU'RE THE GUARDIANS OF THE GALAXY!
YOU'RE FROM SPACE?
FROM EARTH. WAKANDA. BUT I'M NOT REALLY HERE... I'M ASTRAL-PROJECTING. I'M LOOKING FOR MY BROTHER. I DON'T KNOW HOW I FOUND YOU INSTEAD.
OR, YOU KNOW, HOW I ENDED UP LITERALLY INSIDE YOUR HEAD AND CONTROLLING YOUR BODY. SORRY ABOUT THAT. BUT WHILE I'M HERE...

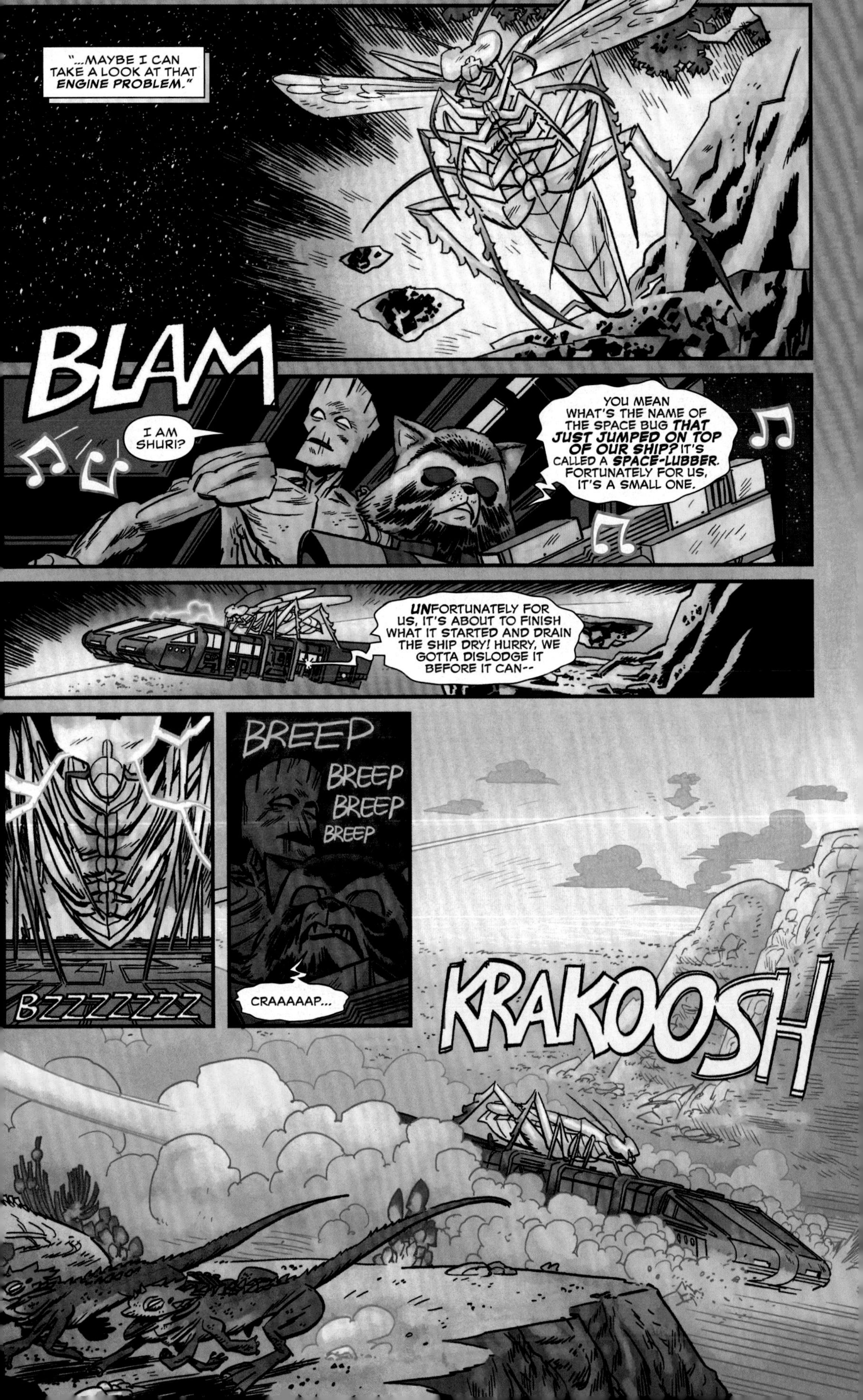

"...MAYBE I CAN TAKE A LOOK AT THAT ENGINE PROBLEM."
BLAM
I AM SHURI?
YOU MEAN WHAT'S THE NAME OF THE SPACE BUG THAT JUST JUMPED ON TOP OF OUR SHIP? IT'S CALLED A SPACE-LUBBER. FORTUNATELY FOR US, IT'S A SMALL ONE.
UNFORTUNATELY FOR US, IT'S ABOUT TO FINISH WHAT IT STARTED AND DRAIN THE SHIP DRY! HURRY, WE GOTTA DISLODGE IT BEFORE IT CAN--
BZZZZZZZZ
BREEP
BREEP
BREEP
BREEP
CRAAAAAP...
KRAKOOSH

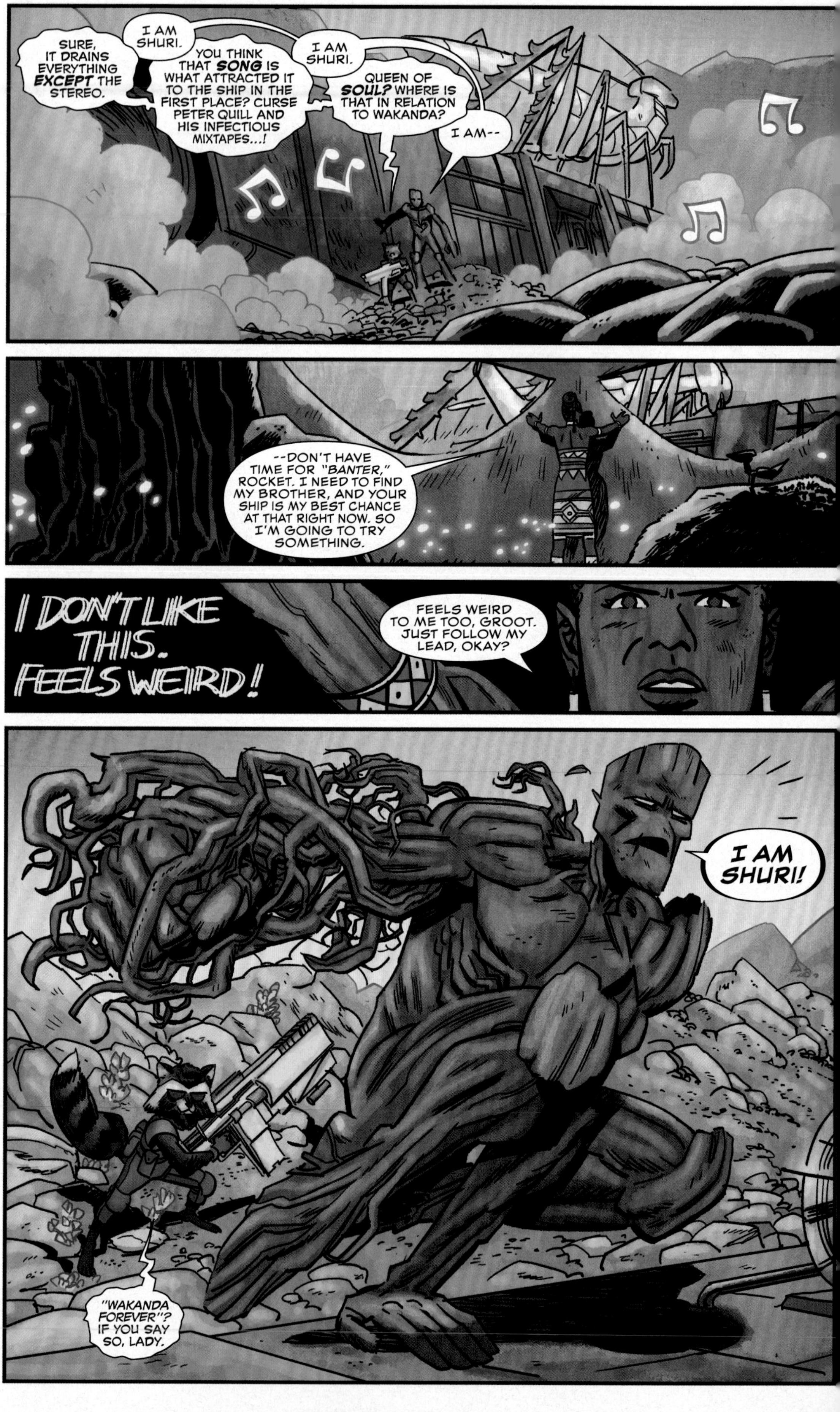

SURE, IT DRAINS EVERYTHING EXCEPT THE STEREO.
I AM SHURI.
YOU THINK THAT SONG IS WHAT ATTRACTED IT TO THE SHIP IN THE FIRST PLACE? CURSE PETER QUILL AND HIS INFECTIOUS MIXTAPES...!
I AM SHURI.
QUEEN OF SOUL? WHERE IS THAT IN RELATION TO WAKANDA?
I AM--
--DON'T HAVE TIME FOR "BANTER," ROCKET. I NEED TO FIND MY BROTHER, AND YOUR SHIP IS MY BEST CHANCE AT THAT RIGHT NOW. SO I'M GOING TO TRY SOMETHING.
I DON'T LIKE THIS.. FEELS WEIRD!
FEELS WEIRD TO ME TOO, GROOT. JUST FOLLOW MY LEAD, OKAY?
I AM SHURI!
"WAKANDA FOREVER"? IF YOU SAY SO, LADY.

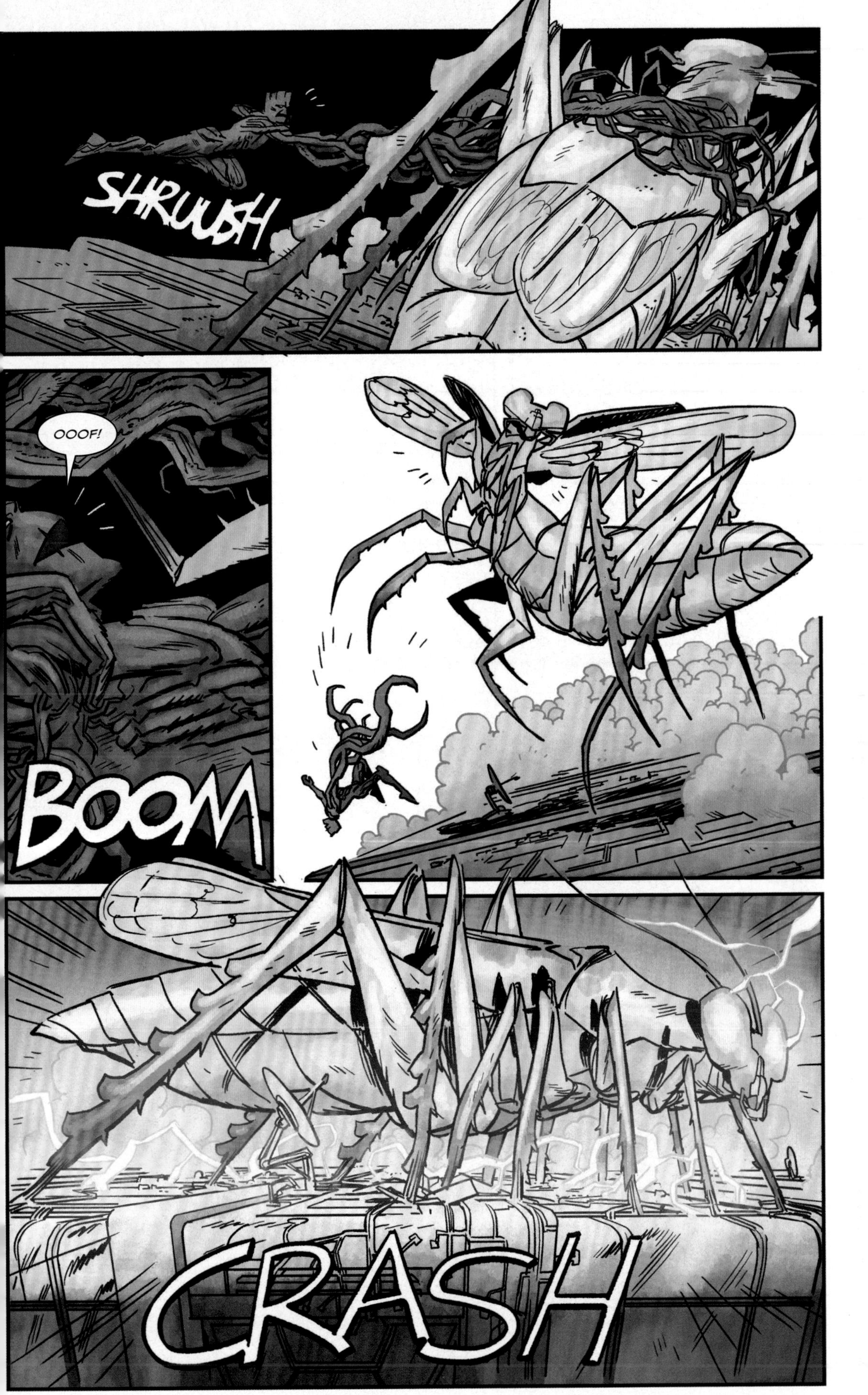
SHRUUSH
OOOF!
BOOM
CRASH

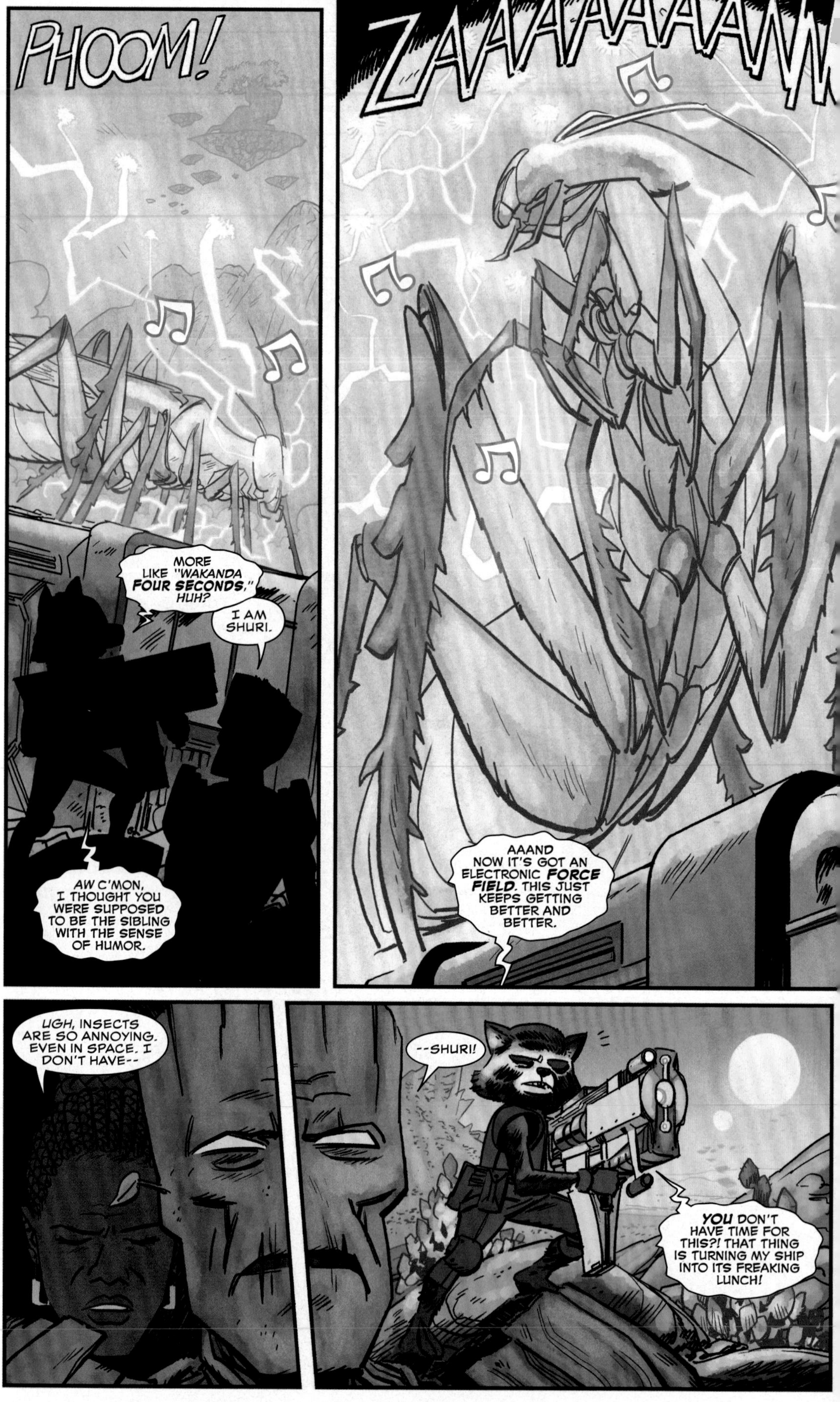
PHOOM!
MORE LIKE "WAKANDA FOUR SECONDS," HUH?
I AM SHURI.
AW C'MON, I THOUGHT YOU WERE SUPPOSED TO BE THE SIBLING WITH THE SENSE OF HUMOR.
ZAAAAAAAAAANN
AAAND NOW IT'S GOT AN ELECTRONIC FORCE FIELD. THIS JUST KEEPS GETTING BETTER AND BETTER.
UGH, INSECTS ARE SO ANNOYING. EVEN IN SPACE. I DON'T HAVE--
--SHURI!
YOU DON'T HAVE TIME FOR THIS?! THAT THING IS TURNING MY SHIP INTO ITS FREAKING LUNCH!

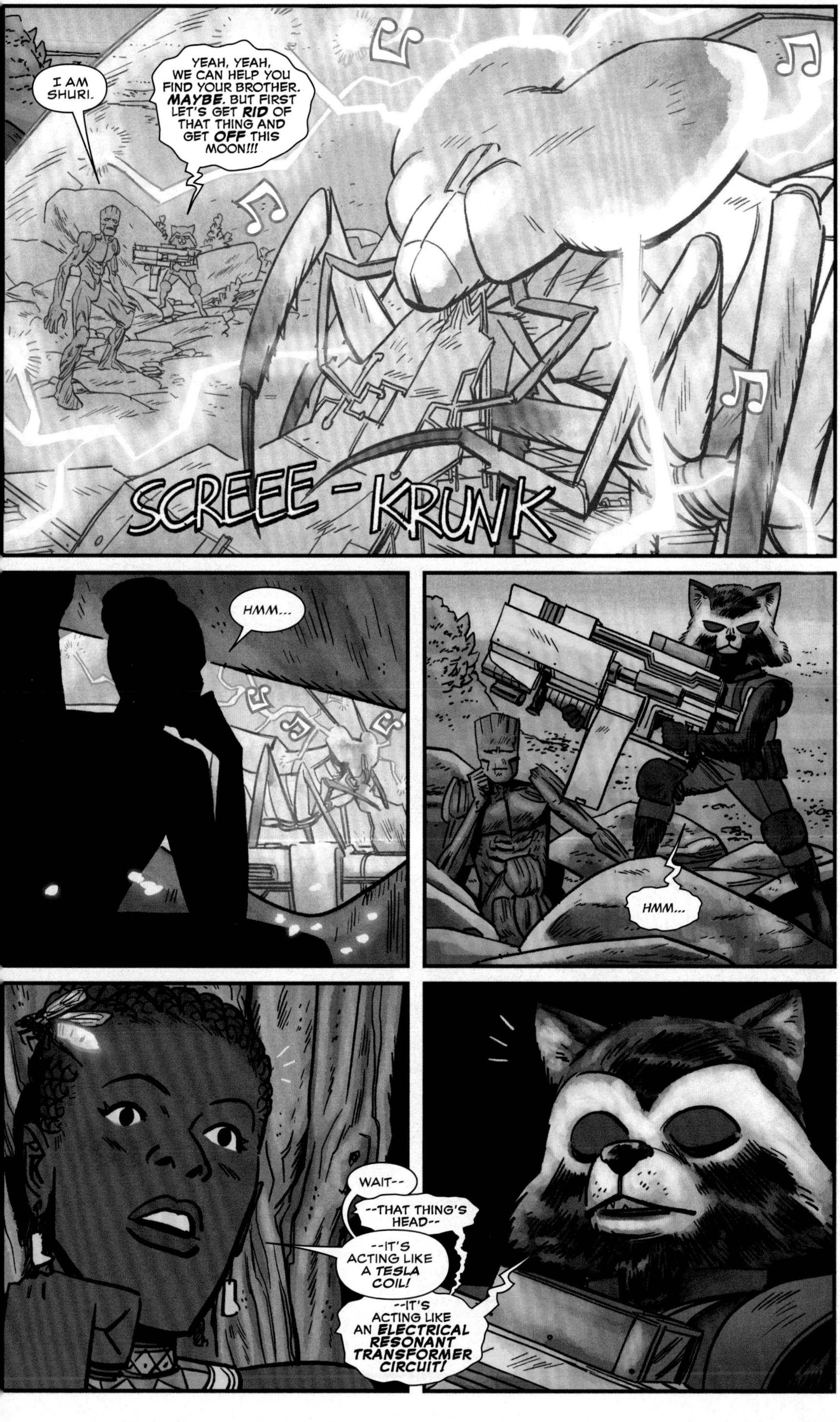
I AM SHURI.
YEAH, YEAH, WE CAN HELP YOU FIND YOUR BROTHER. MAYBE. BUT FIRST LET'S GET RID OF THAT THING AND GET OFF THIS MOON!!!
SCREEE-KRUNK
HMM...
HMM...
WAIT--
--THAT THING'S HEAD--
--IT'S ACTING LIKE A TESLA COIL!
--IT'S ACTING LIKE AN ELECTRICAL RESONANT TRANSFORMER CIRCUIT!

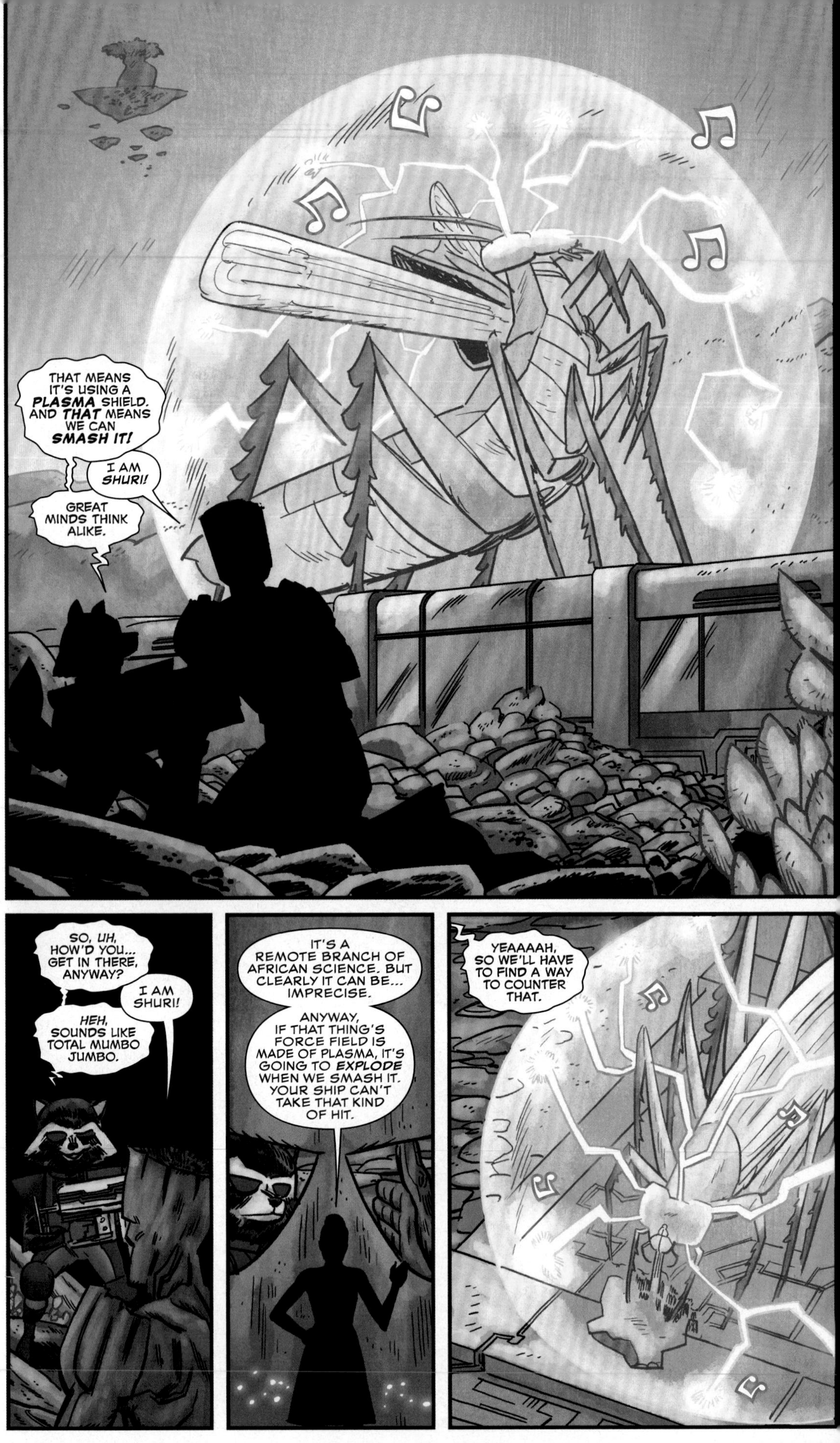
THAT MEANS IT'S USING A PLASMA SHIELD. AND THAT MEANS WE CAN SMASH IT!
I AM SHURI!
GREAT MINDS THINK ALIKE.
SO, UH, HOW'D YOU... GET IN THERE, ANYWAY?
I AM SHURI!
HEH, SOUNDS LIKE TOTAL MUMBO JUMBO.
IT'S A REMOTE BRANCH OF AFRICAN SCIENCE. BUT CLEARLY IT CAN BE... IMPRECISE.
ANYWAY, IF THAT THING'S FORCE FIELD IS MADE OF PLASMA, IT'S GOING TO EXPLODE WHEN WE SMASH IT. YOUR SHIP CAN'T TAKE THAT KIND OF HIT.
YEAAAAH, SO WE'LL HAVE TO FIND A WAY TO COUNTER THAT.

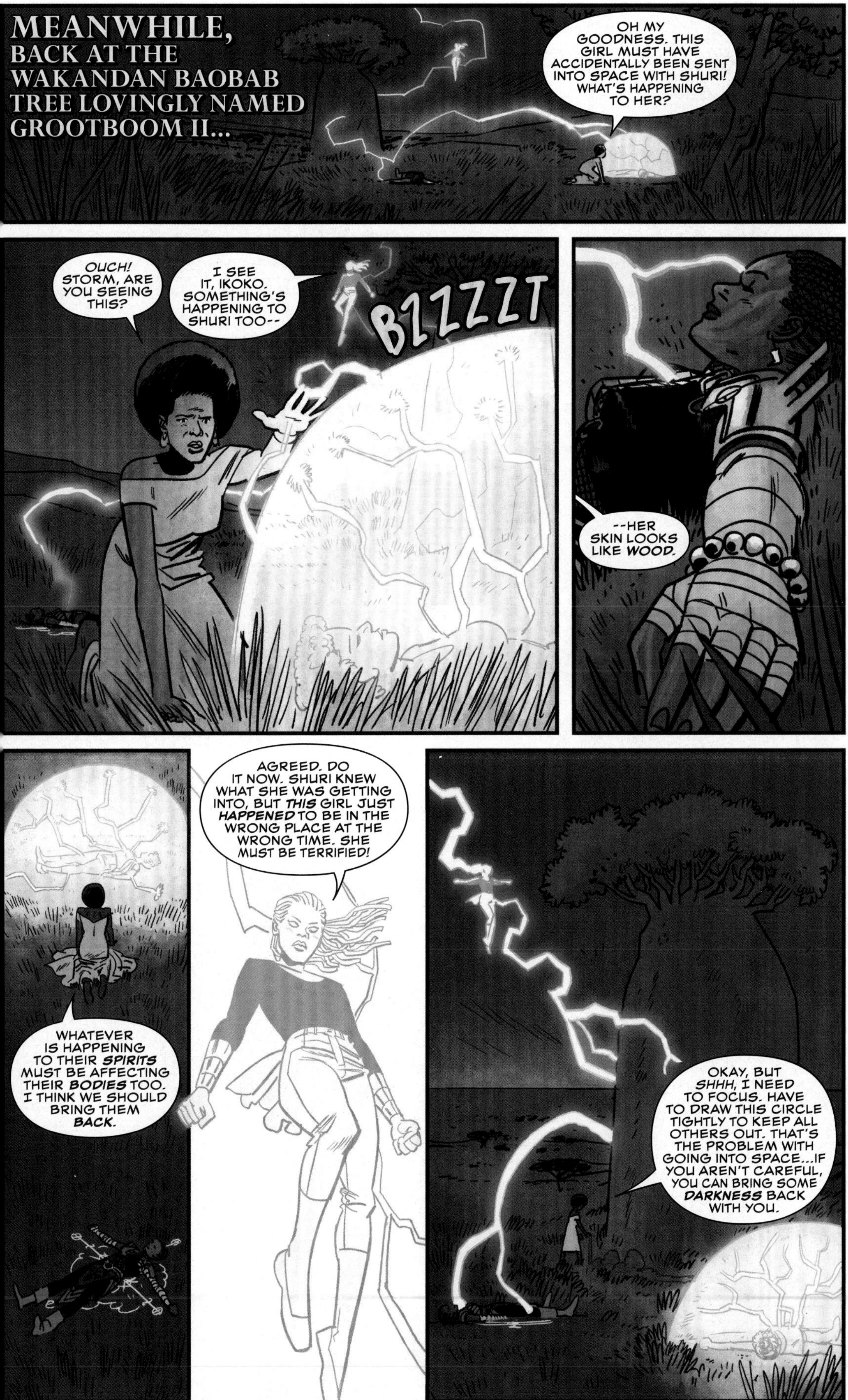
MEANWHILE, BACK AT THE WAKANDAN BAOBAB TREE LOVINGLY NAMED GROOTBOOM II...
OH MY GOODNESS. THIS GIRL MUST HAVE ACCIDENTALLY BEEN SENT INTO SPACE WITH SHURI! WHAT'S HAPPENING TO HER?
OUCH! STORM, ARE YOU SEEING THIS?
I SEE IT, IKOKO. SOMETHING'S HAPPENING TO SHURI TOO--
BZZZZT
--HER SKIN LOOKS LIKE WOOD.
WHATEVER IS HAPPENING TO THEIR SPIRITS MUST BE AFFECTING THEIR BODIES TOO. I THINK WE SHOULD BRING THEM BACK.
AGREED. DO IT NOW. SHURI KNEW WHAT SHE WAS GETTING INTO, BUT THIS GIRL JUST HAPPENED TO BE IN THE WRONG PLACE AT THE WRONG TIME. SHE MUST BE TERRIFIED!
OKAY, BUT SHHH, I NEED TO FOCUS. HAVE TO DRAW THIS CIRCLE TIGHTLY TO KEEP ALL OTHERS OUT. THAT'S THE PROBLEM WITH GOING INTO SPACE...IF YOU AREN'T CAREFUL, YOU CAN BRING SOME DARKNESS BACK WITH YOU.

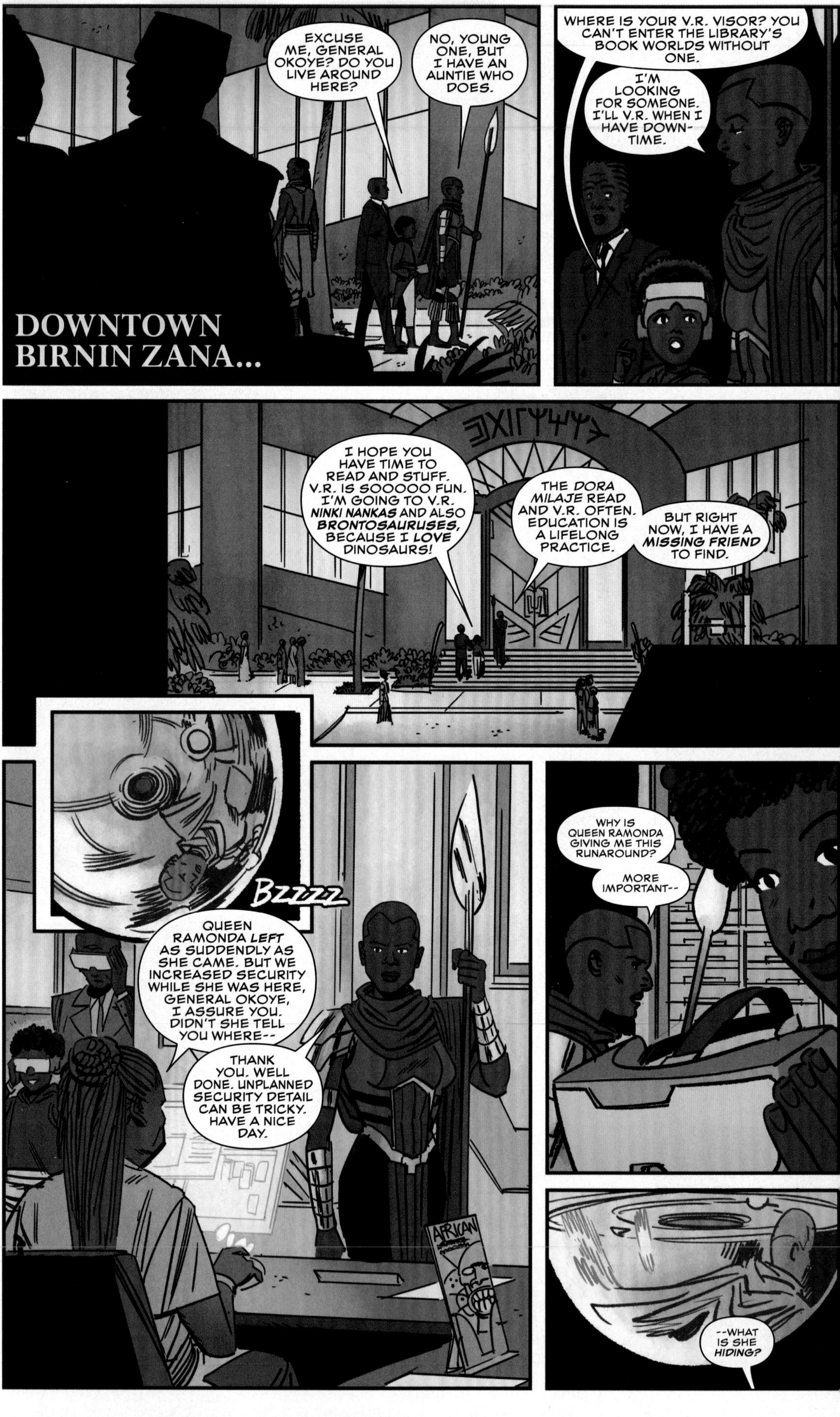
DOWNTOWN BIRNIN ZANA...
EXCUSE ME, GENERAL OKOYE? DO YOU LIVE AROUND HERE?
NO, YOUNG ONE, BUT I HAVE AN AUNTIE WHO DOES.
WHERE IS YOUR V.R. VISOR? YOU CAN'T ENTER THE LIBRARY'S BOOK WORLDS WITHOUT ONE.
I'M LOOKING FOR SOMEONE. I'LL V.R. WHEN I HAVE DOWN-TIME.
I HOPE YOU HAVE TIME TO READ AND STUFF. V.R. IS SOOOOO FUN. I'M GOING TO V.R. NINKI NANKAS AND ALSO BRONTOSAURUSES, BECAUSE I LOVE DINOSAURS!
THE DORA MILAJE READ AND V.R. OFTEN. EDUCATION IS A LIFELONG PRACTICE.
BUT RIGHT NOW, I HAVE A MISSING FRIEND TO FIND.
BZZZZZ
QUEEN RAMONDA LEFT AS SUDDENLY AS SHE CAME. BUT WE INCREASED SECURITY WHILE SHE WAS HERE, GENERAL OKOYE, I ASSURE YOU. DIDN'T SHE TELL YOU WHERE--
THANK YOU. WELL DONE. UNPLANNED SECURITY DETAIL CAN BE TRICKY. HAVE A NICE DAY.
AFRICAN
WHY IS QUEEN RAMONDA GIVING ME THIS RUNAROUND?
MORE IMPORTANT--
--WHAT IS SHE HIDING?

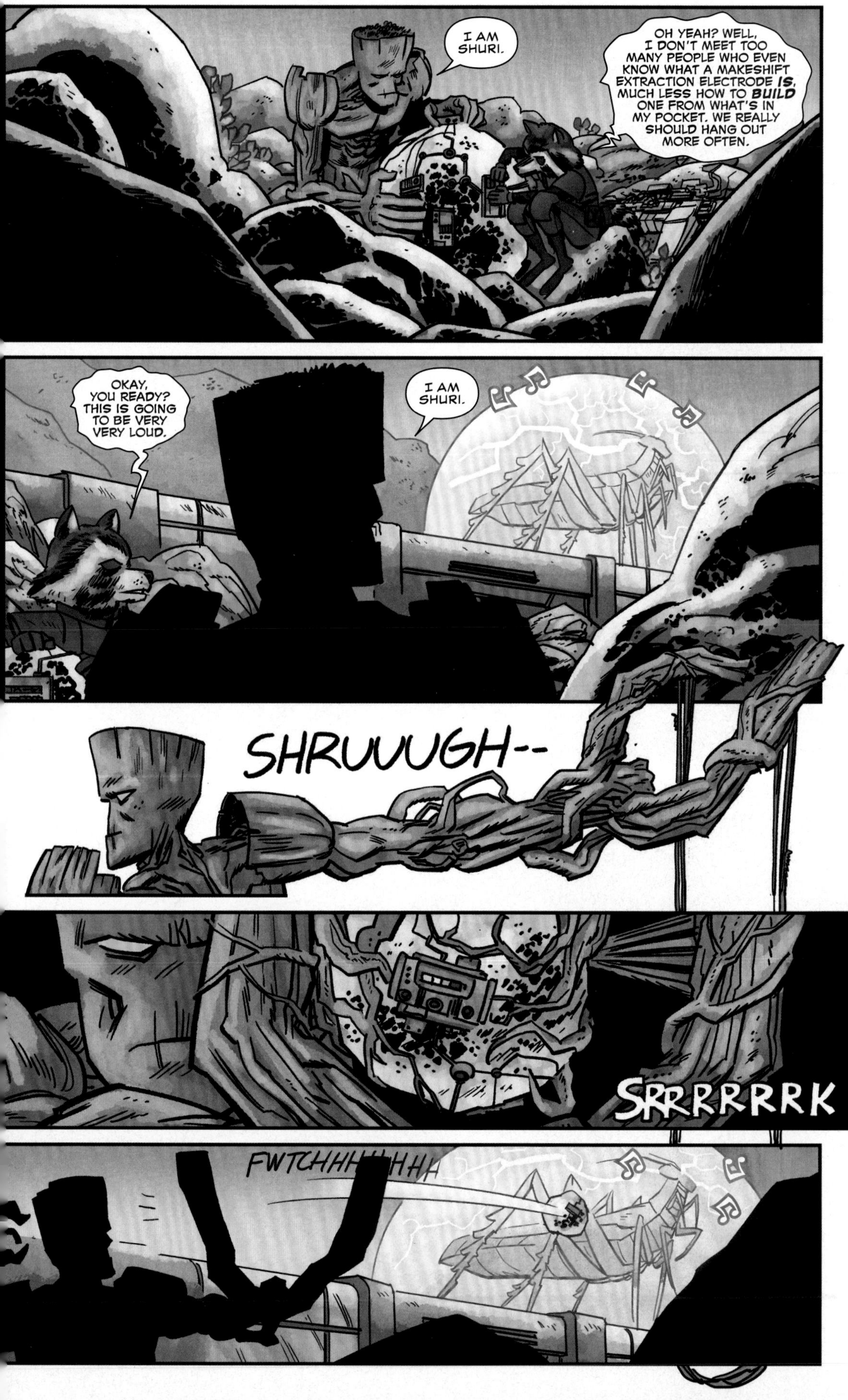
I AM SHURI.
OH YEAH? WELL, I DON'T MEET TOO MANY PEOPLE WHO EVEN KNOW WHAT A MAKESHIFT EXTRACTION ELECTRODE IS, MUCH LESS HOW TO BUILD ONE FROM WHAT'S IN MY POCKET. WE REALLY SHOULD HANG OUT MORE OFTEN.
OKAY, YOU READY? THIS IS GOING TO BE VERY VERY LOUD.
I AM SHURI.
SHRUUUGH--
SRRRRRRK
FWTCHHHHHHHH

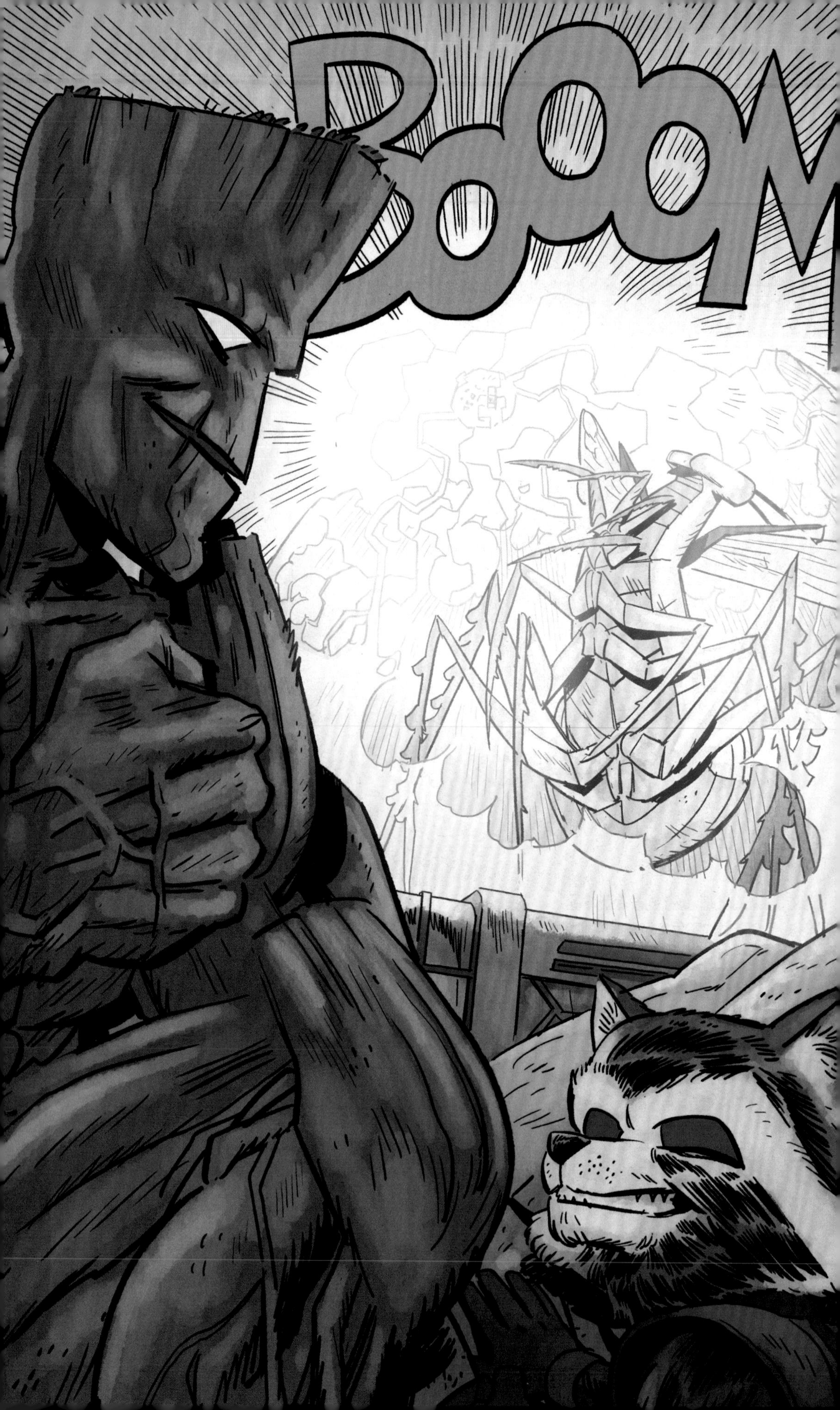
BOOOM

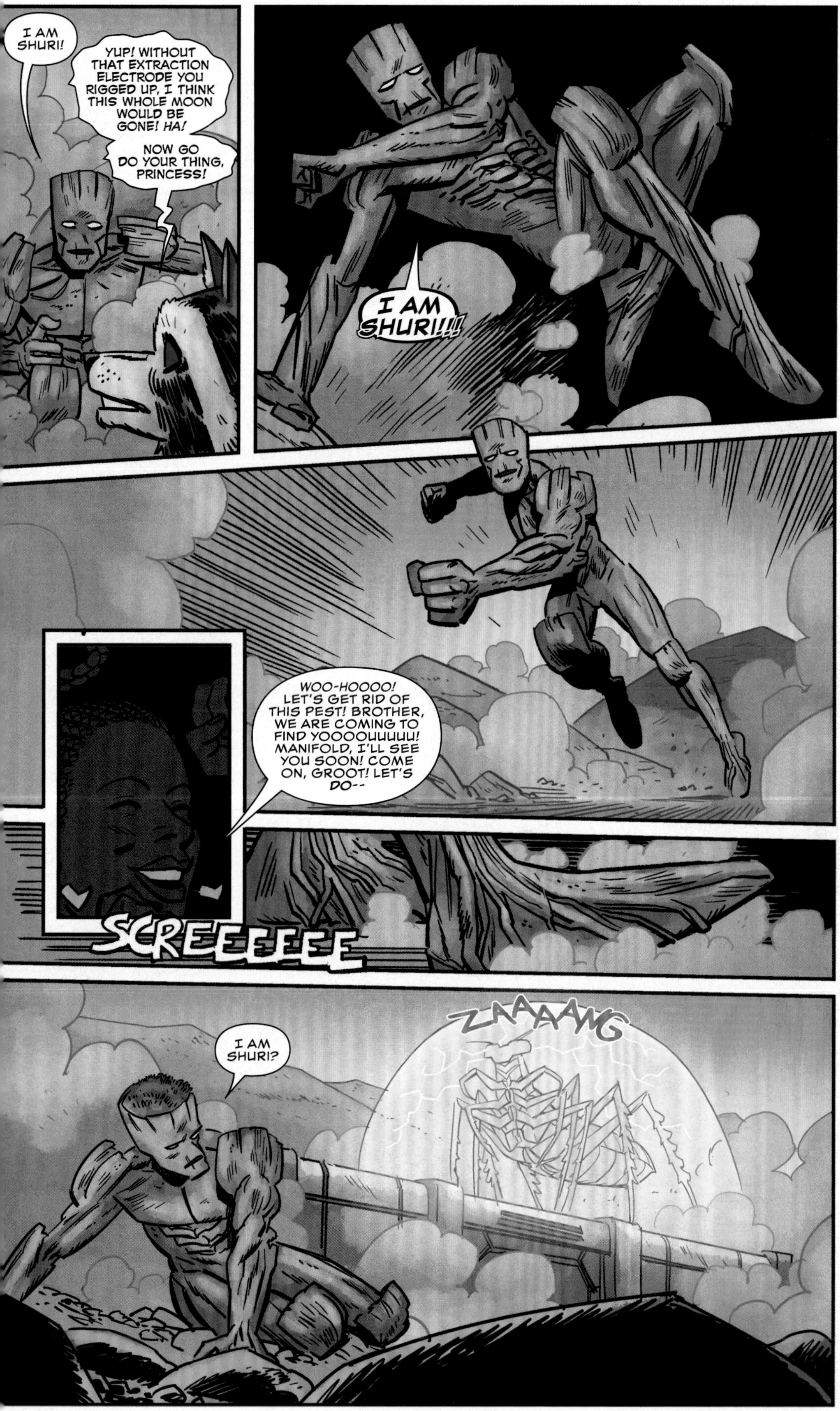

I AM SHURI!
YUP! WITHOUT THAT EXTRACTION ELECTRODE YOU RIGGED UP, I THINK THIS WHOLE MOON WOULD BE GONE! HA!
NOW GO DO YOUR THING, PRINCESS!
I AM SHURI!!!
WOO-HOOOO! LET'S GET RID OF THIS PEST! BROTHER, WE ARE COMING TO FIND YOOOOUUUUU! MANIFOLD, I'LL SEE YOU SOON! COME ON, GROOT! LET'S DO--
SCREEEEEEE
ZAAAANG
I AM SHURI?

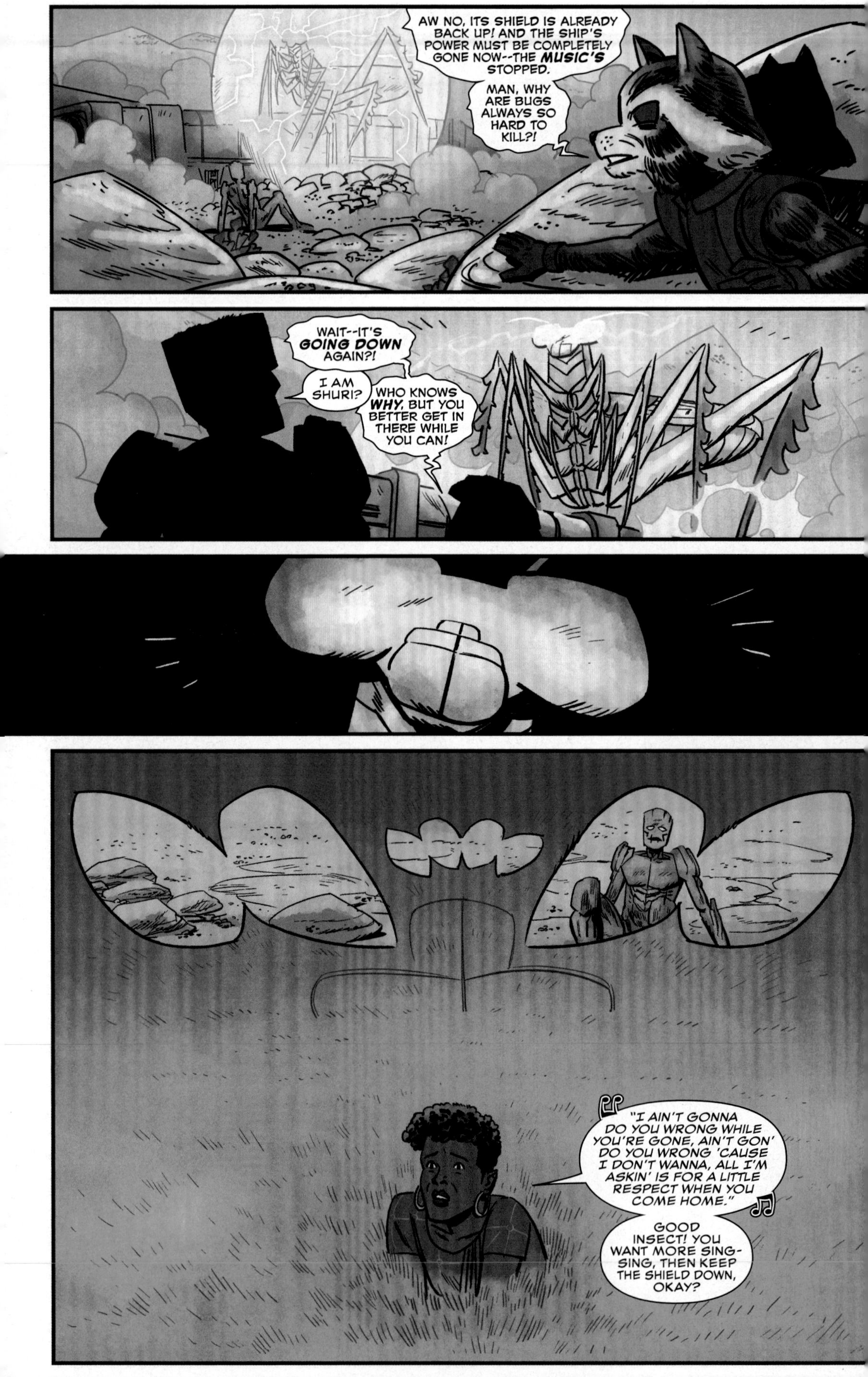

AW NO, ITS SHIELD IS ALREADY BACK UP! AND THE SHIP'S POWER MUST BE COMPLETELY GONE NOW--THE MUSIC'S STOPPED.
MAN, WHY ARE BUGS ALWAYS SO HARD TO KILL?!
WAIT--IT'S GOING DOWN AGAIN?!
I AM SHURI?
WHO KNOWS WHY, BUT YOU BETTER GET IN THERE WHILE YOU CAN!
"I AIN'T GONNA DO YOU WRONG WHILE YOU'RE GONE, AIN'T GON' DO YOU WRONG 'CAUSE I DON'T WANNA, ALL I'M ASKIN' IS FOR A LITTLE RESPECT WHEN YOU COME HOME."
GOOD INSECT! YOU WANT MORE SING-SING, THEN KEEP THE SHIELD DOWN, OKAY?

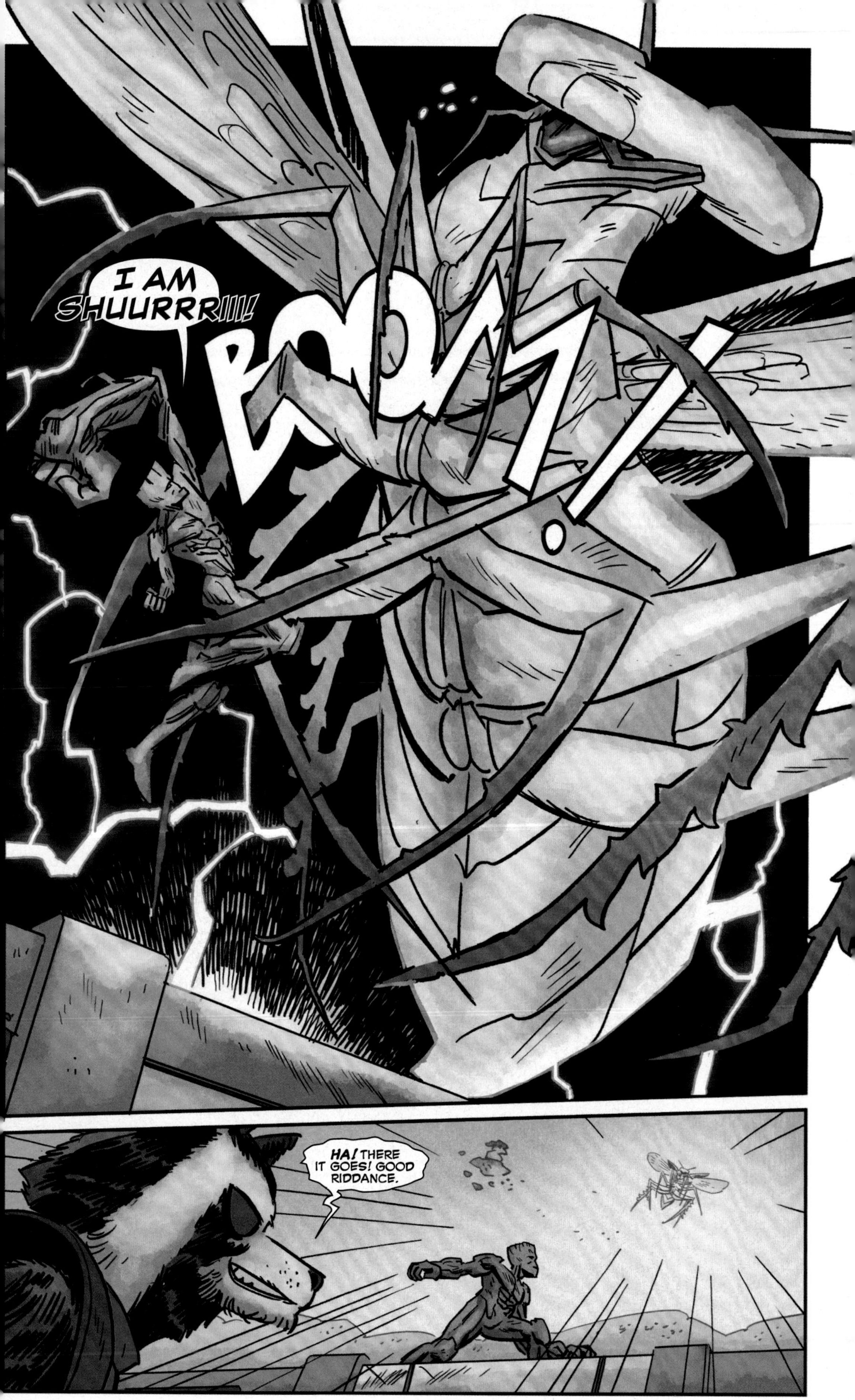
I AM SHUURRRIIII!
BOOM!
HA! THERE IT GOES! GOOD RIDDANCE.

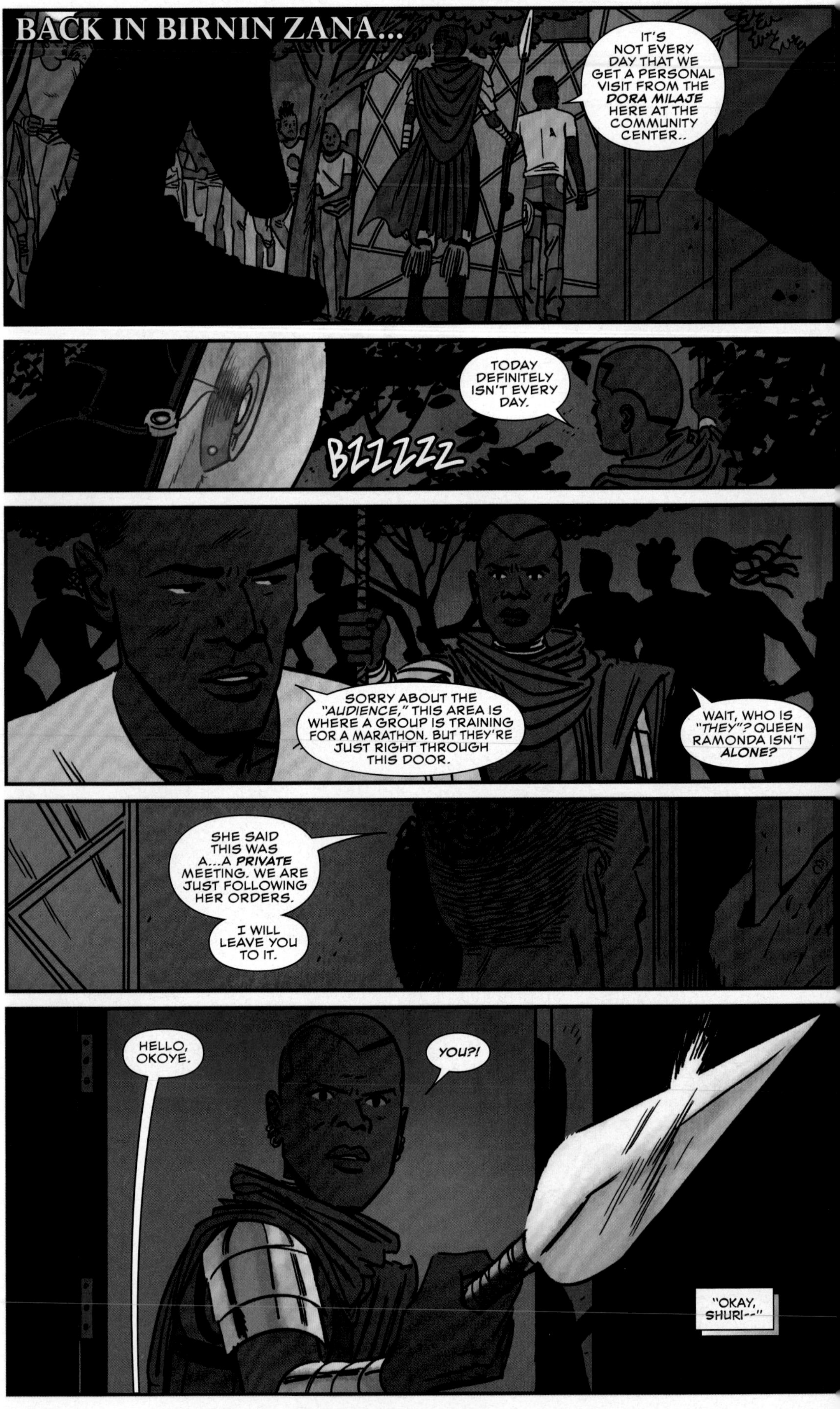
BACK IN BIRNIN ZANA...
IT'S NOT EVERY DAY THAT WE GET A PERSONAL VISIT FROM THE DORA MILAJE HERE AT THE COMMUNITY CENTER..
TODAY DEFINITELY ISN'T EVERY DAY.
BZZZZZ
SORRY ABOUT THE "AUDIENCE," THIS AREA IS WHERE A GROUP IS TRAINING FOR A MARATHON. BUT THEY'RE JUST RIGHT THROUGH THIS DOOR.
WAIT, WHO IS "THEY"? QUEEN RAMONDA ISN'T ALONE?
SHE SAID THIS WAS A...A PRIVATE MEETING. WE ARE JUST FOLLOWING HER ORDERS.
I WILL LEAVE YOU TO IT.
HELLO, OKOYE.
YOU?!
"OKAY, SHURI--"

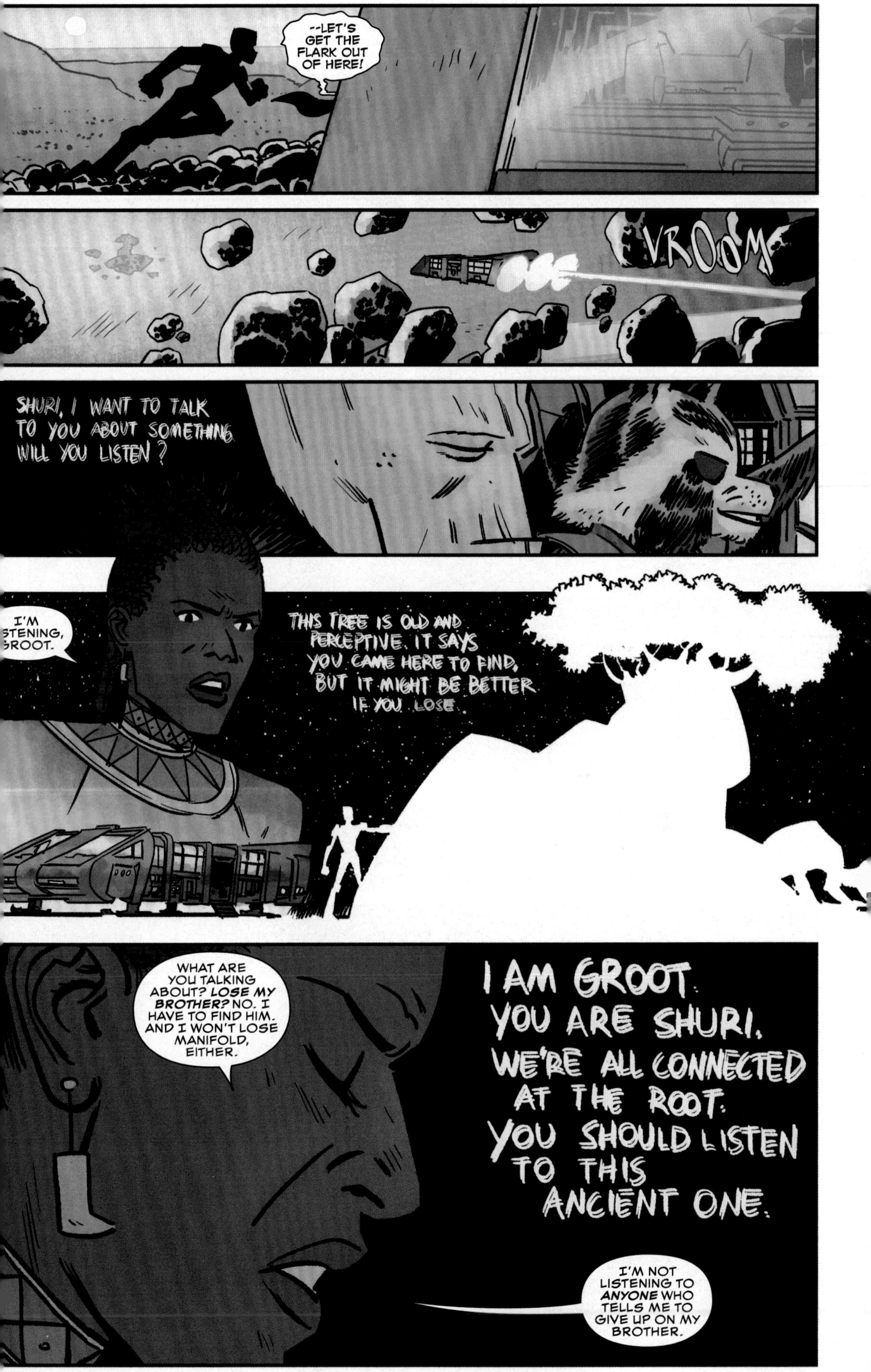
--LET'S GET THE FLARK OUT OF HERE!
VROOM
SHURI, I WANT TO TALK TO YOU ABOUT SOMETHING. WILL YOU LISTEN?
I'M LISTENING, GROOT.
THIS TREE IS OLD AND PERCEPTIVE. IT SAYS YOU CAME HERE TO FIND, BUT IT MIGHT BE BETTER IF YOU... LOSE.
WHAT ARE YOU TALKING ABOUT? LOSE MY BROTHER? NO. I HAVE TO FIND HIM. AND I WON'T LOSE MANIFOLD, EITHER.
I AM GROOT. YOU ARE SHURI. WE'RE ALL CONNECTED AT THE ROOT. YOU SHOULD LISTEN TO THIS ANCIENT ONE.
I'M NOT LISTENING TO ANYONE WHO TELLS ME TO GIVE UP ON MY BROTHER.

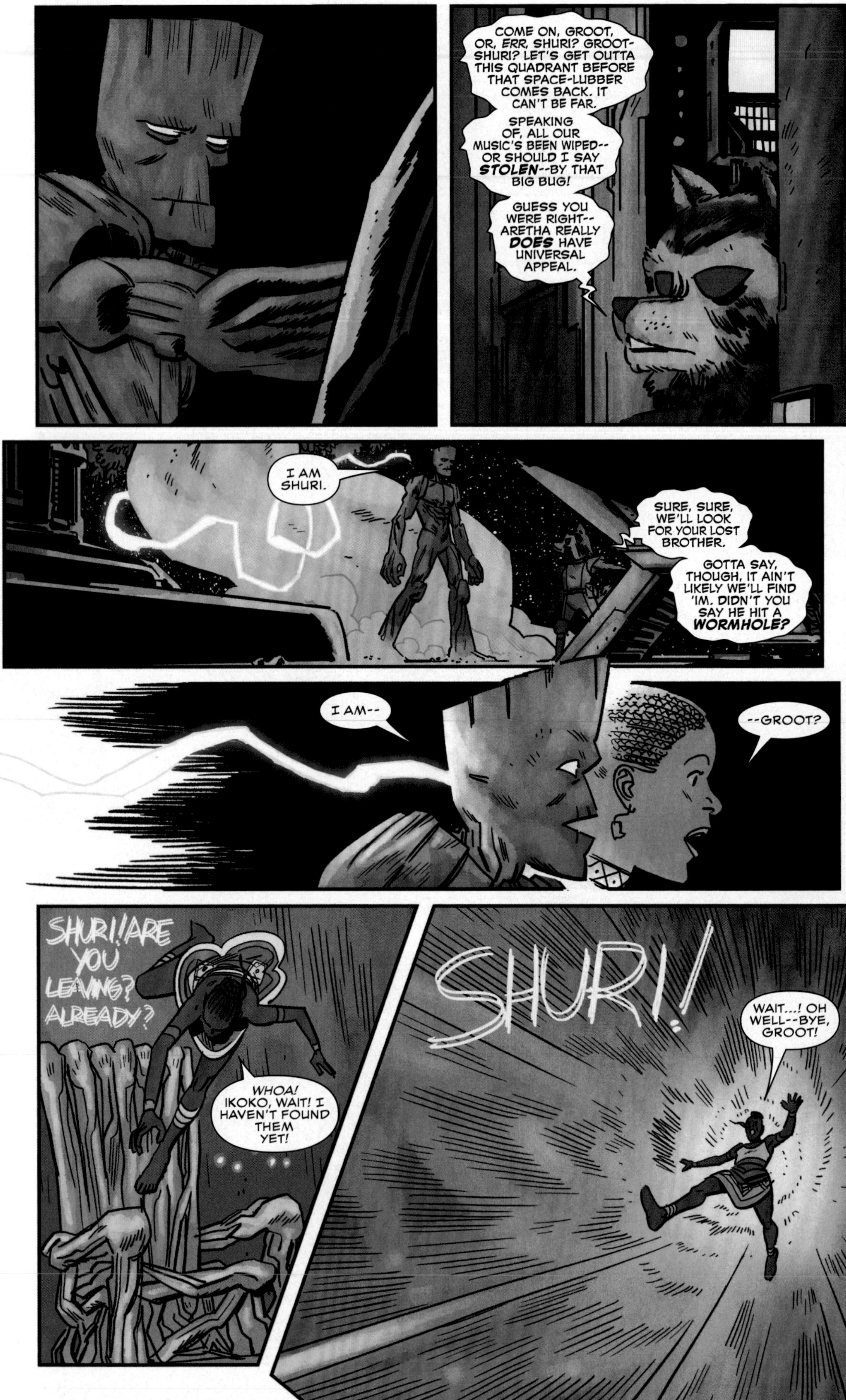
COME ON, GROOT, OR, ERR, SHURI? GROOT-SHURI? LET'S GET OUTTA THIS QUADRANT BEFORE THAT SPACE-LUBBER COMES BACK. IT CAN'T BE FAR.
SPEAKING OF, ALL OUR MUSIC'S BEEN WIPED--OR SHOULD I SAY STOLEN--BY THAT BIG BUG!
GUESS YOU WERE RIGHT--ARETHA REALLY DOES HAVE UNIVERSAL APPEAL.
I AM SHURI.
SURE, SURE, WE'LL LOOK FOR YOUR LOST BROTHER.
GOTTA SAY, THOUGH, IT AIN'T LIKELY WE'LL FIND 'IM. DIDN'T YOU SAY HE HIT A WORMHOLE?
I AM--
--GROOT?
SHURI! ARE YOU LEAVING? ALREADY?
WHOA! IKOKO, WAIT! I HAVEN'T FOUND THEM YET!
SHURI!
WAIT...! OH WELL--BYE, GROOT!

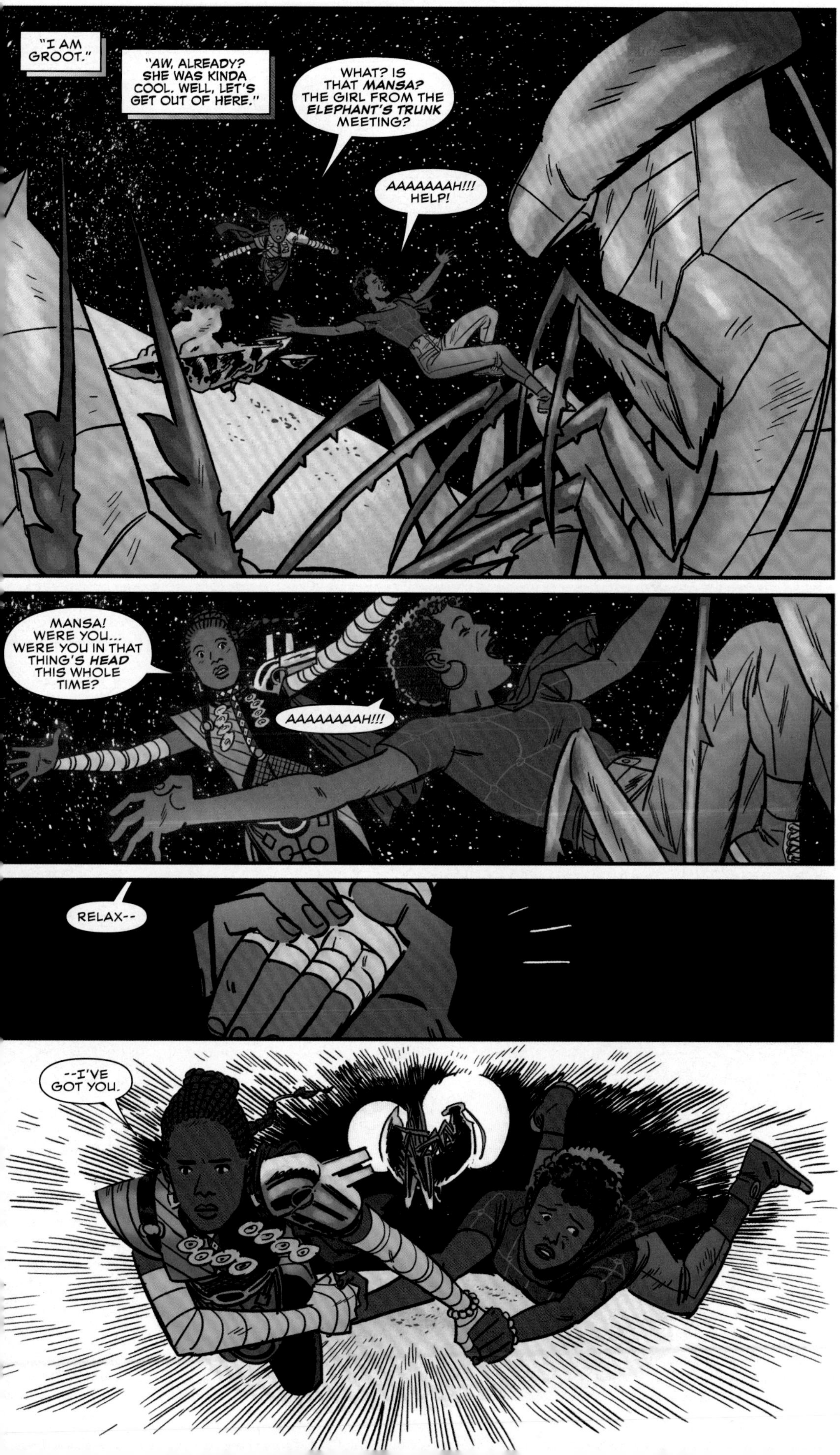
"I AM GROOT."
"AW, ALREADY? SHE WAS KINDA COOL. WELL, LET'S GET OUT OF HERE."
WHAT? IS THAT MANSA? THE GIRL FROM THE ELEPHANT'S TRUNK MEETING?
AAAAAAAH!!! HELP!
MANSA! WERE YOU... WERE YOU IN THAT THING'S HEAD THIS WHOLE TIME?
AAAAAAAAH!!!
RELAX--
--I'VE GOT YOU.

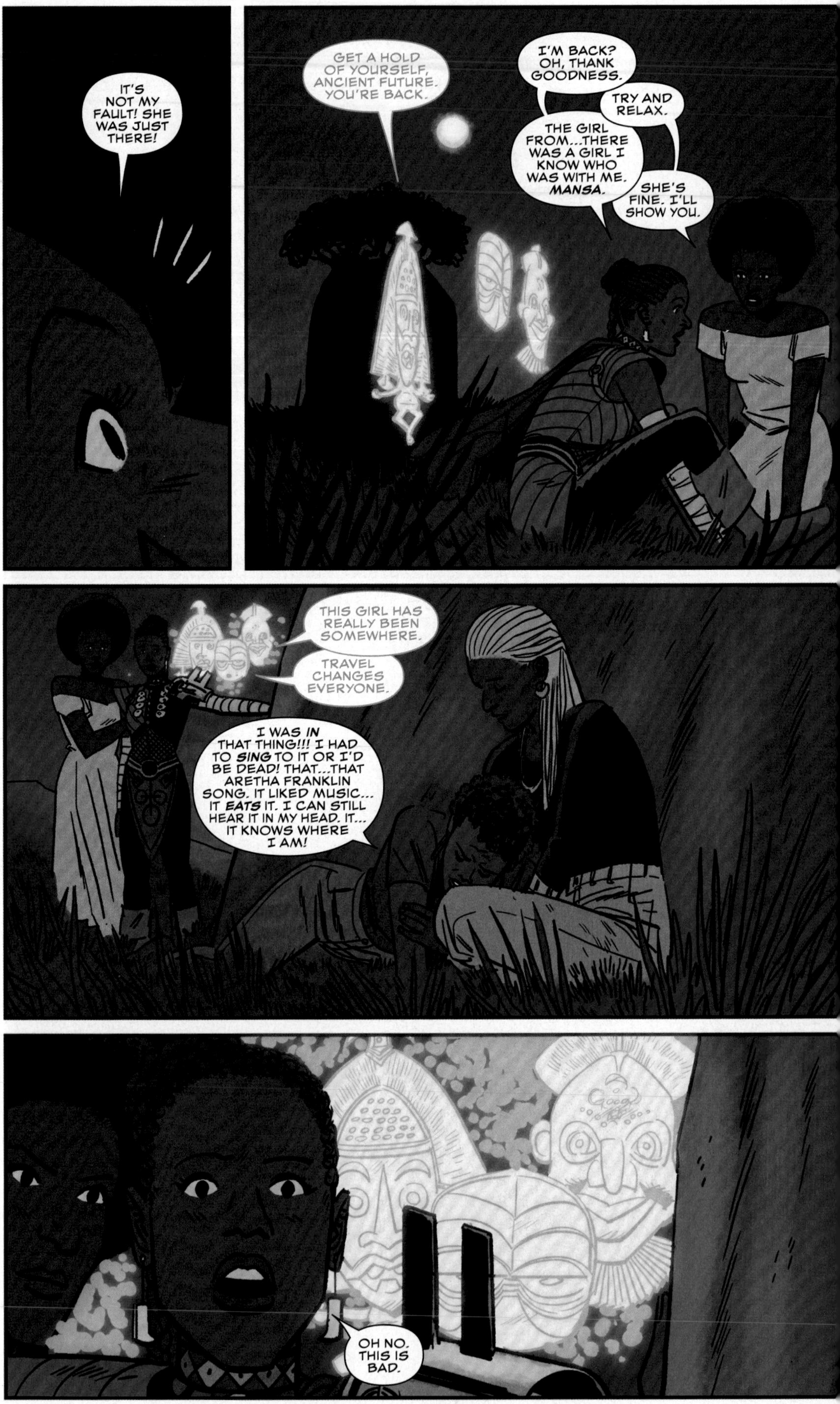

IT'S NOT MY FAULT! SHE WAS JUST THERE!
GET A HOLD OF YOURSELF, ANCIENT FUTURE. YOU'RE BACK.
I'M BACK? OH, THANK GOODNESS.
TRY AND RELAX.
THE GIRL FROM...THERE WAS A GIRL I KNOW WHO WAS WITH ME. MANSA.
SHE'S FINE. I'LL SHOW YOU.
THIS GIRL HAS REALLY BEEN SOMEWHERE.
TRAVEL CHANGES EVERYONE.
I WAS IN THAT THING!!! I HAD TO SING TO IT OR I'D BE DEAD! THAT...THAT ARETHA FRANKLIN SONG. IT LIKED MUSIC... IT EATS IT. I CAN STILL HEAR IT IN MY HEAD. IT... IT KNOWS WHERE I AM!
OH NO. THIS IS BAD.

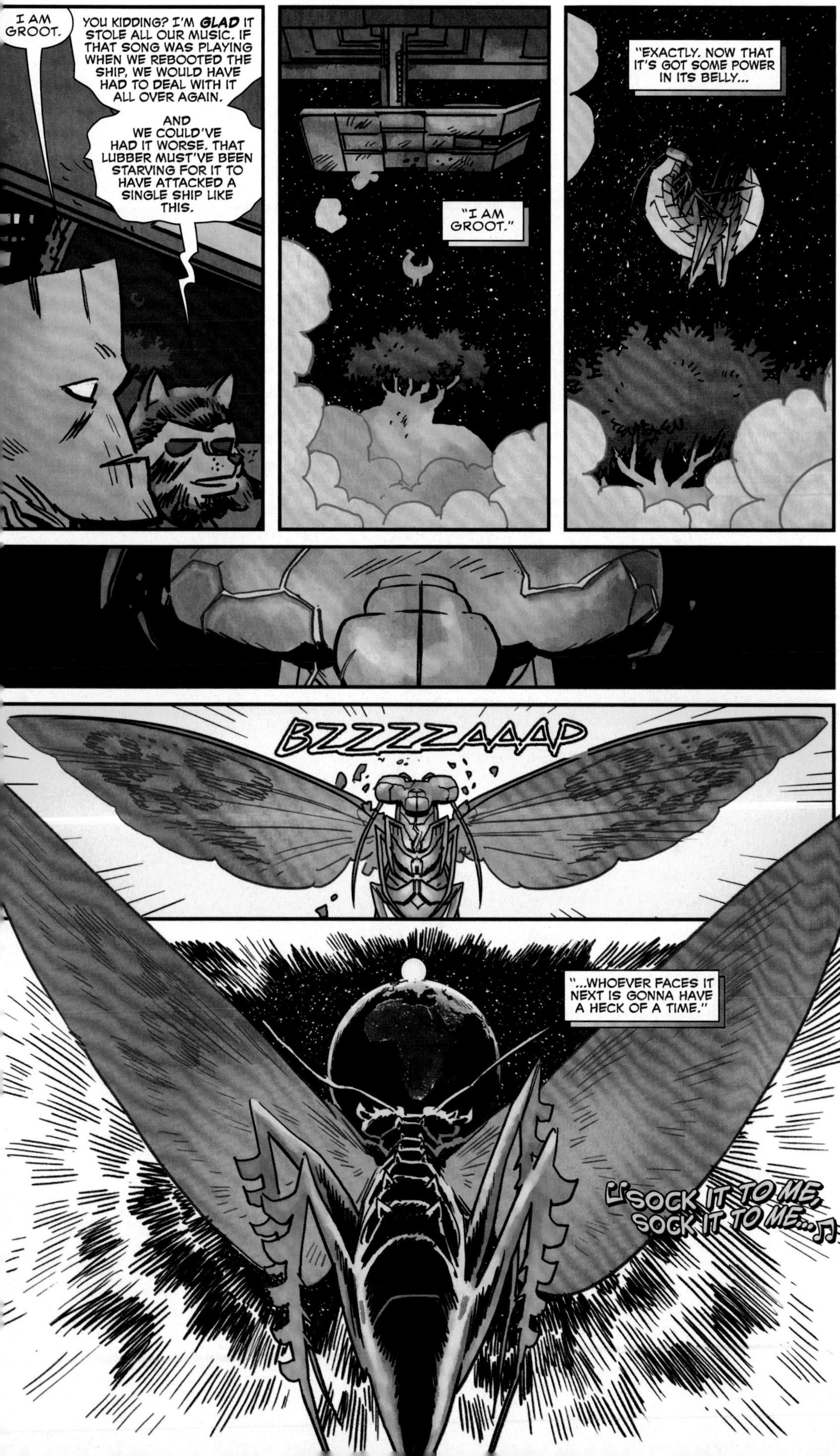
I AM GROOT.
YOU KIDDING? I'M *GLAD* IT STOLE ALL OUR MUSIC. IF THAT SONG WAS PLAYING WHEN WE REBOOTED THE SHIP, WE WOULD HAVE HAD TO DEAL WITH IT ALL OVER AGAIN.
AND WE COULD'VE HAD IT WORSE. THAT LUBBER MUST'VE BEEN STARVING FOR IT TO HAVE ATTACKED A SINGLE SHIP LIKE THIS.
"I AM GROOT."
"EXACTLY. NOW THAT IT'S GOT SOME POWER IN ITS BELLY...
BZZZZZAAAAP
"...WHOEVER FACES IT NEXT IS GONNA HAVE A HECK OF A TIME."
♫SOCK IT TO ME, SOCK IT TO ME...♫

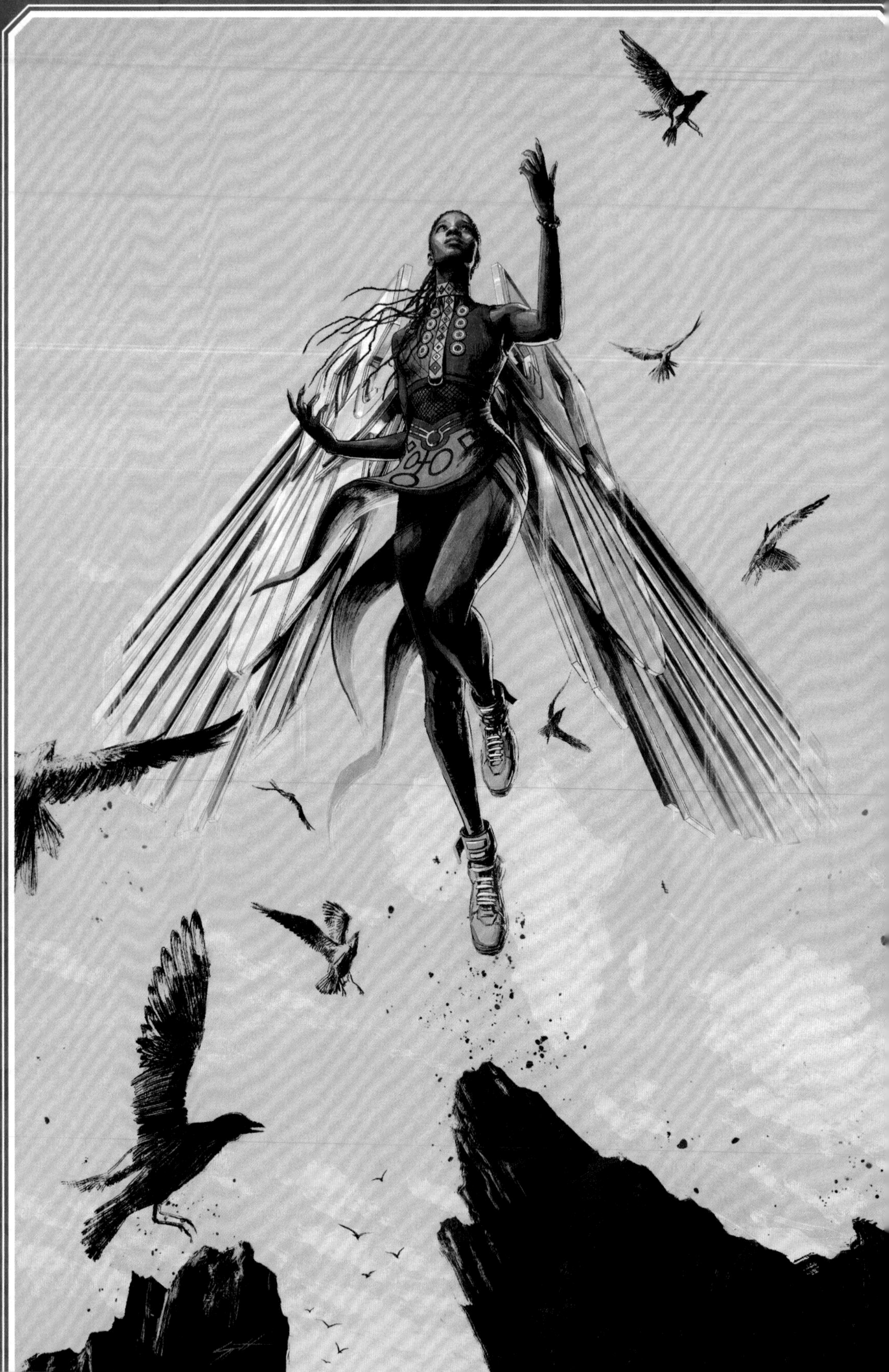

4 – TIMBUKTU

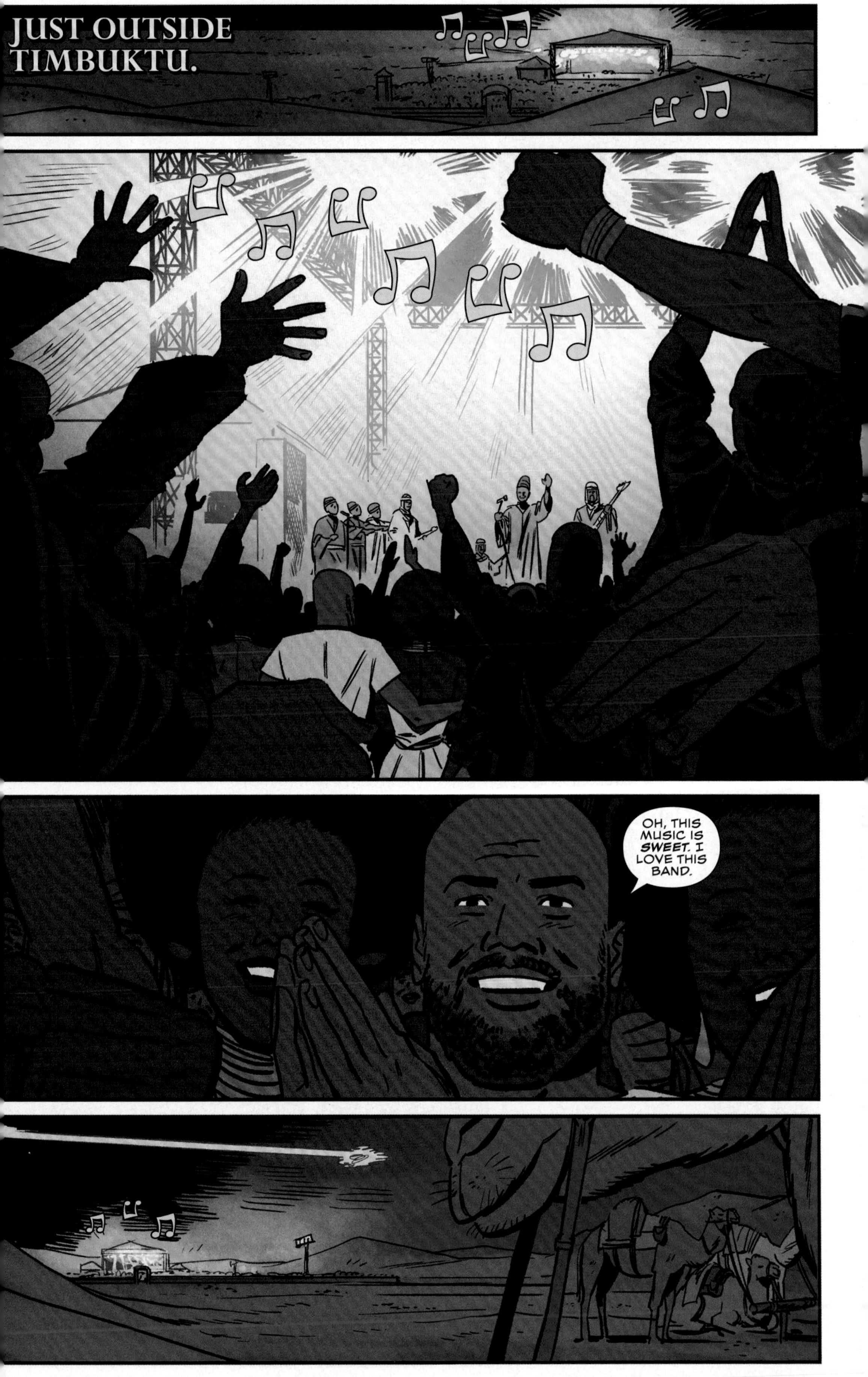
JUST OUTSIDE TIMBUKTU.
OH, THIS MUSIC IS SWEET. I LOVE THIS BAND.

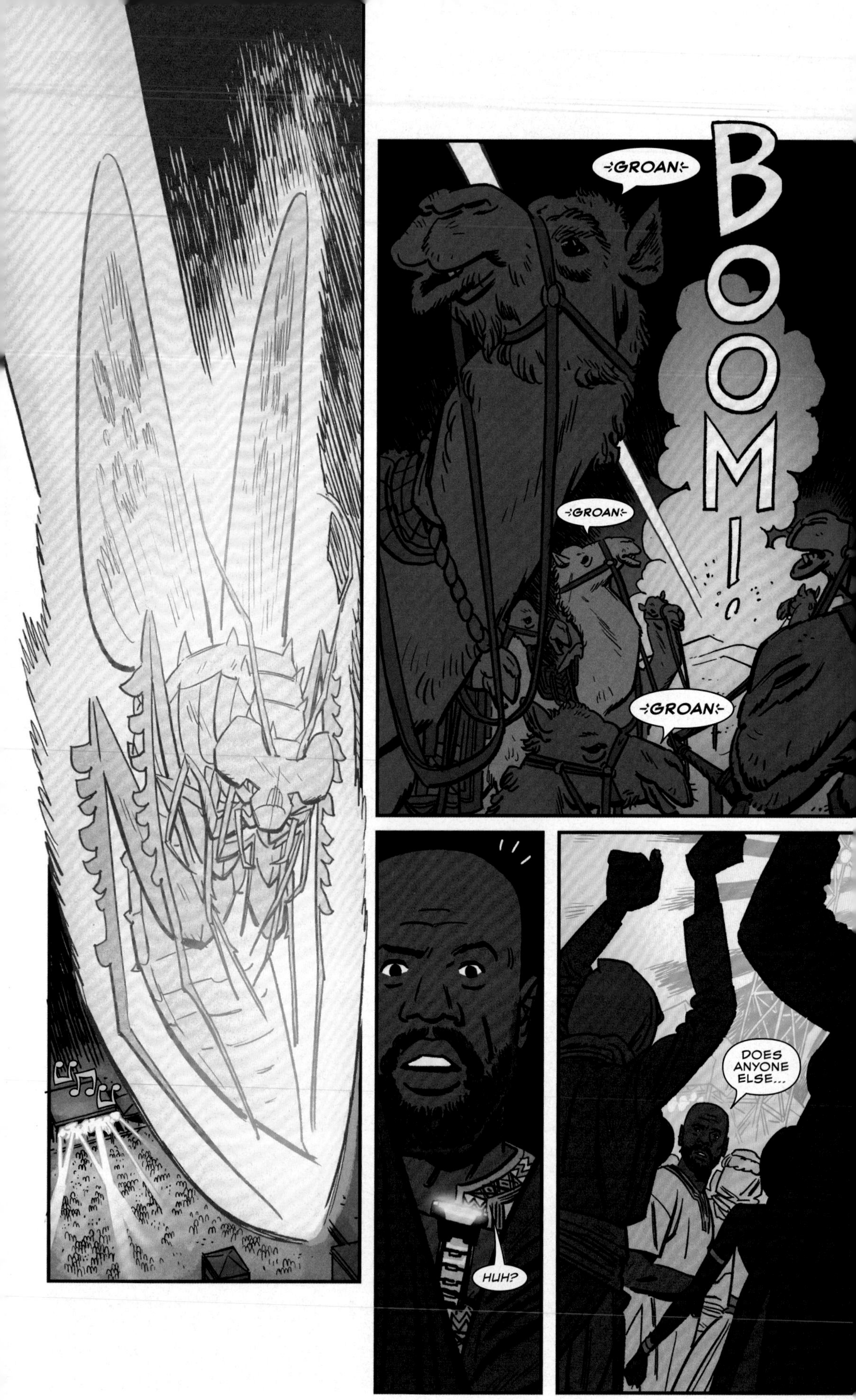

-GROAN-
BOOM!
-GROAN-
-GROAN-
HUH?
DOES ANYONE ELSE...

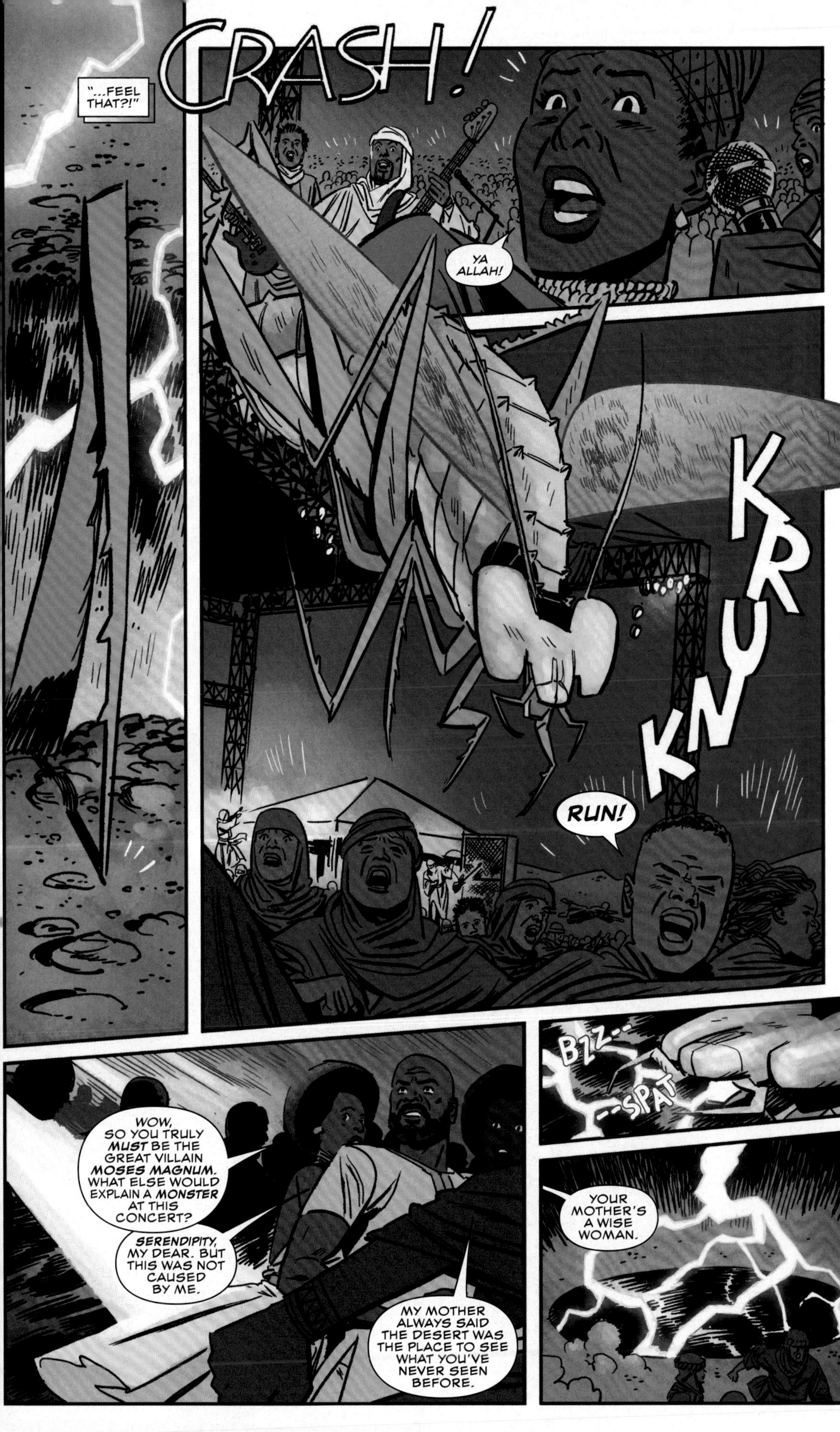

CRASH!
"...FEEL THAT?!"
YA ALLAH!
KRUNK
RUN!
WOW, SO YOU TRULY MUST BE THE GREAT VILLAIN MOSES MAGNUM. WHAT ELSE WOULD EXPLAIN A MONSTER AT THIS CONCERT?
SERENDIPITY, MY DEAR. BUT THIS WAS NOT CAUSED BY ME.
MY MOTHER ALWAYS SAID THE DESERT WAS THE PLACE TO SEE WHAT YOU'VE NEVER SEEN BEFORE.
BZZ--
--SPAT
YOUR MOTHER'S A WISE WOMAN.

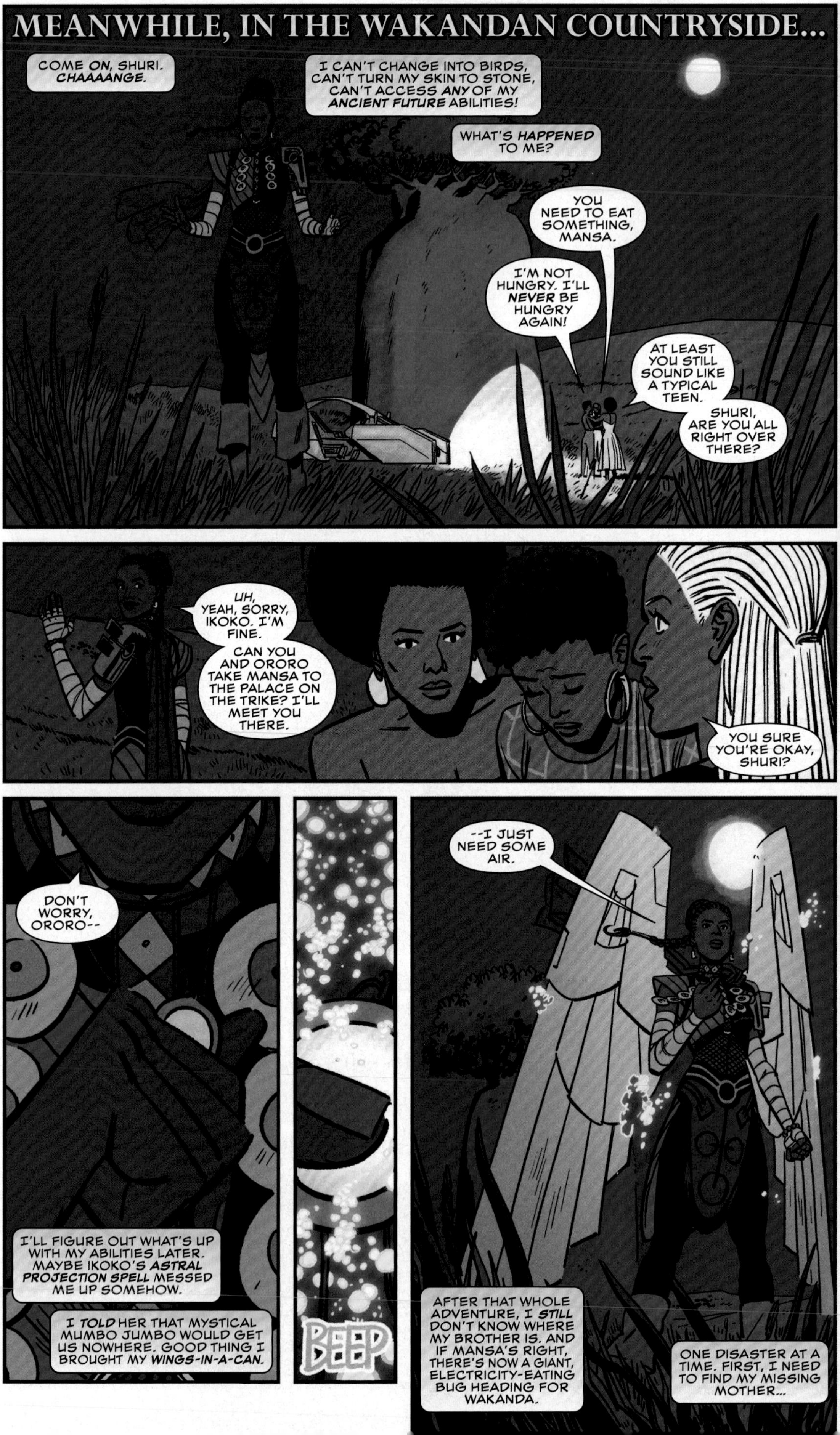
MEANWHILE, IN THE WAKANDAN COUNTRYSIDE...
COME ON, SHURI. CHAAAANGE.
I CAN'T CHANGE INTO BIRDS, CAN'T TURN MY SKIN TO STONE, CAN'T ACCESS ANY OF MY ANCIENT FUTURE ABILITIES!
WHAT'S HAPPENED TO ME?
YOU NEED TO EAT SOMETHING, MANSA.
I'M NOT HUNGRY. I'LL NEVER BE HUNGRY AGAIN!
AT LEAST YOU STILL SOUND LIKE A TYPICAL TEEN.
SHURI, ARE YOU ALL RIGHT OVER THERE?
UH, YEAH, SORRY, IKOKO. I'M FINE.
CAN YOU AND ORORO TAKE MANSA TO THE PALACE ON THE TRIKE? I'LL MEET YOU THERE.
YOU SURE YOU'RE OKAY, SHURI?
DON'T WORRY, ORORO--
I'LL FIGURE OUT WHAT'S UP WITH MY ABILITIES LATER. MAYBE IKOKO'S ASTRAL PROJECTION SPELL MESSED ME UP SOMEHOW.
I TOLD HER THAT MYSTICAL MUMBO JUMBO WOULD GET US NOWHERE. GOOD THING I BROUGHT MY WINGS-IN-A-CAN.
BEEP
--I JUST NEED SOME AIR.
AFTER THAT WHOLE ADVENTURE, I STILL DON'T KNOW WHERE MY BROTHER IS. AND IF MANSA'S RIGHT, THERE'S NOW A GIANT, ELECTRICITY-EATING BUG HEADING FOR WAKANDA.
ONE DISASTER AT A TIME. FIRST, I NEED TO FIND MY MISSING MOTHER...

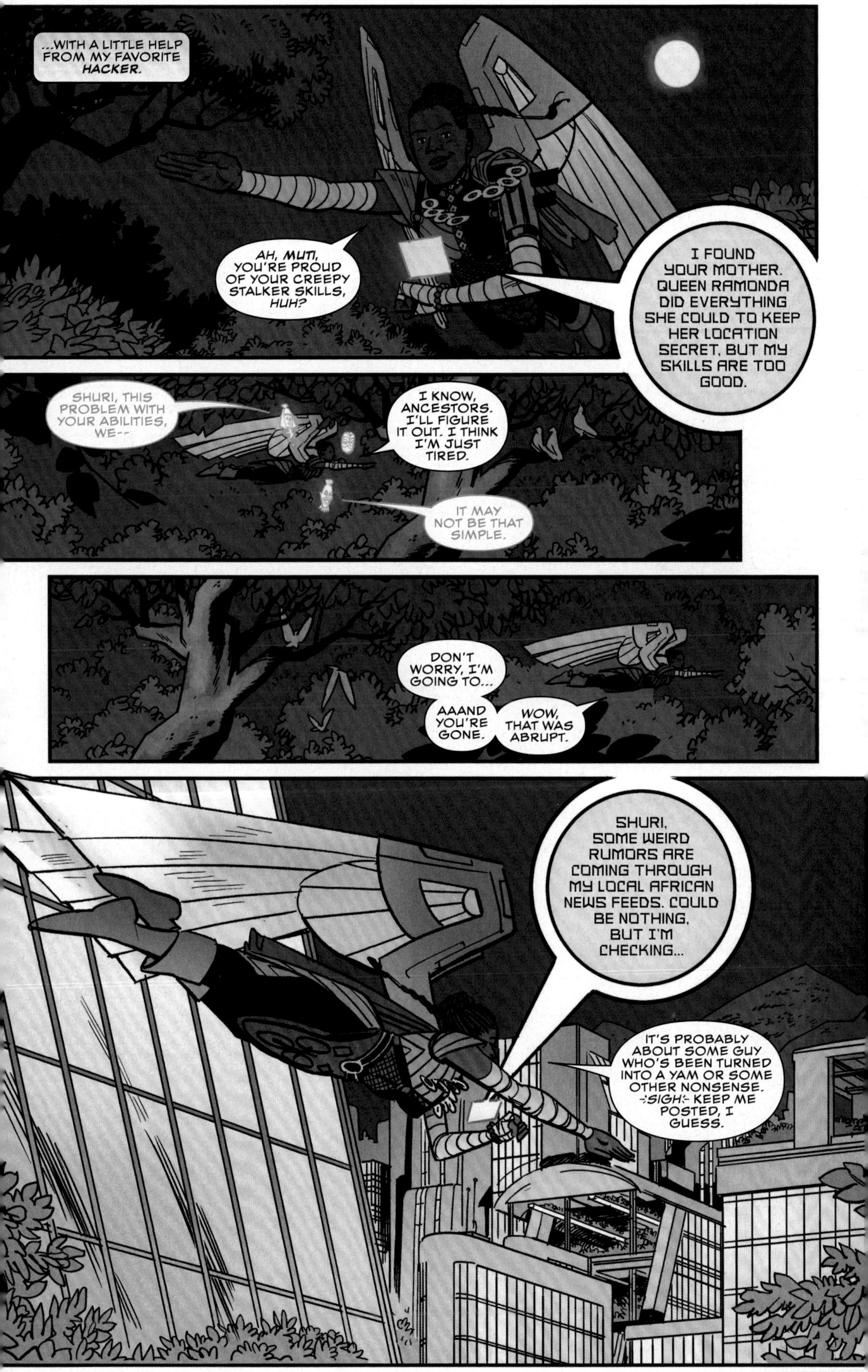
...WITH A LITTLE HELP FROM MY FAVORITE HACKER.
AH, MUTI, YOU'RE PROUD OF YOUR CREEPY STALKER SKILLS, HUH?
I FOUND YOUR MOTHER. QUEEN RAMONDA DID EVERYTHING SHE COULD TO KEEP HER LOCATION SECRET, BUT MY SKILLS ARE TOO GOOD.
SHURI, THIS PROBLEM WITH YOUR ABILITIES, WE--
I KNOW, ANCESTORS. I'LL FIGURE IT OUT. I THINK I'M JUST TIRED.
IT MAY NOT BE THAT SIMPLE.
DON'T WORRY, I'M GOING TO...
AAAND YOU'RE GONE.
WOW, THAT WAS ABRUPT.
SHURI, SOME WEIRD RUMORS ARE COMING THROUGH MY LOCAL AFRICAN NEWS FEEDS. COULD BE NOTHING, BUT I'M CHECKING...
IT'S PROBABLY ABOUT SOME GUY WHO'S BEEN TURNED INTO A YAM OR SOME OTHER NONSENSE. -SIGH- KEEP ME POSTED, I GUESS.

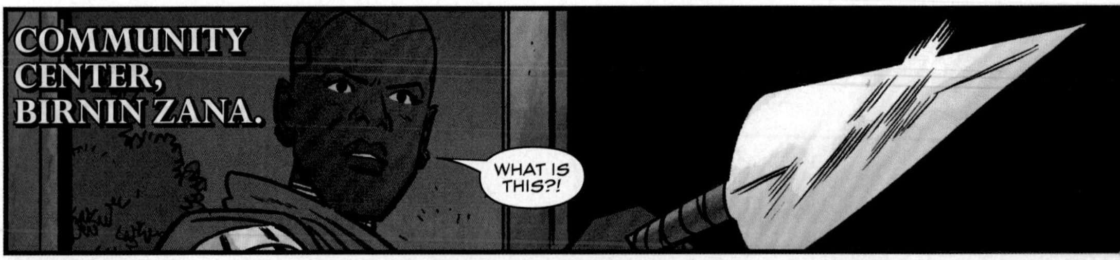
COMMUNITY CENTER, BIRNIN ZANA.
WHAT IS THIS?!

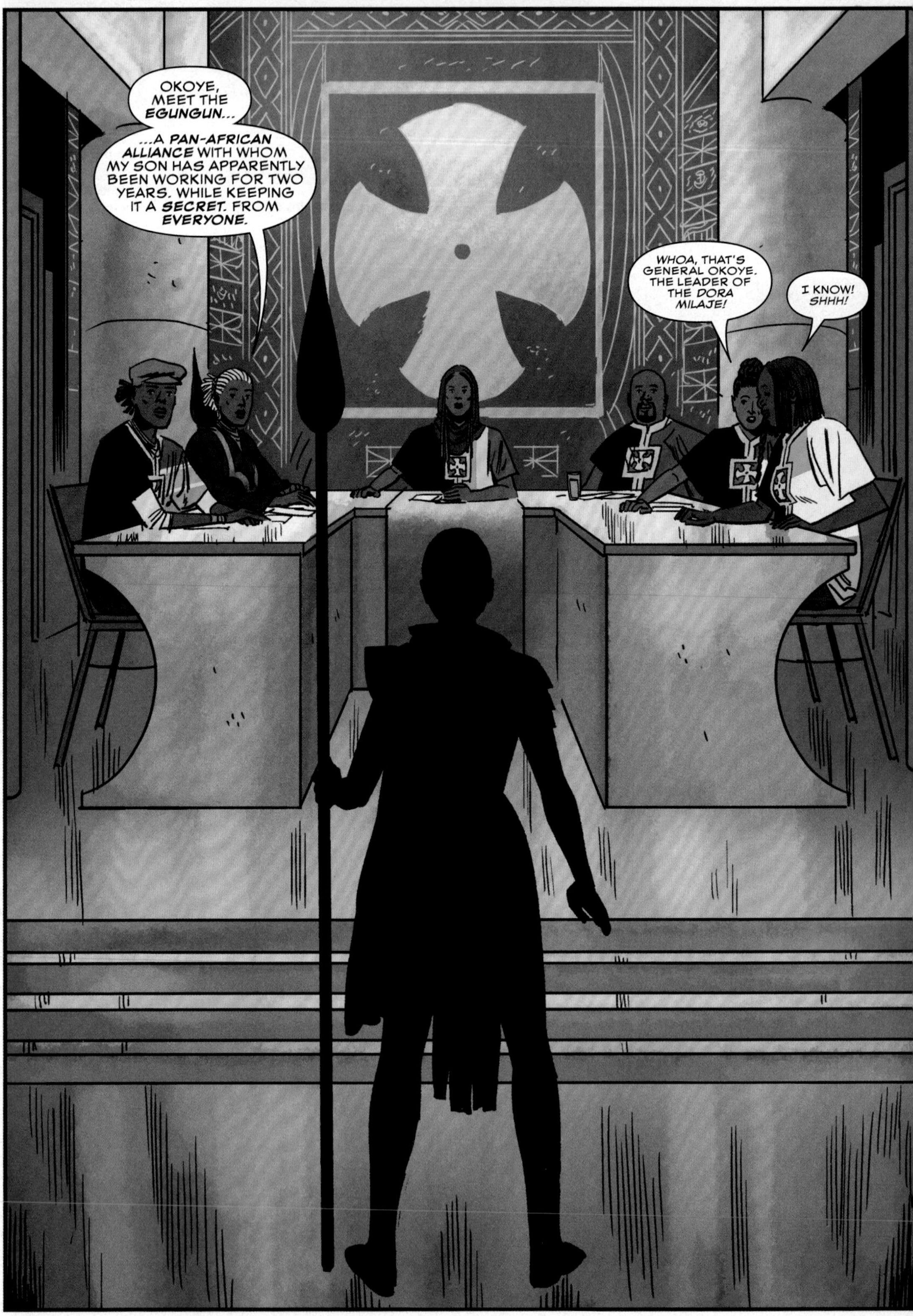
OKOYE, MEET THE EGUNGUN...
...A PAN-AFRICAN ALLIANCE WITH WHOM MY SON HAS APPARENTLY BEEN WORKING FOR TWO YEARS. WHILE KEEPING IT A SECRET. FROM EVERYONE.
WHOA, THAT'S GENERAL OKOYE. THE LEADER OF THE DORA MILAJE!
I KNOW! SHHH!

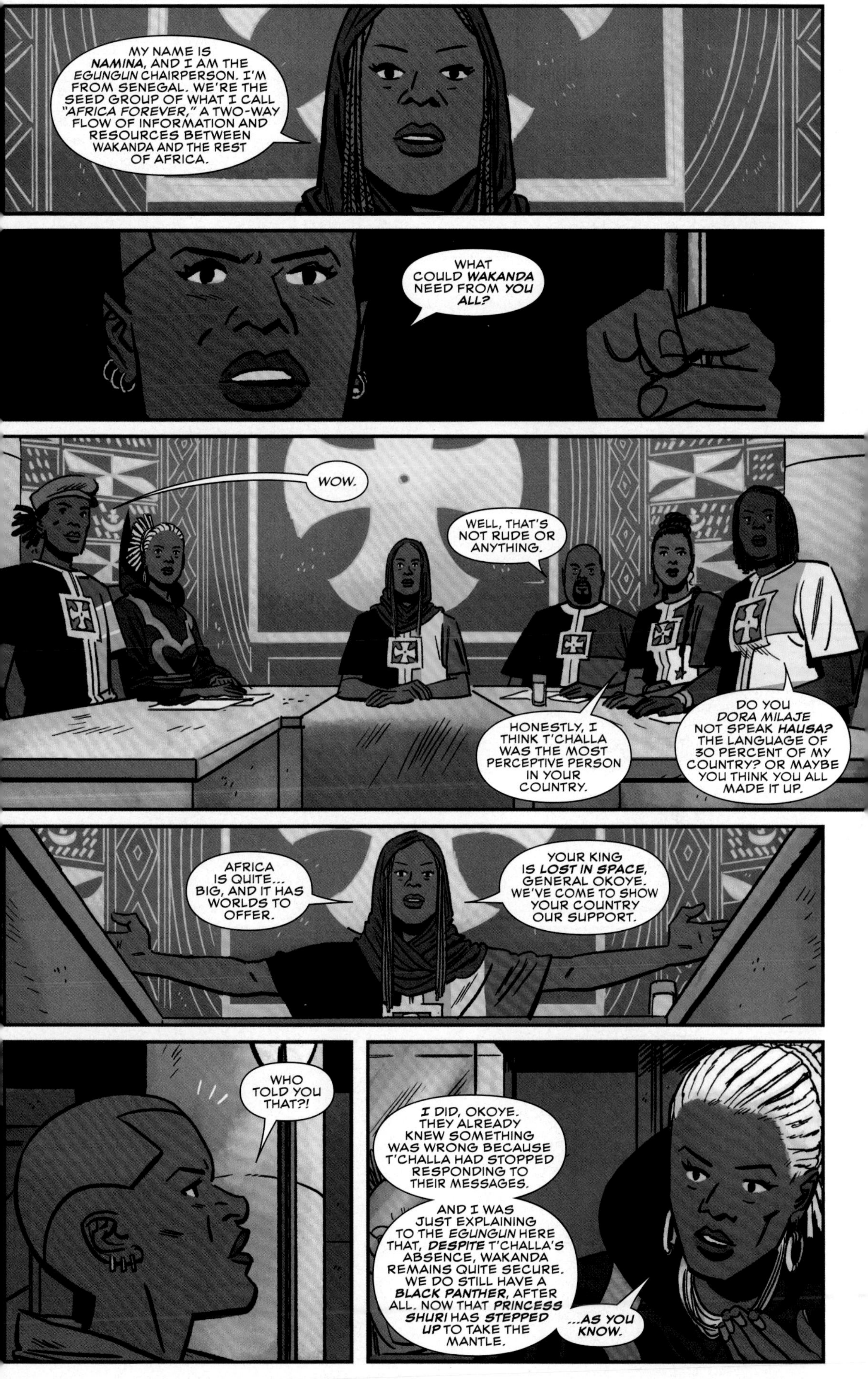
MY NAME IS NAMINA, AND I AM THE EGUNGUN CHAIRPERSON. I'M FROM SENEGAL. WE'RE THE SEED GROUP OF WHAT I CALL "AFRICA FOREVER," A TWO-WAY FLOW OF INFORMATION AND RESOURCES BETWEEN WAKANDA AND THE REST OF AFRICA.
WHAT COULD WAKANDA NEED FROM YOU ALL?
WOW.
WELL, THAT'S NOT RUDE OR ANYTHING.
HONESTLY, I THINK T'CHALLA WAS THE MOST PERCEPTIVE PERSON IN YOUR COUNTRY.
DO YOU DORA MILAJE NOT SPEAK HAUSA? THE LANGUAGE OF 30 PERCENT OF MY COUNTRY? OR MAYBE YOU THINK YOU ALL MADE IT UP.
AFRICA IS QUITE... BIG, AND IT HAS WORLDS TO OFFER.
YOUR KING IS LOST IN SPACE, GENERAL OKOYE. WE'VE COME TO SHOW YOUR COUNTRY OUR SUPPORT.
WHO TOLD YOU THAT?!
I DID, OKOYE. THEY ALREADY KNEW SOMETHING WAS WRONG BECAUSE T'CHALLA HAD STOPPED RESPONDING TO THEIR MESSAGES.
AND I WAS JUST EXPLAINING TO THE EGUNGUN HERE THAT, DESPITE T'CHALLA'S ABSENCE, WAKANDA REMAINS QUITE SECURE. WE DO STILL HAVE A BLACK PANTHER, AFTER ALL. NOW THAT PRINCESS SHURI HAS STEPPED UP TO TAKE THE MANTLE.
...AS YOU KNOW.

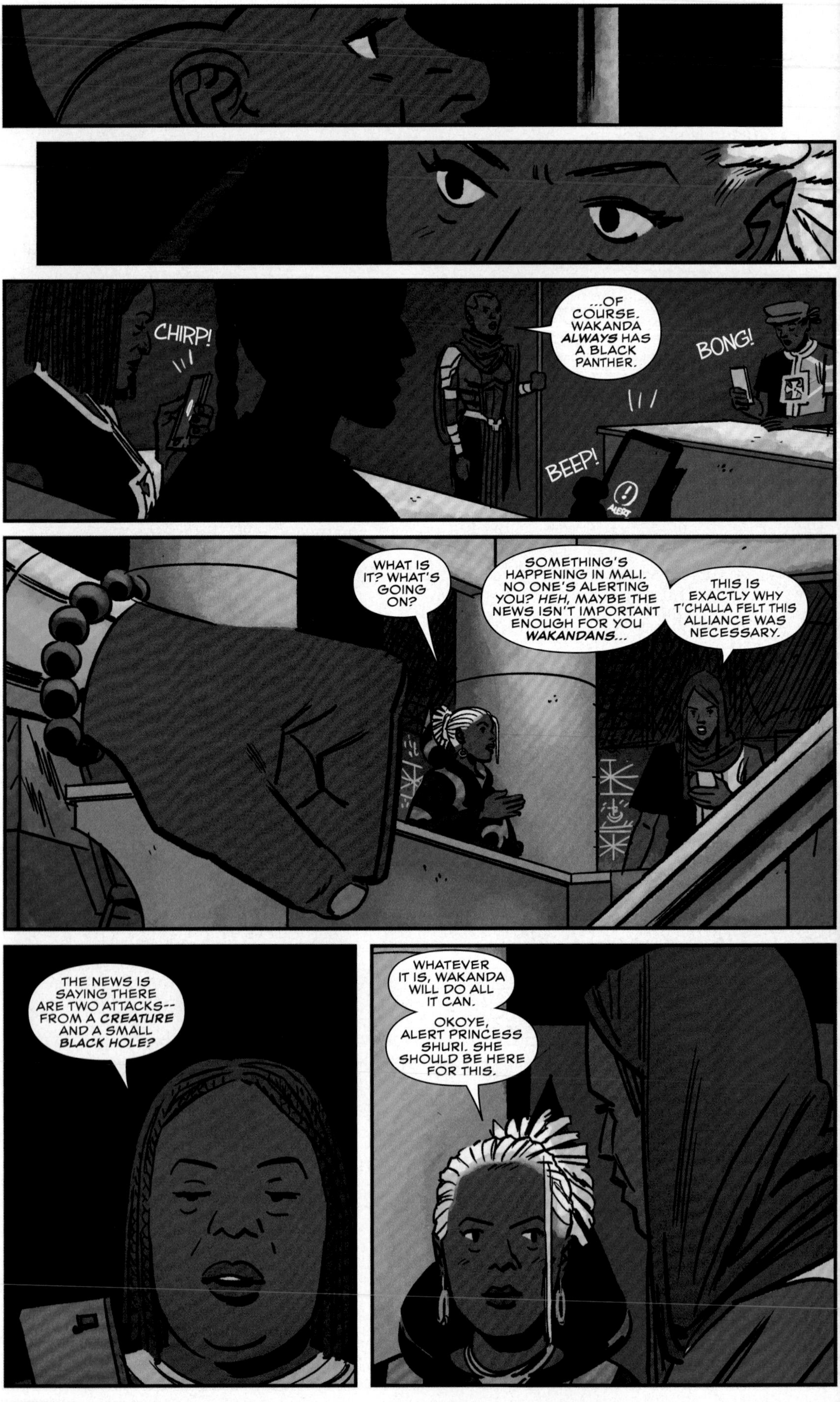
CHIRP!
...OF COURSE. WAKANDA ALWAYS HAS A BLACK PANTHER.
BONG!
BEEP!
ALERT
WHAT IS IT? WHAT'S GOING ON?
SOMETHING'S HAPPENING IN MALI. NO ONE'S ALERTING YOU? HEH, MAYBE THE NEWS ISN'T IMPORTANT ENOUGH FOR YOU WAKANDANS...
THIS IS EXACTLY WHY T'CHALLA FELT THIS ALLIANCE WAS NECESSARY.
THE NEWS IS SAYING THERE ARE TWO ATTACKS-- FROM A CREATURE AND A SMALL BLACK HOLE?
WHATEVER IT IS, WAKANDA WILL DO ALL IT CAN.
OKOYE, ALERT PRINCESS SHURI. SHE SHOULD BE HERE FOR THIS.

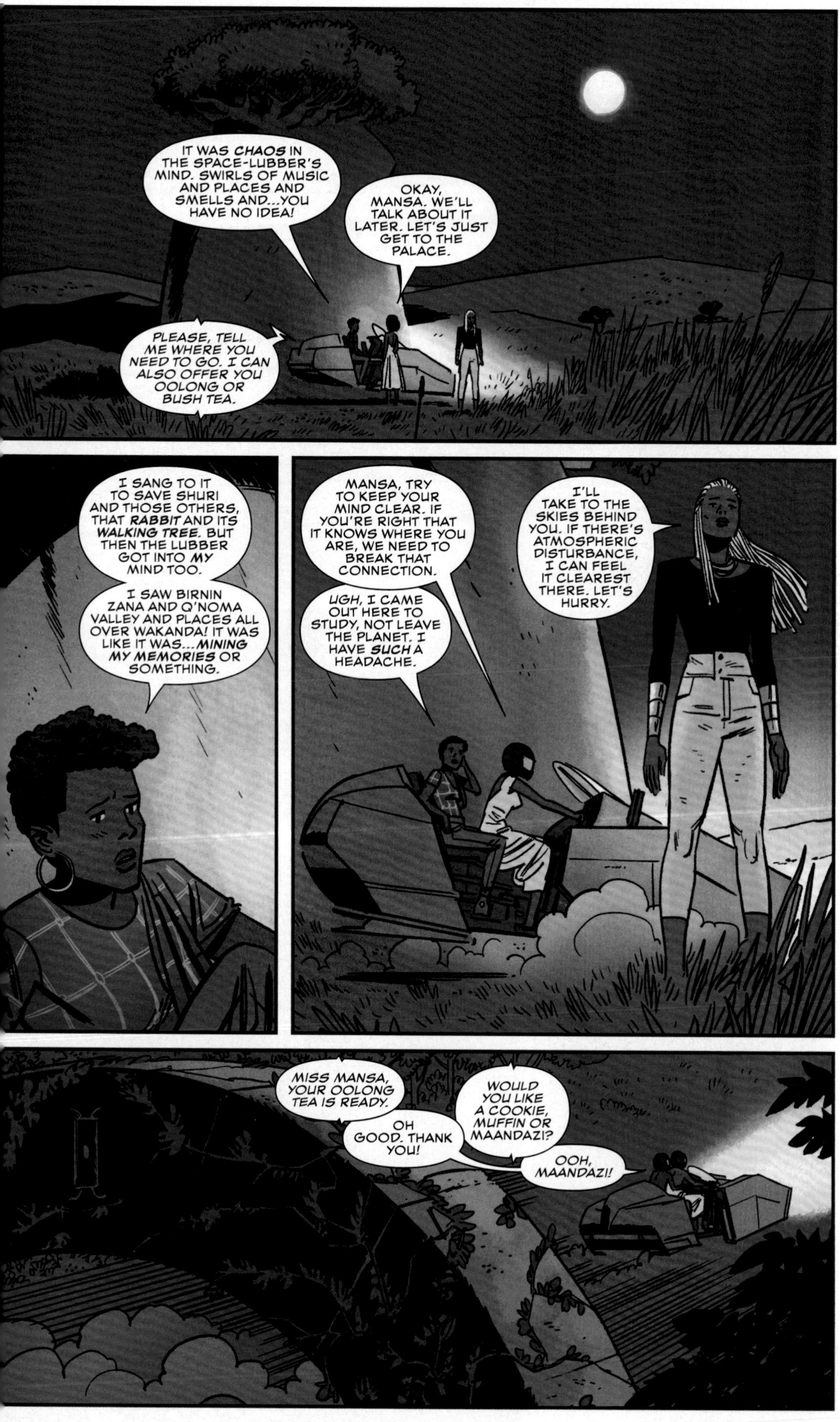
IT WAS CHAOS IN THE SPACE-LUBBER'S MIND. SWIRLS OF MUSIC AND PLACES AND SMELLS AND...YOU HAVE NO IDEA!
OKAY, MANSA. WE'LL TALK ABOUT IT LATER. LET'S JUST GET TO THE PALACE.
PLEASE, TELL ME WHERE YOU NEED TO GO. I CAN ALSO OFFER YOU OOLONG OR BUSH TEA.
I SANG TO IT TO SAVE SHURI AND THOSE OTHERS, THAT RABBIT AND ITS WALKING TREE. BUT THEN THE LUBBER GOT INTO MY MIND TOO.
I SAW BIRNIN ZANA AND Q'NOMA VALLEY AND PLACES ALL OVER WAKANDA! IT WAS LIKE IT WAS...MINING MY MEMORIES OR SOMETHING.
MANSA, TRY TO KEEP YOUR MIND CLEAR. IF YOU'RE RIGHT THAT IT KNOWS WHERE YOU ARE, WE NEED TO BREAK THAT CONNECTION.
UGH, I CAME OUT HERE TO STUDY, NOT LEAVE THE PLANET. I HAVE SUCH A HEADACHE.
I'LL TAKE TO THE SKIES BEHIND YOU. IF THERE'S ATMOSPHERIC DISTURBANCE, I CAN FEEL IT CLEAREST THERE. LET'S HURRY.
MISS MANSA, YOUR OOLONG TEA IS READY.
OH GOOD. THANK YOU!
WOULD YOU LIKE A COOKIE, MUFFIN OR MAANDAZI?
OOH, MAANDAZI!

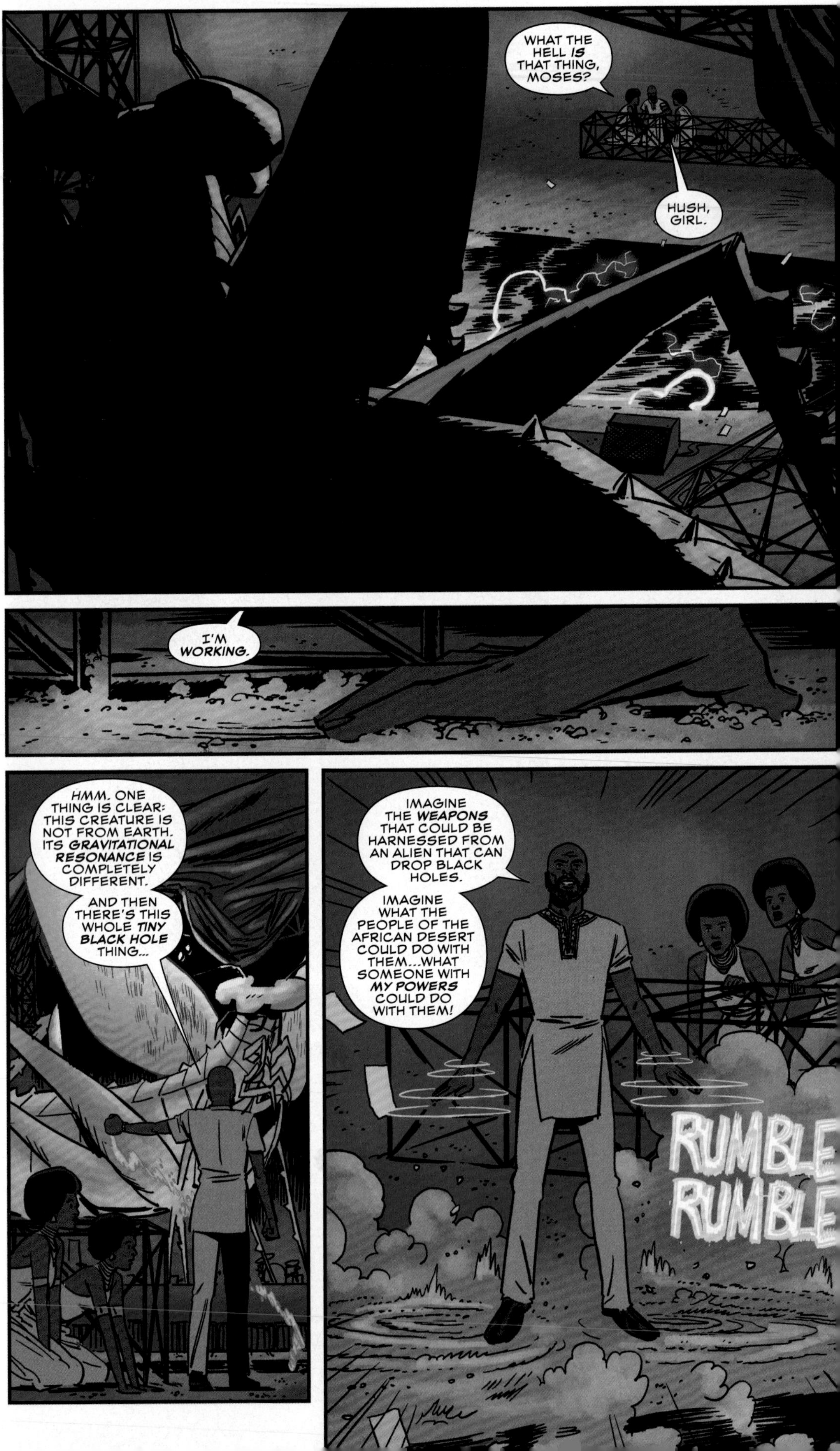
WHAT THE HELL *IS* THAT THING, MOSES?
HUSH, GIRL.
I'M *WORKING.*
HMM. ONE THING IS CLEAR: THIS CREATURE IS NOT FROM EARTH. ITS *GRAVITATIONAL RESONANCE* IS COMPLETELY DIFFERENT.
AND THEN THERE'S THIS WHOLE *TINY BLACK HOLE* THING...
IMAGINE THE *WEAPONS* THAT COULD BE HARNESSED FROM AN ALIEN THAT CAN DROP BLACK HOLES.
IMAGINE WHAT THE PEOPLE OF THE AFRICAN DESERT COULD DO WITH THEM...WHAT SOMEONE WITH *MY POWERS* COULD DO WITH THEM!
RUMBLE RUMBLE

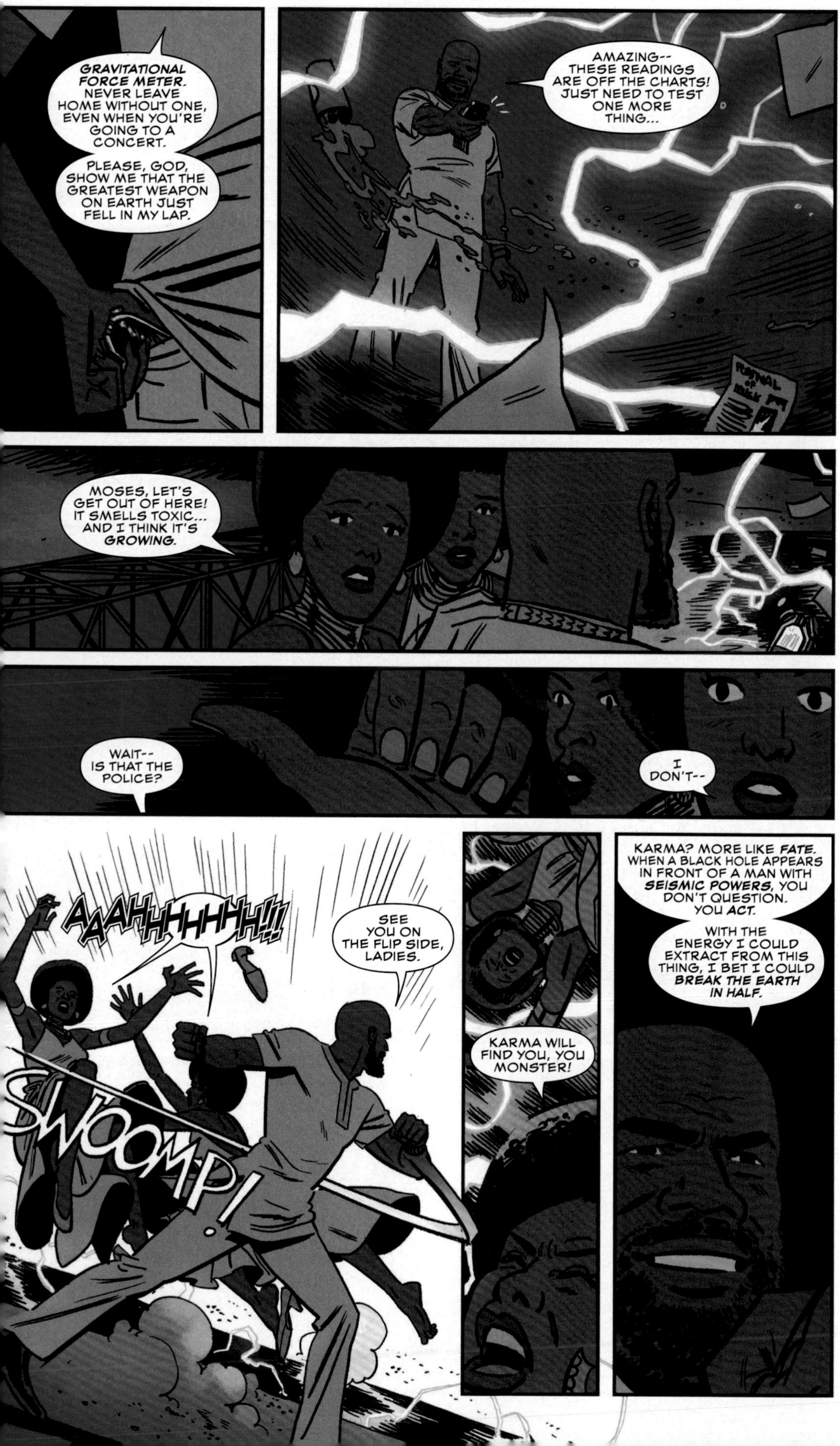

GRAVITATIONAL FORCE METER. NEVER LEAVE HOME WITHOUT ONE, EVEN WHEN YOU'RE GOING TO A CONCERT.
PLEASE, GOD, SHOW ME THAT THE GREATEST WEAPON ON EARTH JUST FELL IN MY LAP.
AMAZING-- THESE READINGS ARE OFF THE CHARTS! JUST NEED TO TEST ONE MORE THING...
MOSES, LET'S GET OUT OF HERE! IT SMELLS TOXIC... AND I THINK IT'S GROWING.
WAIT-- IS THAT THE POLICE?
I DON'T--
AAAHHHHHH!!!
SEE YOU ON THE FLIP SIDE, LADIES.
SWOOMP!
KARMA WILL FIND YOU, YOU MONSTER!
KARMA? MORE LIKE FATE. WHEN A BLACK HOLE APPEARS IN FRONT OF A MAN WITH SEISMIC POWERS, YOU DON'T QUESTION. YOU ACT.
WITH THE ENERGY I COULD EXTRACT FROM THIS THING, I BET I COULD BREAK THE EARTH IN HALF.

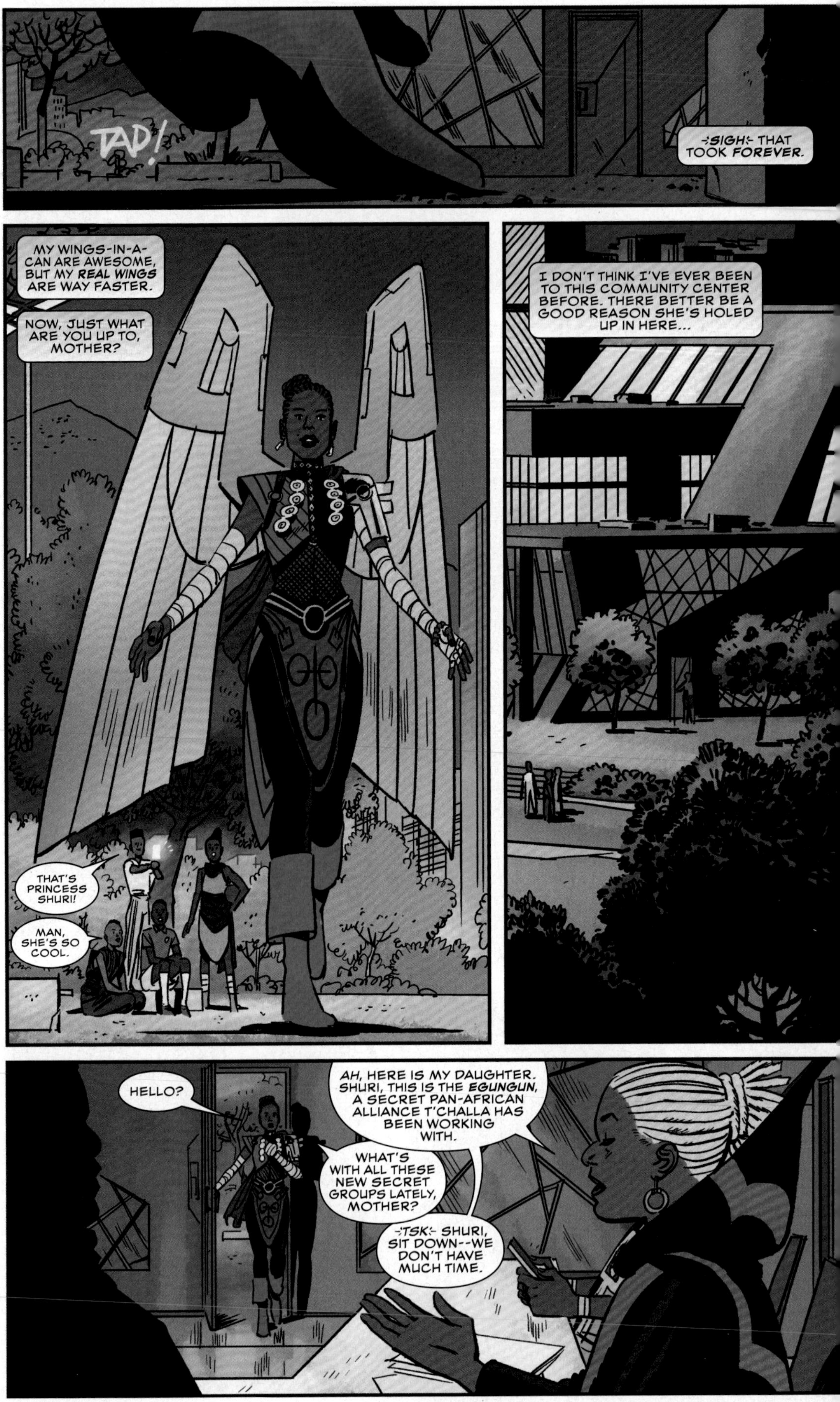
TAP!
-SIGH- THAT TOOK FOREVER.
MY WINGS-IN-A-CAN ARE AWESOME, BUT MY REAL WINGS ARE WAY FASTER.
NOW, JUST WHAT ARE YOU UP TO, MOTHER?
THAT'S PRINCESS SHURI!
MAN, SHE'S SO COOL.
I DON'T THINK I'VE EVER BEEN TO THIS COMMUNITY CENTER BEFORE. THERE BETTER BE A GOOD REASON SHE'S HOLED UP IN HERE...
HELLO?
AH, HERE IS MY DAUGHTER. SHURI, THIS IS THE EGUNGUN, A SECRET PAN-AFRICAN ALLIANCE T'CHALLA HAS BEEN WORKING WITH.
WHAT'S WITH ALL THESE NEW SECRET GROUPS LATELY, MOTHER?
-TSK- SHURI, SIT DOWN--WE DON'T HAVE MUCH TIME.

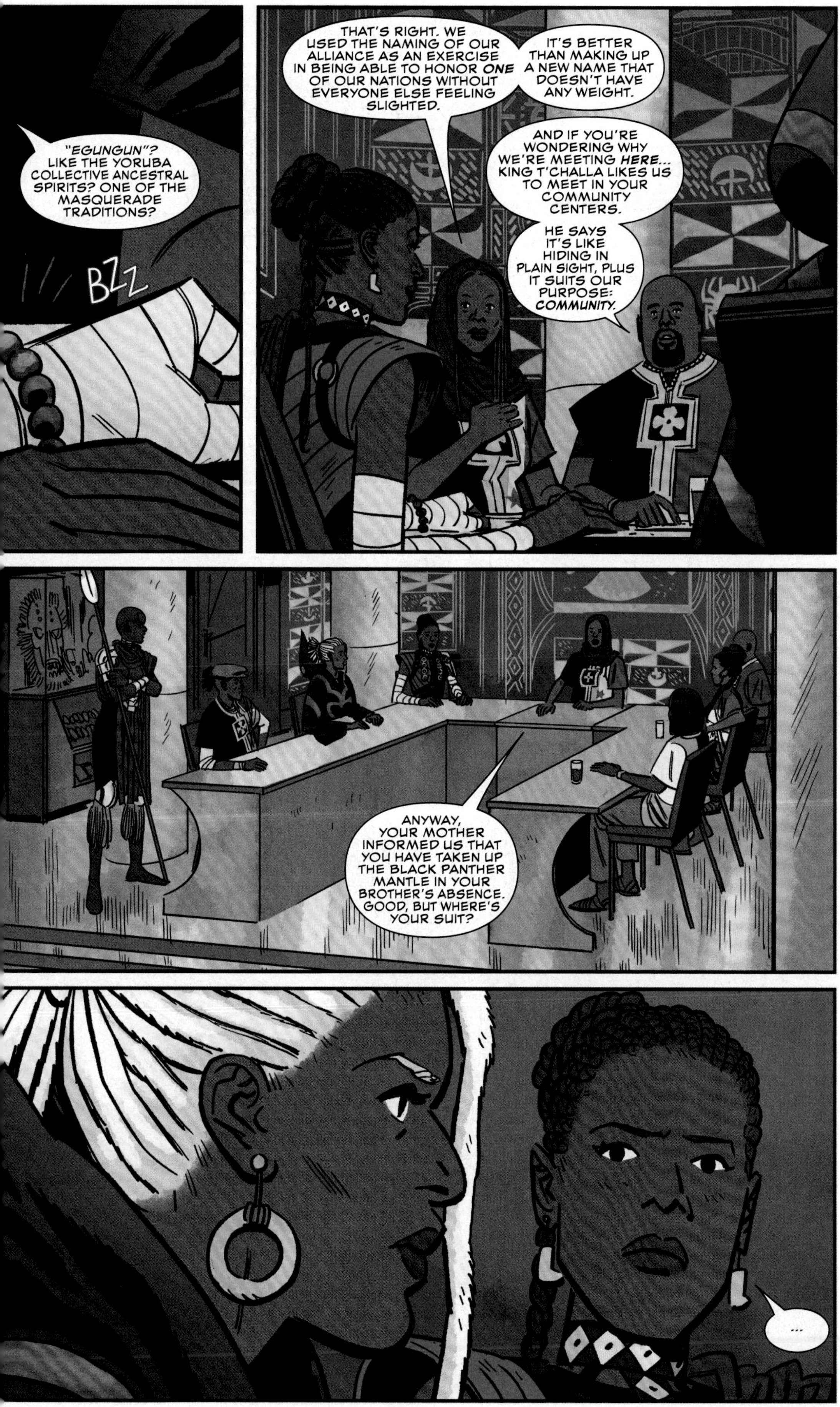
"EGUNGUN"? LIKE THE YORUBA COLLECTIVE ANCESTRAL SPIRITS? ONE OF THE MASQUERADE TRADITIONS?
BZZ
THAT'S RIGHT. WE USED THE NAMING OF OUR ALLIANCE AS AN EXERCISE IN BEING ABLE TO HONOR ONE OF OUR NATIONS WITHOUT EVERYONE ELSE FEELING SLIGHTED.
IT'S BETTER THAN MAKING UP A NEW NAME THAT DOESN'T HAVE ANY WEIGHT.
AND IF YOU'RE WONDERING WHY WE'RE MEETING HERE... KING T'CHALLA LIKES US TO MEET IN YOUR COMMUNITY CENTERS.
HE SAYS IT'S LIKE HIDING IN PLAIN SIGHT, PLUS IT SUITS OUR PURPOSE: COMMUNITY.
ANYWAY, YOUR MOTHER INFORMED US THAT YOU HAVE TAKEN UP THE BLACK PANTHER MANTLE IN YOUR BROTHER'S ABSENCE. GOOD, BUT WHERE'S YOUR SUIT?
...

OH, I, UH, ONLY SUIT UP WHEN STUFF IS GOING DOWN. PLUS, I'M MAKING SOME...CHANGES TO IT. YOU'LL, UH, SEE, HEH.

AND WHAT'S GOING ON WITH YOUR BRACELET?

HUH? OH, I HADN'T...NO, THAT CAN'T BE.

AH, YOU ARE GETTING THE NEWS. I'M GLAD SOMEONE IN WAKANDA IS AWARE OF WHAT'S HAPPENING IN OTHER PARTS OF AFRICA.

SHURI! THERE'S SOME KIND OF HUGE BUG CAUSING CHAOS IN TIMBUKTU! PEOPLE IN MALI ARE CALLING IT A DJINN! IT'S STILL THERE!

BZZ-BZZ-BZZ-

THIS SOUNDS SERIOUS. I BETTER GO CHECK IT OUT.

GOOD TO HEAR THAT. WE WILL LET THE MALI AUTHORITIES KNOW YOU'RE COMING.

HA, THIS IS WHAT I EXPECT OF A BLACK PANTHER.

WELL, THAT WAS A SHORT MEETING.

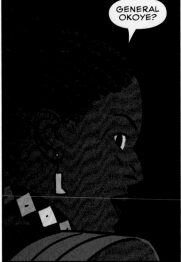

GENERAL OKOYE?

COMING, PRINCESS SH--I MEAN, BLACK PANTHER.

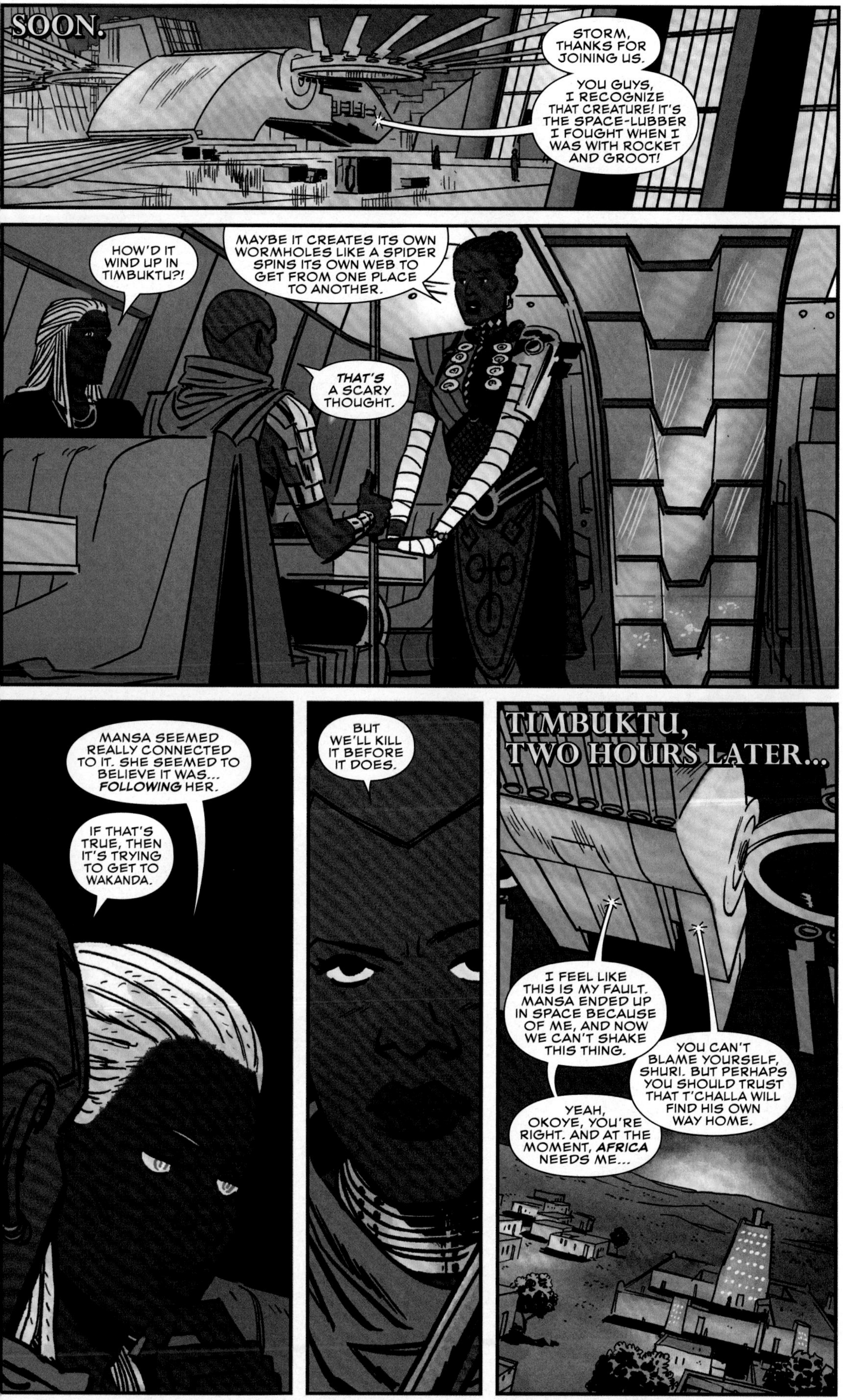
SOON.
STORM, THANKS FOR JOINING US.
YOU GUYS, I RECOGNIZE THAT CREATURE! IT'S THE SPACE-LUBBER I FOUGHT WHEN I WAS WITH ROCKET AND GROOT!
HOW'D IT WIND UP IN TIMBUKTU?!
MAYBE IT CREATES ITS OWN WORMHOLES LIKE A SPIDER SPINS ITS OWN WEB TO GET FROM ONE PLACE TO ANOTHER.
THAT'S A SCARY THOUGHT.
MANSA SEEMED REALLY CONNECTED TO IT. SHE SEEMED TO BELIEVE IT WAS... *FOLLOWING* HER.
IF THAT'S TRUE, THEN IT'S TRYING TO GET TO WAKANDA.
BUT WE'LL KILL IT BEFORE IT DOES.
TIMBUKTU, TWO HOURS LATER...
I FEEL LIKE THIS IS MY FAULT. MANSA ENDED UP IN SPACE BECAUSE OF ME, AND NOW WE CAN'T SHAKE THIS THING.
YOU CAN'T BLAME YOURSELF, SHURI. BUT PERHAPS YOU SHOULD TRUST THAT T'CHALLA WILL FIND HIS OWN WAY HOME.
YEAH, OKOYE, YOU'RE RIGHT. AND AT THE MOMENT, *AFRICA* NEEDS ME...

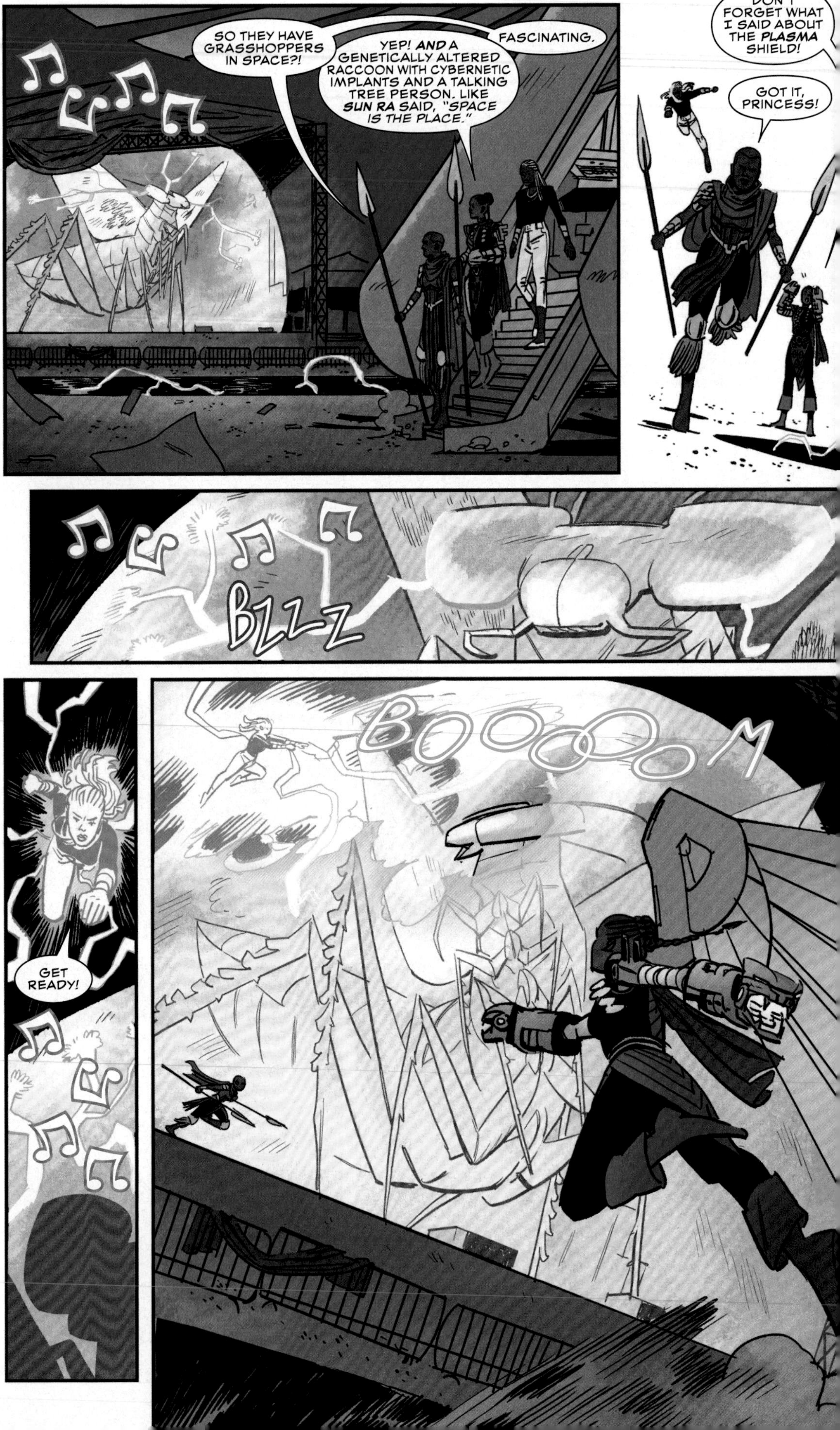

SO THEY HAVE GRASSHOPPERS IN SPACE?!
FASCINATING.
YEP! AND A GENETICALLY ALTERED RACCOON WITH CYBERNETIC IMPLANTS AND A TALKING TREE PERSON. LIKE SUN RA SAID, "SPACE IS THE PLACE."
DON'T FORGET WHAT I SAID ABOUT THE PLASMA SHIELD!
GOT IT, PRINCESS!
BZZZ
GET READY!
BOOOOOOM

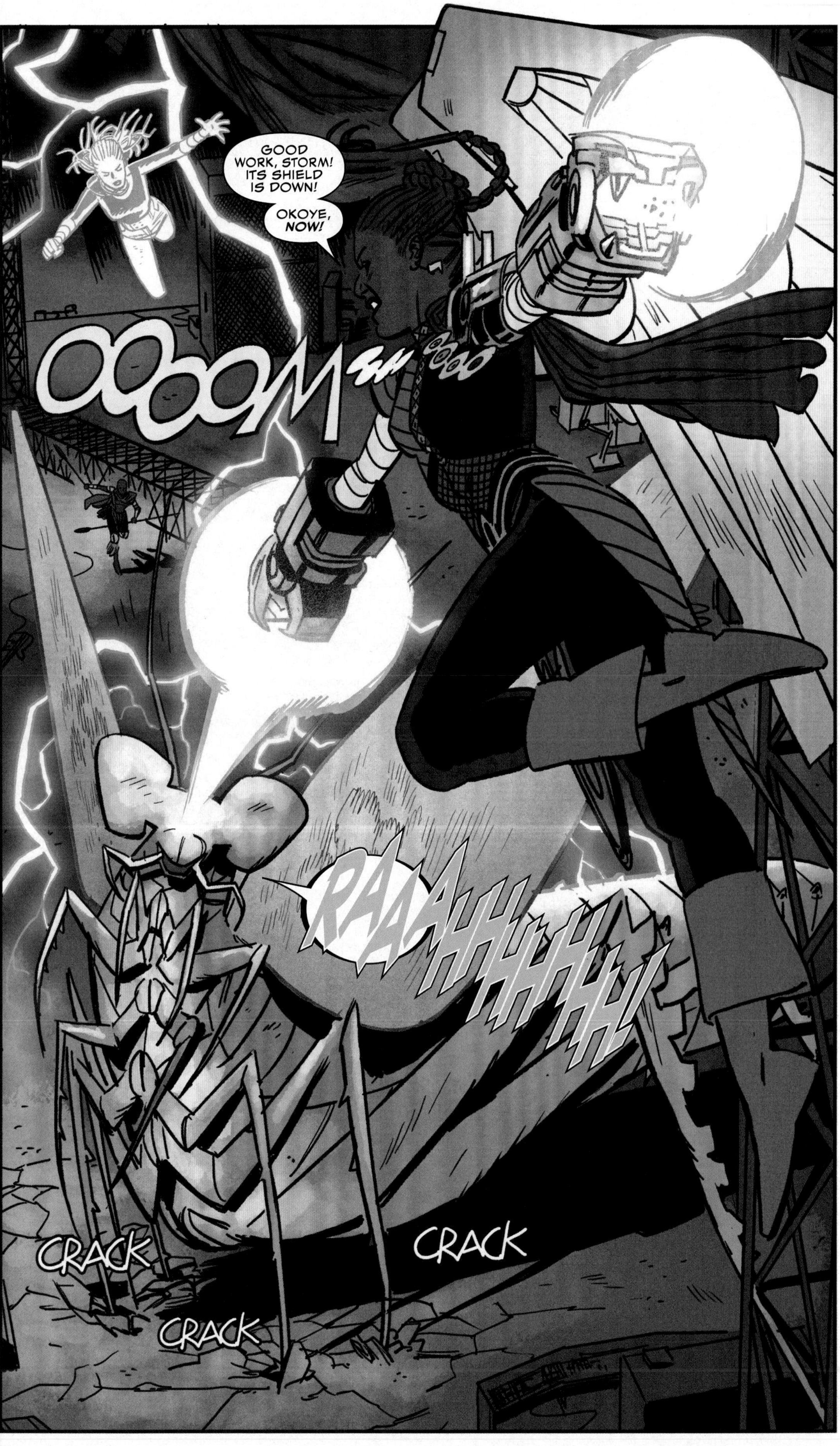
GOOD WORK, STORM! ITS SHIELD IS DOWN!
OKOYE, NOW!
OOOOM
RAAAHHHHHH!
CRACK
CRACK
CRACK

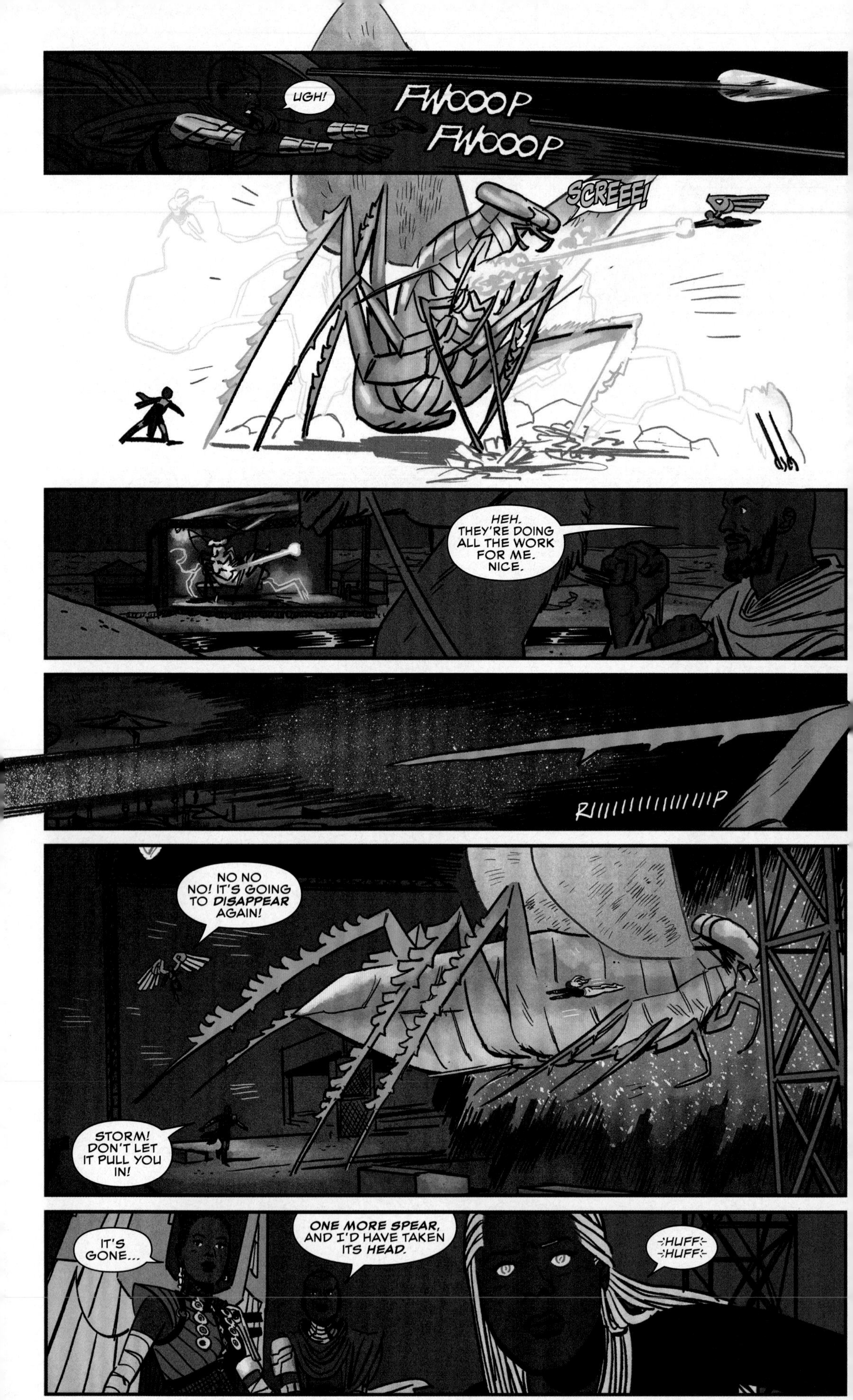
UGH!
FWOOOP
FWOOOP
SCREEE!
HEH. THEY'RE DOING ALL THE WORK FOR ME. NICE.
RIIIIIIIIIIIIIIP
NO NO NO! IT'S GOING TO DISAPPEAR AGAIN!
STORM! DON'T LET IT PULL YOU IN!
IT'S GONE...
ONE MORE SPEAR, AND I'D HAVE TAKEN ITS HEAD.
HUFF
HUFF

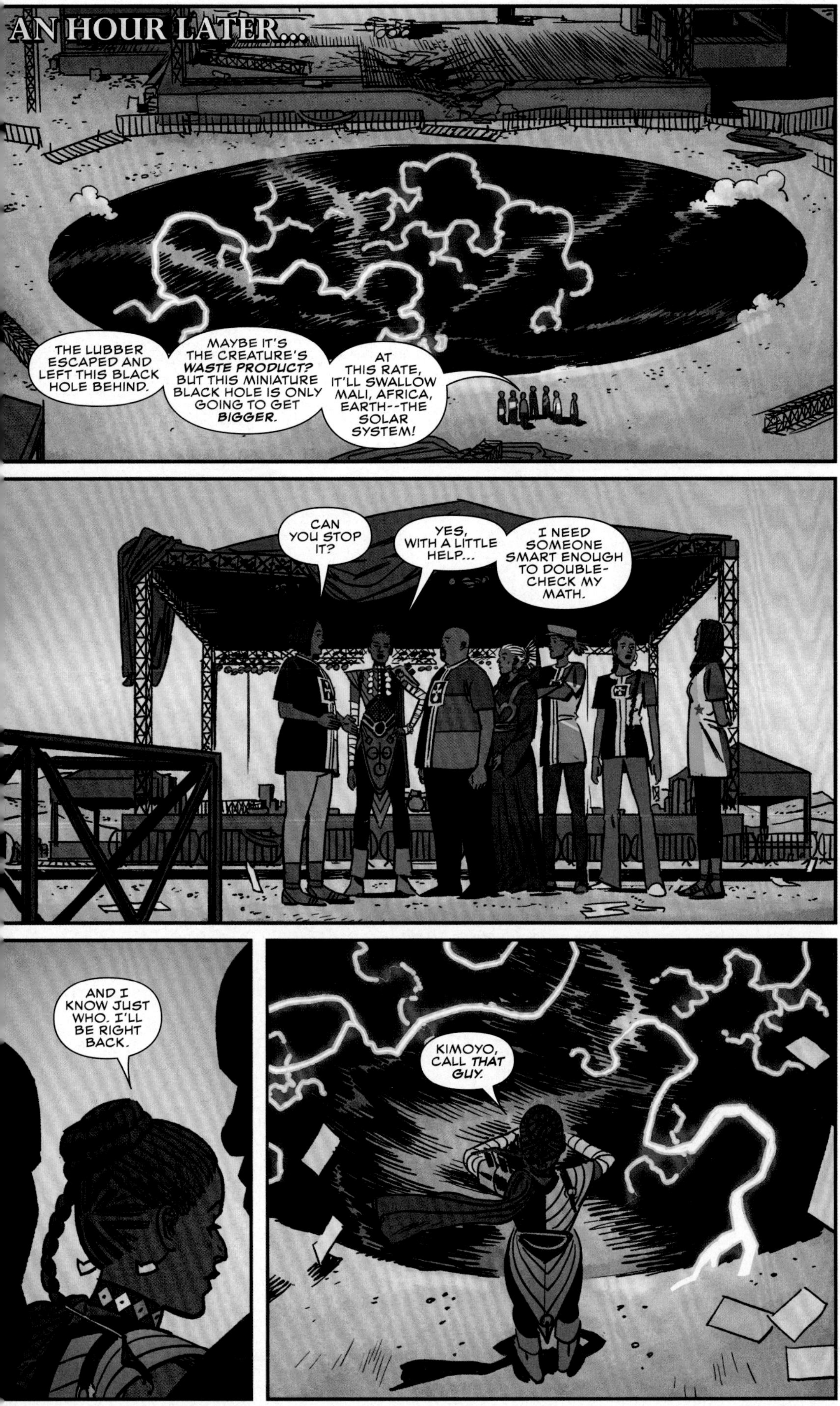
AN HOUR LATER...
THE LUBBER ESCAPED AND LEFT THIS BLACK HOLE BEHIND.
MAYBE IT'S THE CREATURE'S WASTE PRODUCT? BUT THIS MINIATURE BLACK HOLE IS ONLY GOING TO GET BIGGER.
AT THIS RATE, IT'LL SWALLOW MALI, AFRICA, EARTH--THE SOLAR SYSTEM!
CAN YOU STOP IT?
YES, WITH A LITTLE HELP...
I NEED SOMEONE SMART ENOUGH TO DOUBLE-CHECK MY MATH.
AND I KNOW JUST WHO. I'LL BE RIGHT BACK.
KIMOYO, CALL THAT GUY.

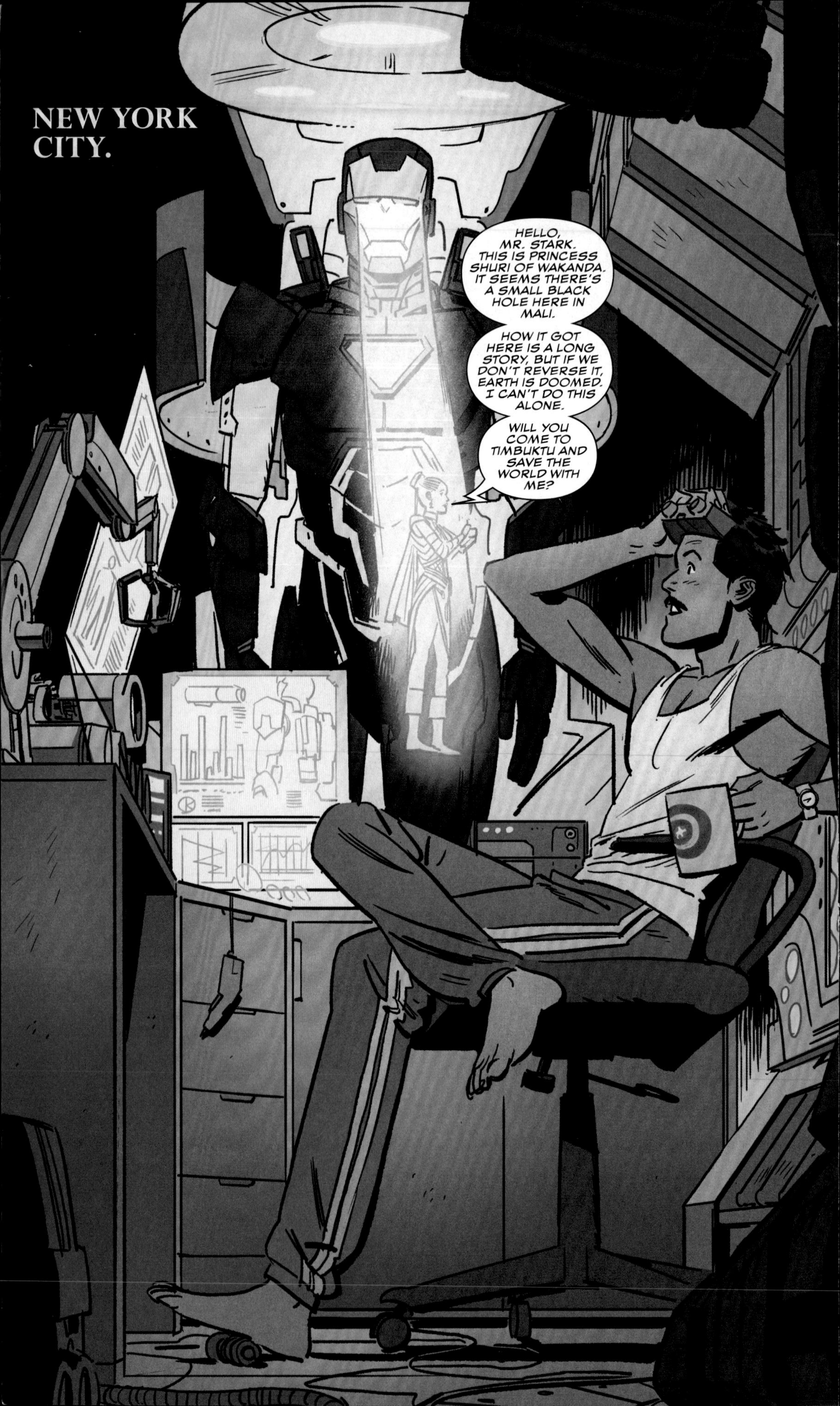
NEW YORK CITY.
HELLO, MR. STARK. THIS IS PRINCESS SHURI OF WAKANDA. IT SEEMS THERE'S A SMALL BLACK HOLE HERE IN MALI.
HOW IT GOT HERE IS A LONG STORY, BUT IF WE DON'T REVERSE IT, EARTH IS DOOMED. I CAN'T DO THIS ALONE.
WILL YOU COME TO TIMBUKTU AND SAVE THE WORLD WITH ME?

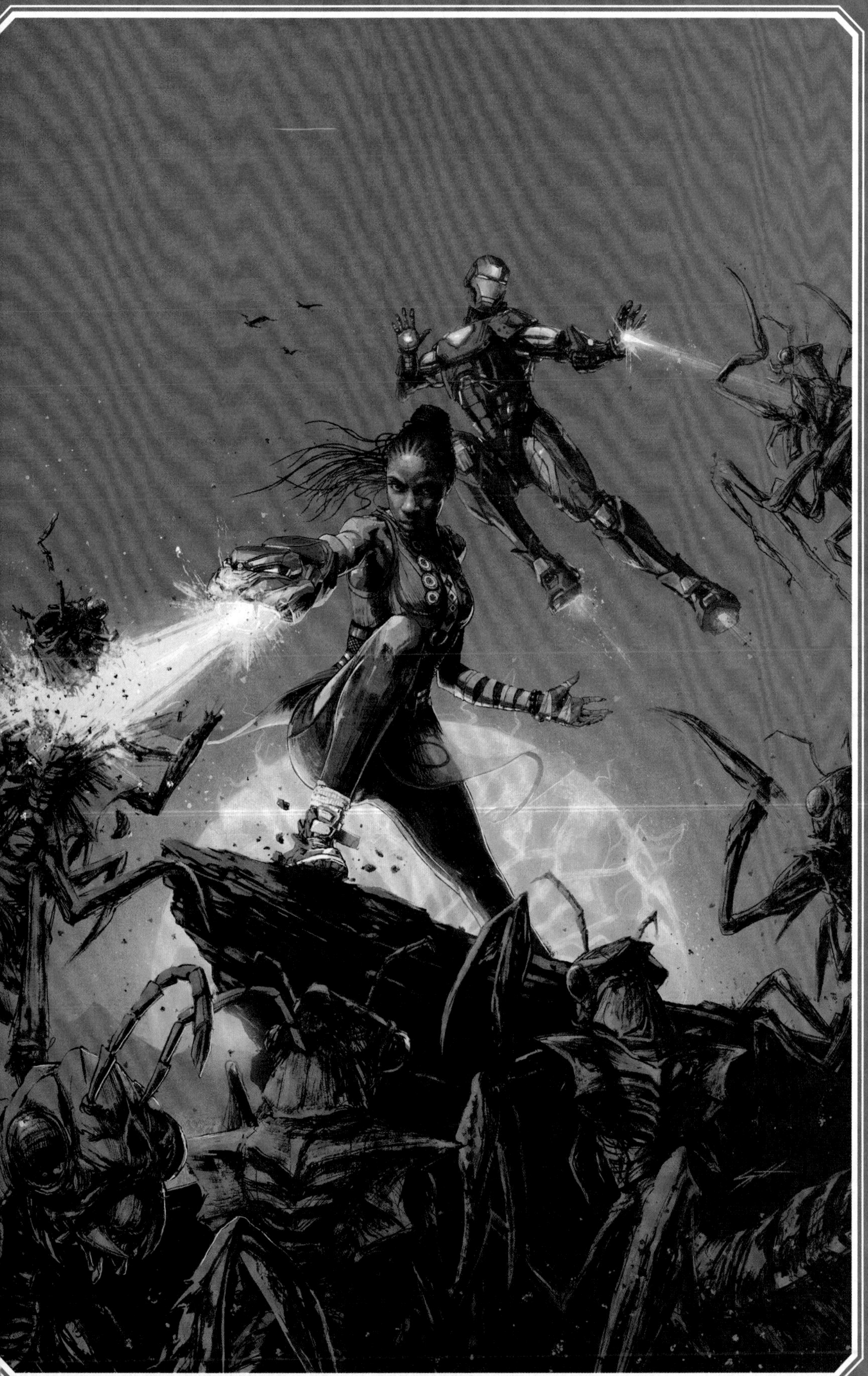

5 – THE END OF THE EARTH

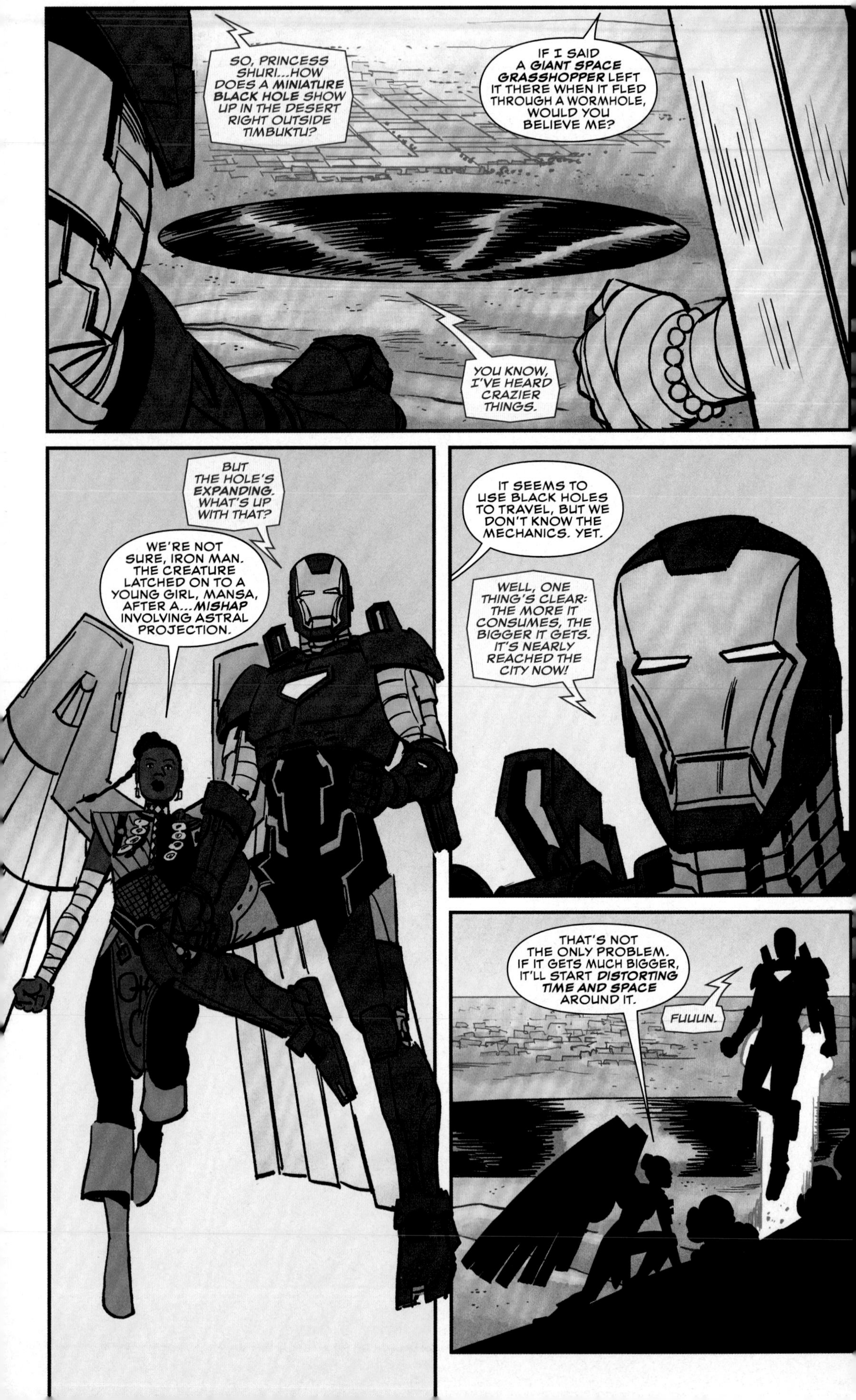
SO, PRINCESS SHURI...HOW DOES A MINIATURE BLACK HOLE SHOW UP IN THE DESERT RIGHT OUTSIDE TIMBUKTU?
IF I SAID A GIANT SPACE GRASSHOPPER LEFT IT THERE WHEN IT FLED THROUGH A WORMHOLE, WOULD YOU BELIEVE ME?
YOU KNOW, I'VE HEARD CRAZIER THINGS.
BUT THE HOLE'S EXPANDING. WHAT'S UP WITH THAT?
WE'RE NOT SURE, IRON MAN. THE CREATURE LATCHED ON TO A YOUNG GIRL, MANSA, AFTER A...MISHAP INVOLVING ASTRAL PROJECTION.
IT SEEMS TO USE BLACK HOLES TO TRAVEL, BUT WE DON'T KNOW THE MECHANICS. YET.
WELL, ONE THING'S CLEAR: THE MORE IT CONSUMES, THE BIGGER IT GETS. IT'S NEARLY REACHED THE CITY NOW!
THAT'S NOT THE ONLY PROBLEM. IF IT GETS MUCH BIGGER, IT'LL START DISTORTING TIME AND SPACE AROUND IT.
FUUUN.

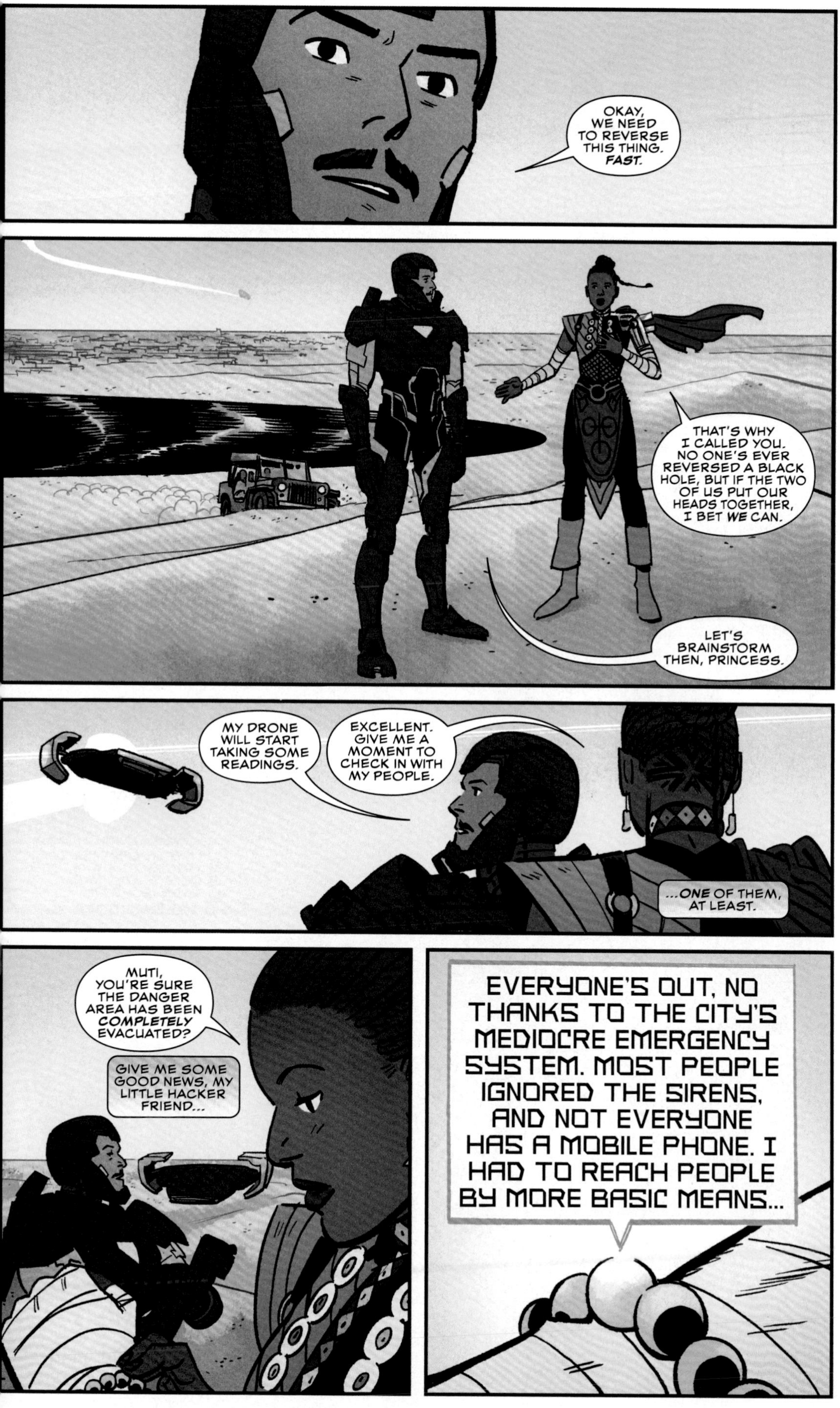
OKAY, WE NEED TO REVERSE THIS THING. FAST.
THAT'S WHY I CALLED YOU. NO ONE'S EVER REVERSED A BLACK HOLE, BUT IF THE TWO OF US PUT OUR HEADS TOGETHER, I BET WE CAN.
LET'S BRAINSTORM THEN, PRINCESS.
MY DRONE WILL START TAKING SOME READINGS.
EXCELLENT. GIVE ME A MOMENT TO CHECK IN WITH MY PEOPLE.
...ONE OF THEM, AT LEAST.
MUTI, YOU'RE SURE THE DANGER AREA HAS BEEN COMPLETELY EVACUATED?
GIVE ME SOME GOOD NEWS, MY LITTLE HACKER FRIEND...
EVERYONE'S OUT, NO THANKS TO THE CITY'S MEDIOCRE EMERGENCY SYSTEM. MOST PEOPLE IGNORED THE SIRENS, AND NOT EVERYONE HAS A MOBILE PHONE. I HAD TO REACH PEOPLE BY MORE BASIC MEANS...

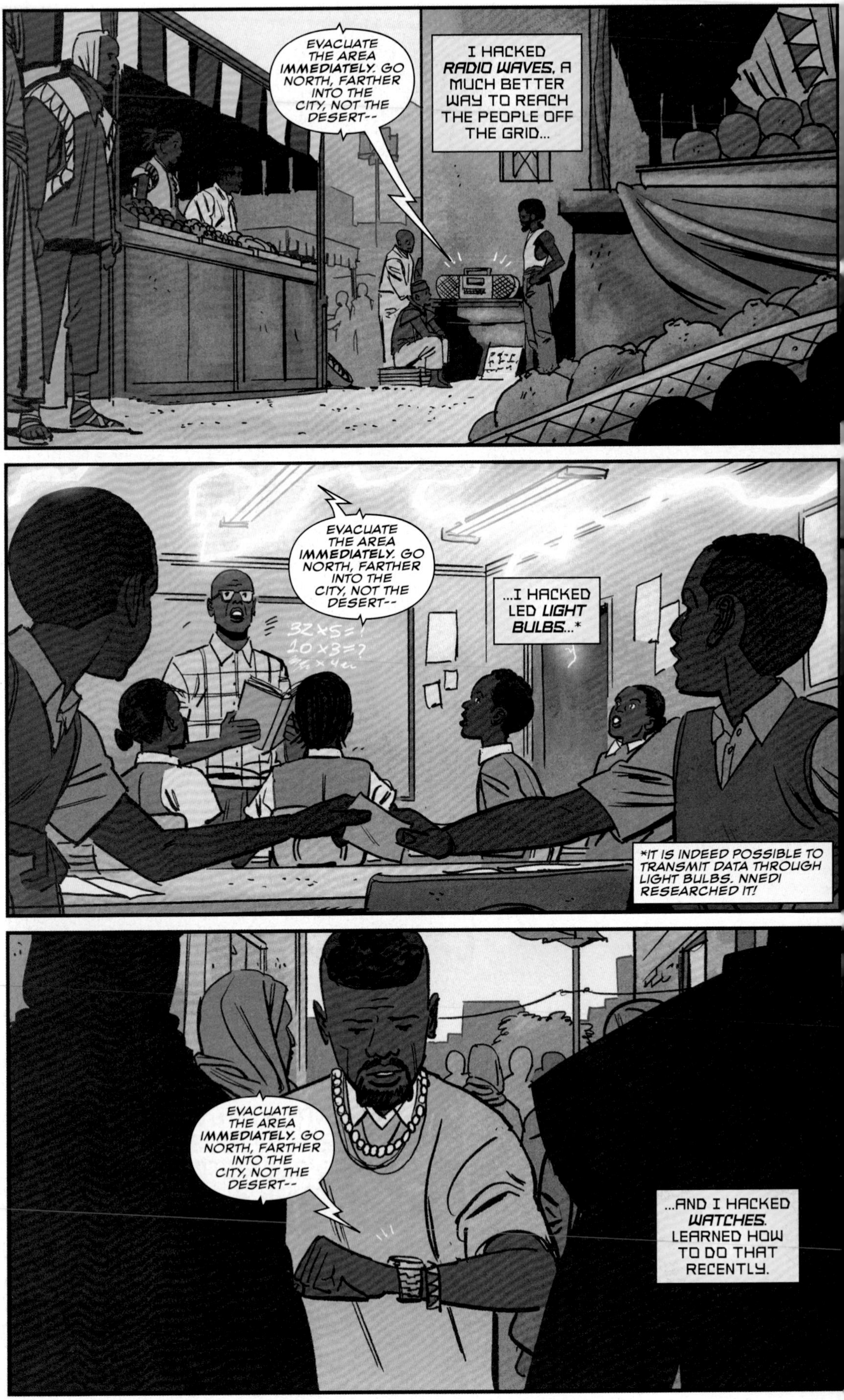
EVACUATE THE AREA IMMEDIATELY. GO NORTH, FARTHER INTO THE CITY, NOT THE DESERT--
I HACKED RADIO WAVES, A MUCH BETTER WAY TO REACH THE PEOPLE OFF THE GRID...
EVACUATE THE AREA IMMEDIATELY. GO NORTH, FARTHER INTO THE CITY, NOT THE DESERT--
...I HACKED LED LIGHT BULBS...*
32×5=?
10×3=?
*IT IS INDEED POSSIBLE TO TRANSMIT DATA THROUGH LIGHT BULBS. NNEDI RESEARCHED IT!
EVACUATE THE AREA IMMEDIATELY. GO NORTH, FARTHER INTO THE CITY, NOT THE DESERT--
...AND I HACKED WATCHES. LEARNED HOW TO DO THAT RECENTLY.

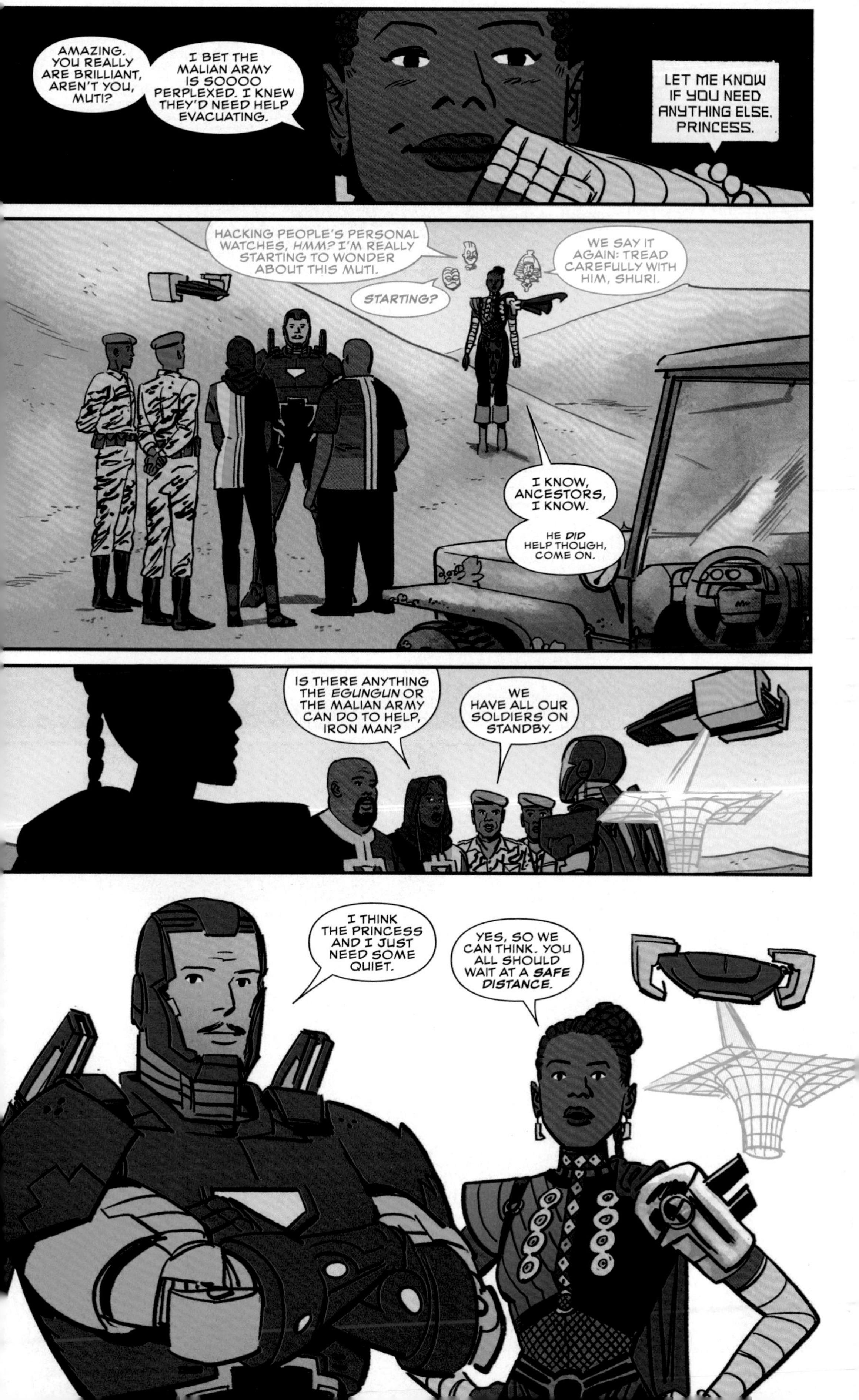

AMAZING. YOU REALLY ARE BRILLIANT, AREN'T YOU, MUTI?
I BET THE MALIAN ARMY IS SOOOO PERPLEXED. I KNEW THEY'D NEED HELP EVACUATING.
LET ME KNOW IF YOU NEED ANYTHING ELSE, PRINCESS.
HACKING PEOPLE'S PERSONAL WATCHES, HMM? I'M REALLY STARTING TO WONDER ABOUT THIS MUTI.
STARTING?
WE SAY IT AGAIN: TREAD CAREFULLY WITH HIM, SHURI.
I KNOW, ANCESTORS, I KNOW.
HE DID HELP THOUGH, COME ON.
IS THERE ANYTHING THE EGUNGUN OR THE MALIAN ARMY CAN DO TO HELP, IRON MAN?
WE HAVE ALL OUR SOLDIERS ON STANDBY.
I THINK THE PRINCESS AND I JUST NEED SOME QUIET.
YES, SO WE CAN THINK. YOU ALL SHOULD WAIT AT A SAFE DISTANCE.

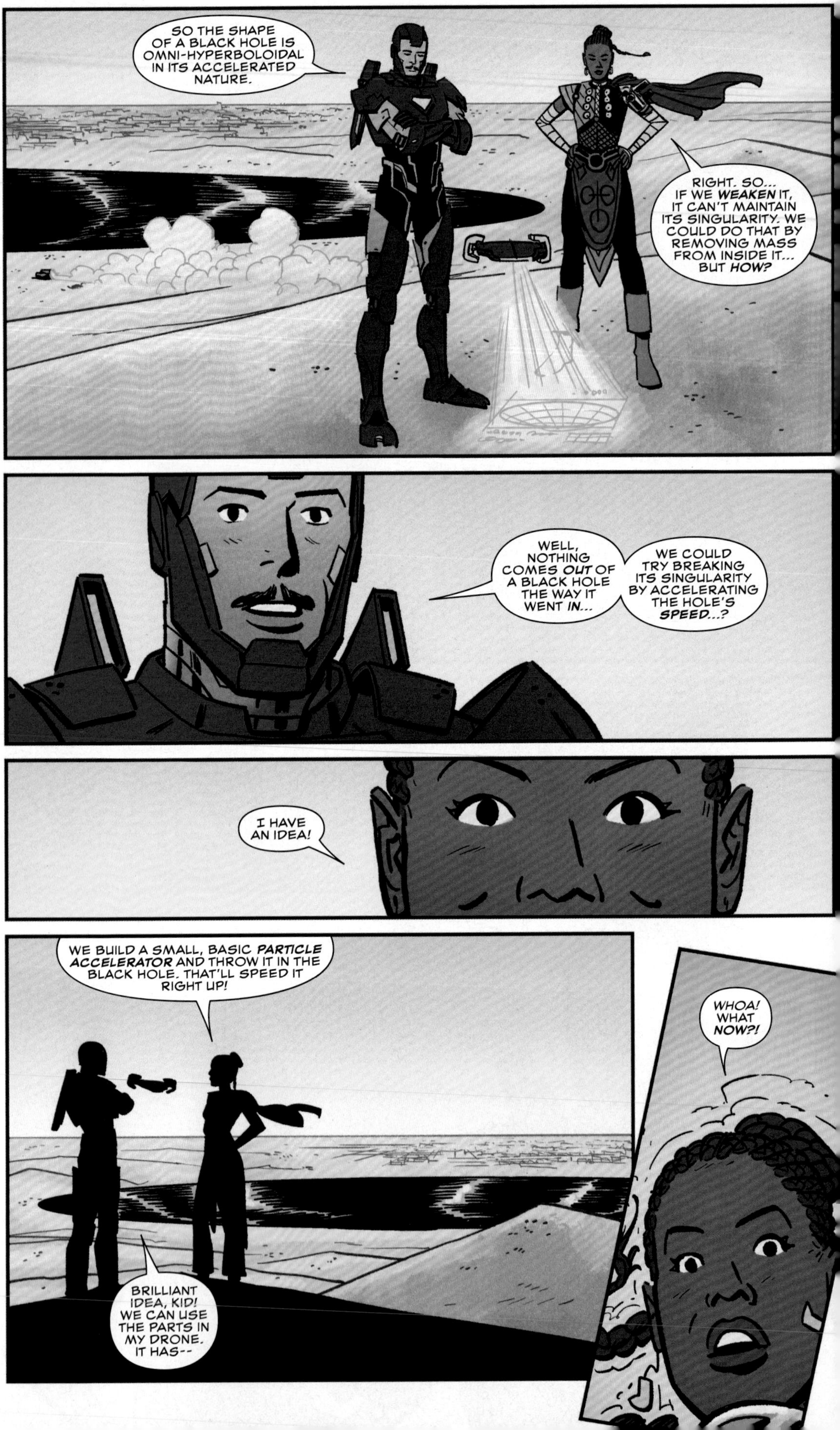
SO THE SHAPE OF A BLACK HOLE IS OMNI-HYPERBOLOIDAL IN ITS ACCELERATED NATURE.
RIGHT. SO... IF WE *WEAKEN* IT, IT CAN'T MAINTAIN ITS SINGULARITY. WE COULD DO THAT BY REMOVING MASS FROM INSIDE IT... BUT *HOW?*
WELL, NOTHING COMES *OUT* OF A BLACK HOLE THE WAY IT WENT *IN*...
WE COULD TRY BREAKING ITS SINGULARITY BY ACCELERATING THE HOLE'S *SPEED*...?
I HAVE AN IDEA!
WE BUILD A SMALL, BASIC *PARTICLE ACCELERATOR* AND THROW IT IN THE BLACK HOLE. THAT'LL SPEED IT RIGHT UP!
BRILLIANT IDEA, KID! WE CAN USE THE PARTS IN MY DRONE. IT HAS--
WHOA! WHAT *NOW?!*

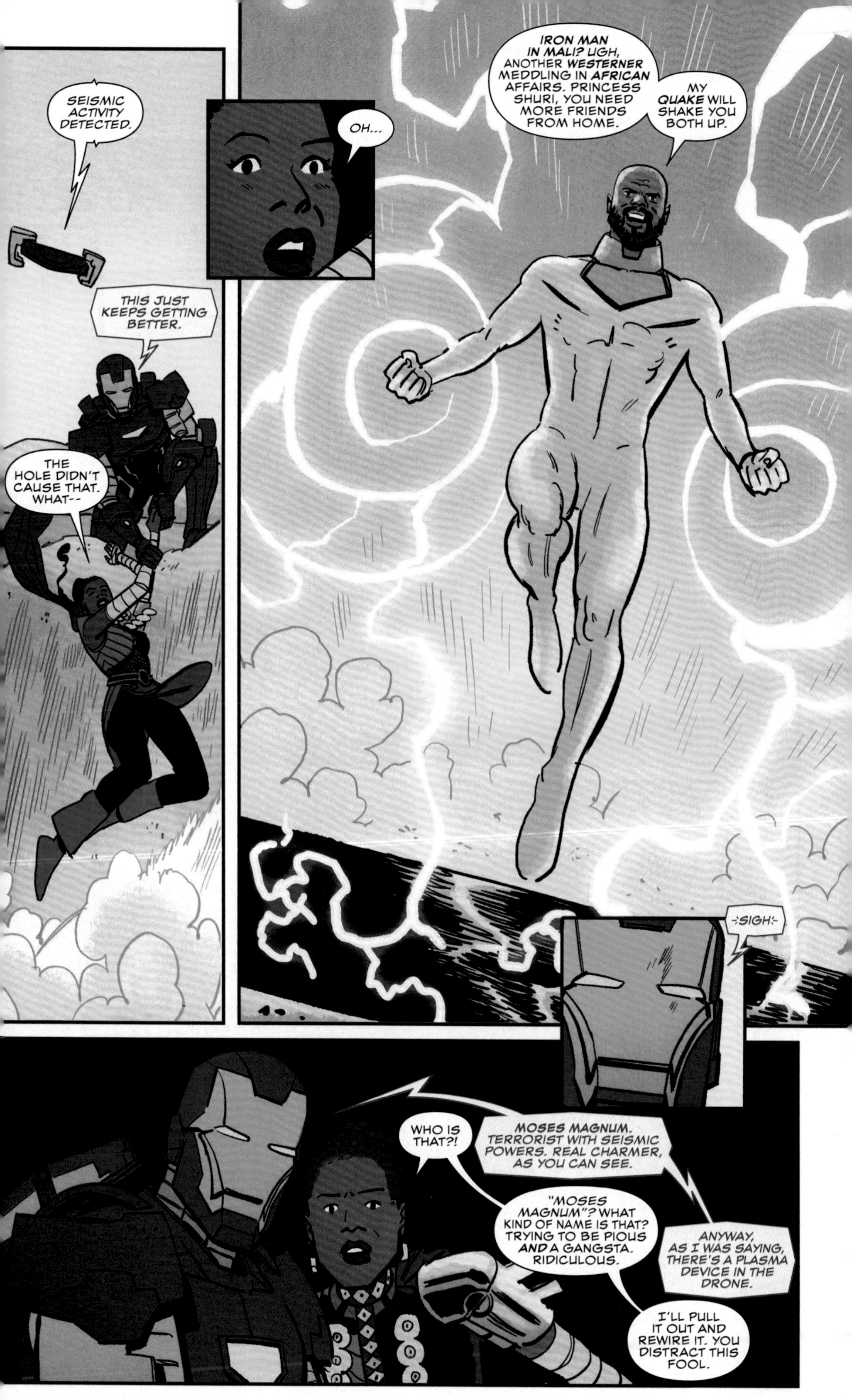

SEISMIC ACTIVITY DETECTED.
THIS JUST KEEPS GETTING BETTER.
THE HOLE DIDN'T CAUSE THAT. WHAT--
OH...
IRON MAN IN MALI? UGH, ANOTHER WESTERNER MEDDLING IN AFRICAN AFFAIRS. PRINCESS SHURI, YOU NEED MORE FRIENDS FROM HOME.
MY QUAKE WILL SHAKE YOU BOTH UP.
-SIGH-
WHO IS THAT?!
MOSES MAGNUM. TERRORIST WITH SEISMIC POWERS. REAL CHARMER, AS YOU CAN SEE.
"MOSES MAGNUM"? WHAT KIND OF NAME IS THAT? TRYING TO BE PIOUS AND A GANGSTA. RIDICULOUS.
ANYWAY, AS I WAS SAYING, THERE'S A PLASMA DEVICE IN THE DRONE.
I'LL PULL IT OUT AND REWIRE IT. YOU DISTRACT THIS FOOL.

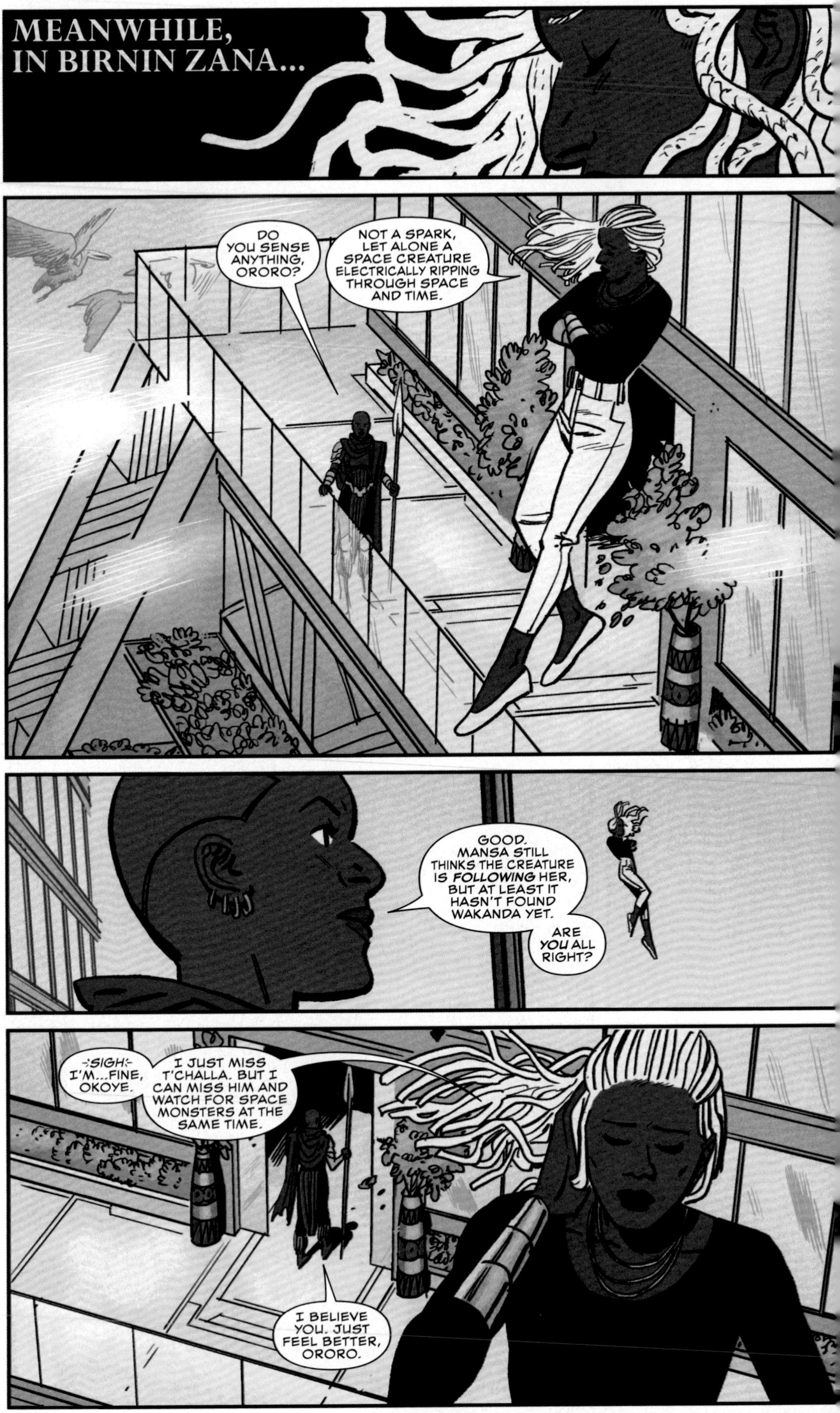
MEANWHILE, IN BIRNIN ZANA...
DO YOU SENSE ANYTHING, ORORO?
NOT A SPARK, LET ALONE A SPACE CREATURE ELECTRICALLY RIPPING THROUGH SPACE AND TIME.
GOOD. MANSA STILL THINKS THE CREATURE IS *FOLLOWING* HER, BUT AT LEAST IT HASN'T FOUND WAKANDA YET.
ARE *YOU* ALL RIGHT?
-SIGH- I'M...FINE, OKOYE.
I JUST MISS T'CHALLA. BUT I CAN MISS HIM AND WATCH FOR SPACE MONSTERS AT THE SAME TIME.
I BELIEVE YOU. JUST FEEL BETTER, ORORO.

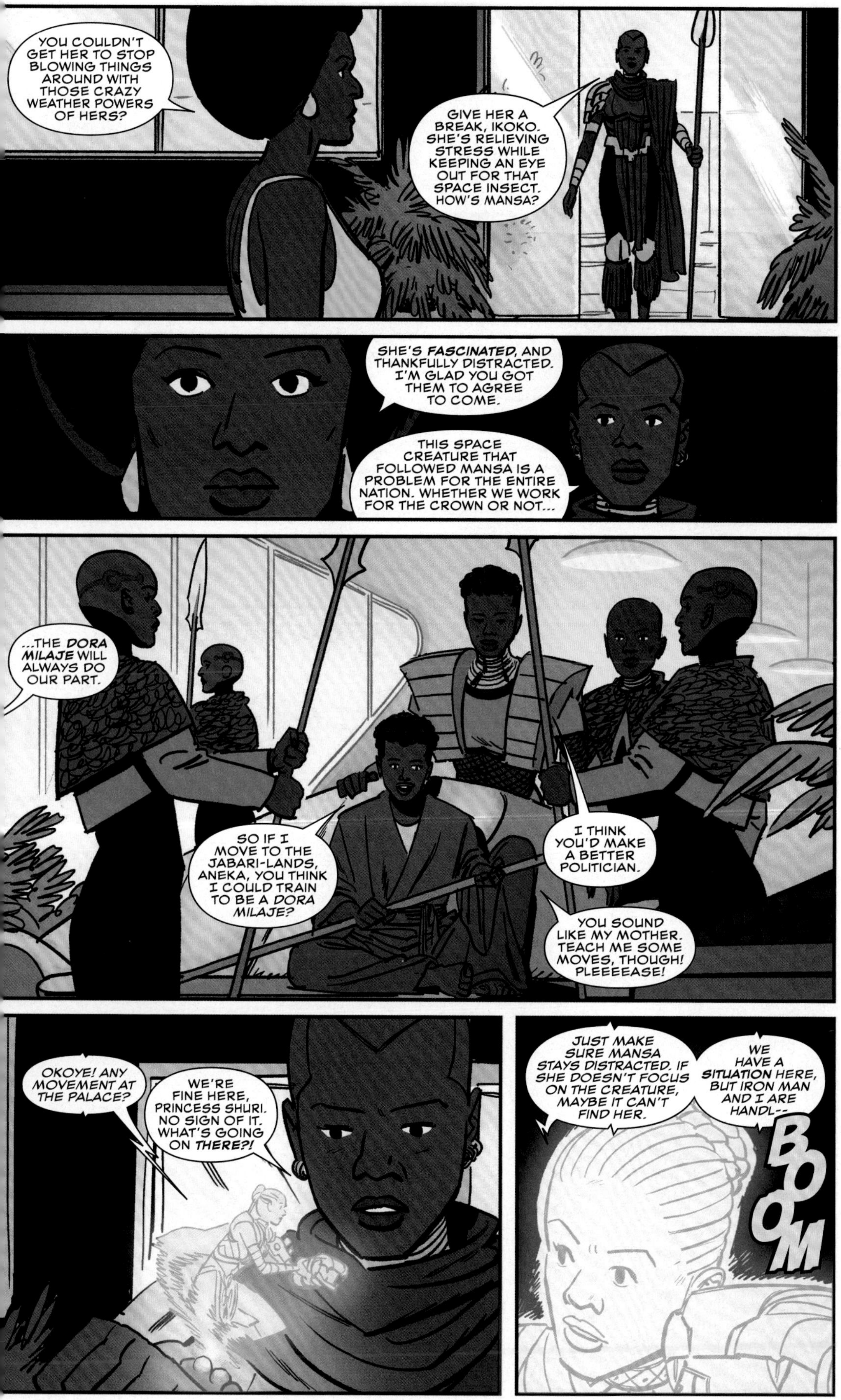

YOU COULDN'T GET HER TO STOP BLOWING THINGS AROUND WITH THOSE CRAZY WEATHER POWERS OF HERS?
GIVE HER A BREAK, IKOKO. SHE'S RELIEVING STRESS WHILE KEEPING AN EYE OUT FOR THAT SPACE INSECT. HOW'S MANSA?
SHE'S *FASCINATED*, AND THANKFULLY DISTRACTED. I'M GLAD YOU GOT THEM TO AGREE TO COME.
THIS SPACE CREATURE THAT FOLLOWED MANSA IS A PROBLEM FOR THE ENTIRE NATION. WHETHER WE WORK FOR THE CROWN OR NOT...
...THE *DORA MILAJE* WILL ALWAYS DO OUR PART.
SO IF I MOVE TO THE JABARI-LANDS, ANEKA, YOU THINK I COULD TRAIN TO BE A *DORA MILAJE*?
I THINK YOU'D MAKE A BETTER POLITICIAN.
YOU SOUND LIKE MY MOTHER. TEACH ME SOME MOVES, THOUGH! PLEEEEASE!
OKOYE! ANY MOVEMENT AT THE PALACE?
WE'RE FINE HERE, PRINCESS SHURI. NO SIGN OF IT. WHAT'S GOING ON *THERE?!*
JUST MAKE SURE MANSA STAYS DISTRACTED. IF SHE DOESN'T FOCUS ON THE CREATURE, MAYBE IT CAN'T FIND HER.
WE HAVE A *SITUATION* HERE, BUT IRON MAN AND I ARE HANDL--
BOOOM

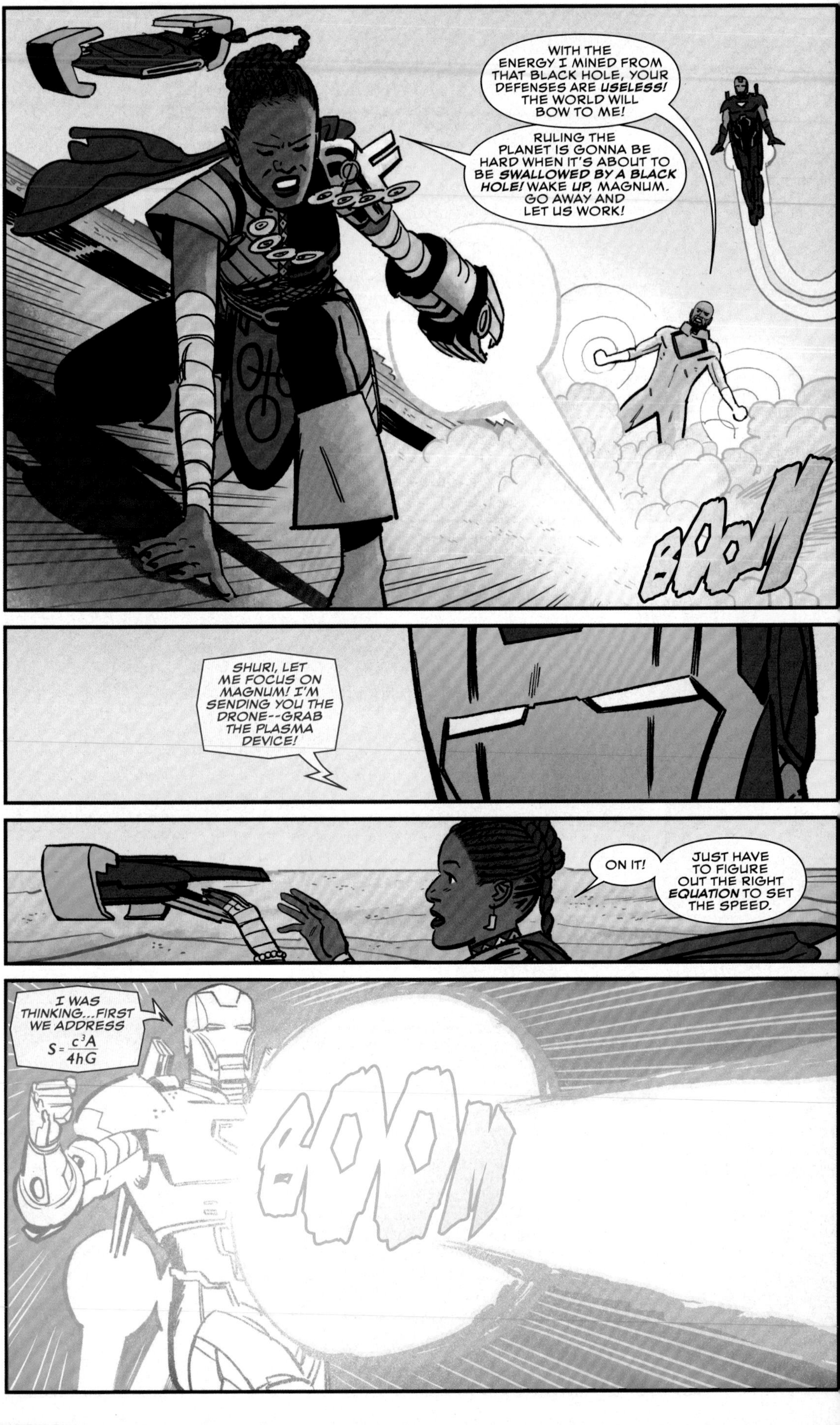
WITH THE ENERGY I MINED FROM THAT BLACK HOLE, YOUR DEFENSES ARE *USELESS!* THE WORLD WILL BOW TO ME!
RULING THE PLANET IS GONNA BE HARD WHEN IT'S ABOUT TO BE *SWALLOWED BY A BLACK HOLE!* WAKE UP, MAGNUM. GO AWAY AND LET US WORK!
BOOM
SHURI, LET ME FOCUS ON MAGNUM! I'M SENDING YOU THE DRONE--GRAB THE PLASMA DEVICE!
ON IT!
JUST HAVE TO FIGURE OUT THE RIGHT *EQUATION* TO SET THE SPEED.
I WAS THINKING...FIRST WE ADDRESS
$S = \frac{c^3A}{4hG}$
BOOM

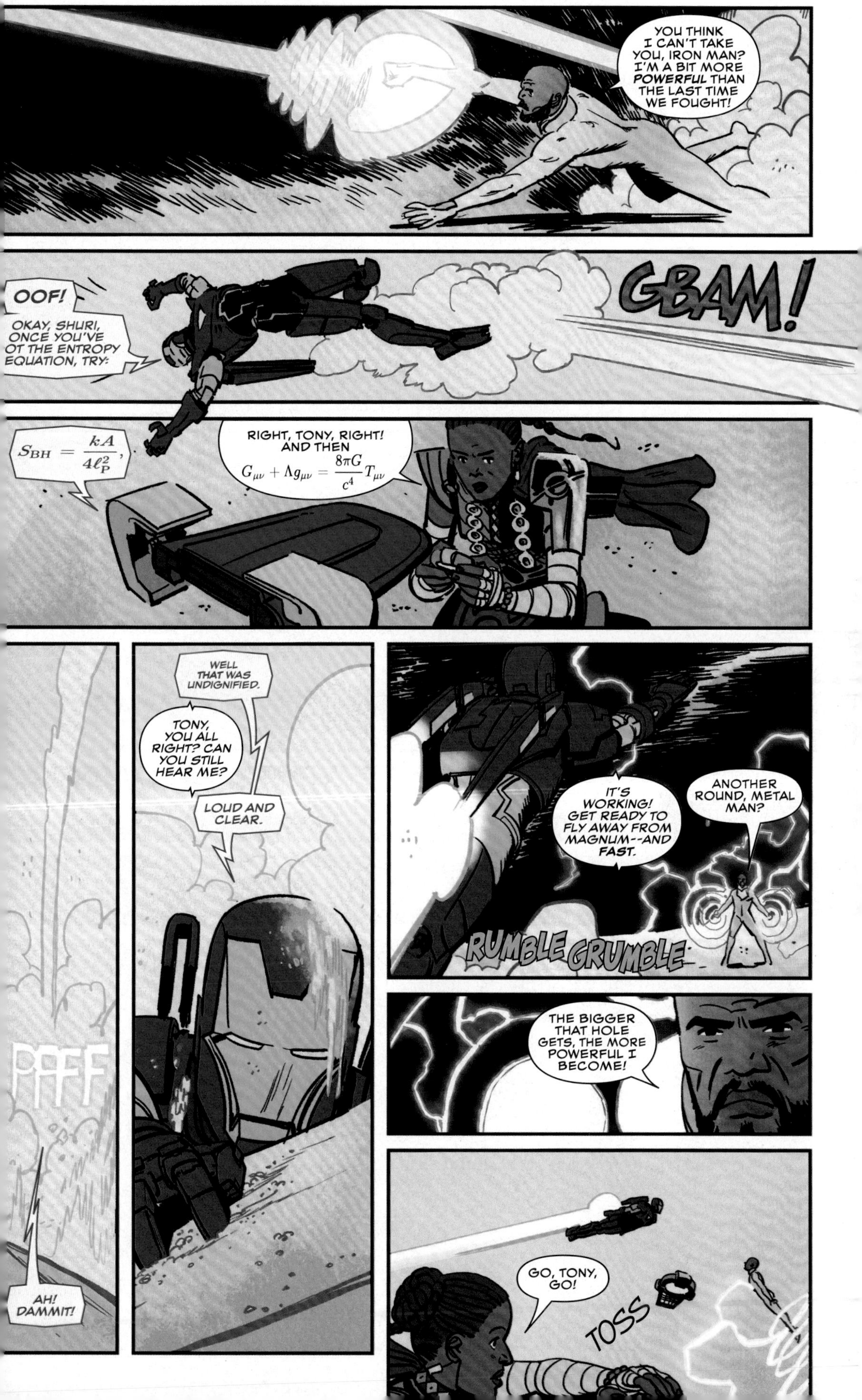

YOU THINK I CAN'T TAKE YOU, IRON MAN? I'M A BIT MORE POWERFUL THAN THE LAST TIME WE FOUGHT!
OOF!
GBAM!
OKAY, SHURI, ONCE YOU'VE OT THE ENTROPY EQUATION, TRY:
$S_{BH} = \frac{kA}{4\ell_P^2}$,
RIGHT, TONY, RIGHT! AND THEN $G_{\mu\nu} + \Lambda g_{\mu\nu} = \frac{8\pi G}{c^4} T_{\mu\nu}$
PFFF
AH! DAMMIT!
WELL THAT WAS UNDIGNIFIED.
TONY, YOU ALL RIGHT? CAN YOU STILL HEAR ME?
LOUD AND CLEAR.
IT'S WORKING! GET READY TO FLY AWAY FROM MAGNUM--AND FAST.
ANOTHER ROUND, METAL MAN?
RUMBLE GRUMBLE
THE BIGGER THAT HOLE GETS, THE MORE POWERFUL I BECOME!
GO, TONY, GO!
TOSS

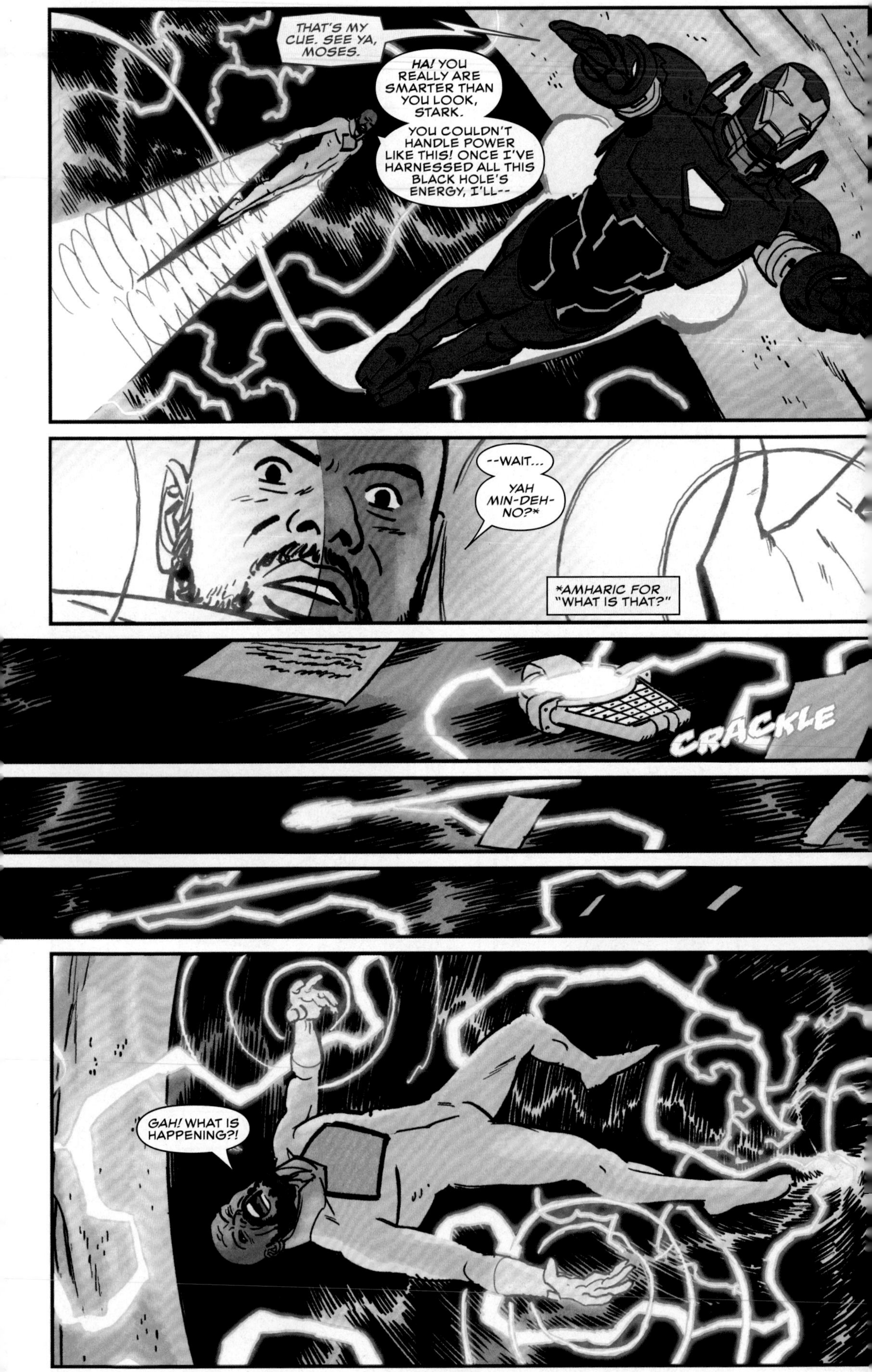
THAT'S MY CUE. SEE YA, MOSES.
HA! YOU REALLY ARE SMARTER THAN YOU LOOK, STARK.
YOU COULDN'T HANDLE POWER LIKE THIS! ONCE I'VE HARNESSED ALL THIS BLACK HOLE'S ENERGY, I'LL--
--WAIT...
YAH MIN-DEH-NO?*
*AMHARIC FOR "WHAT IS THAT?"
CRACKLE
GAH! WHAT IS HAPPENING?!

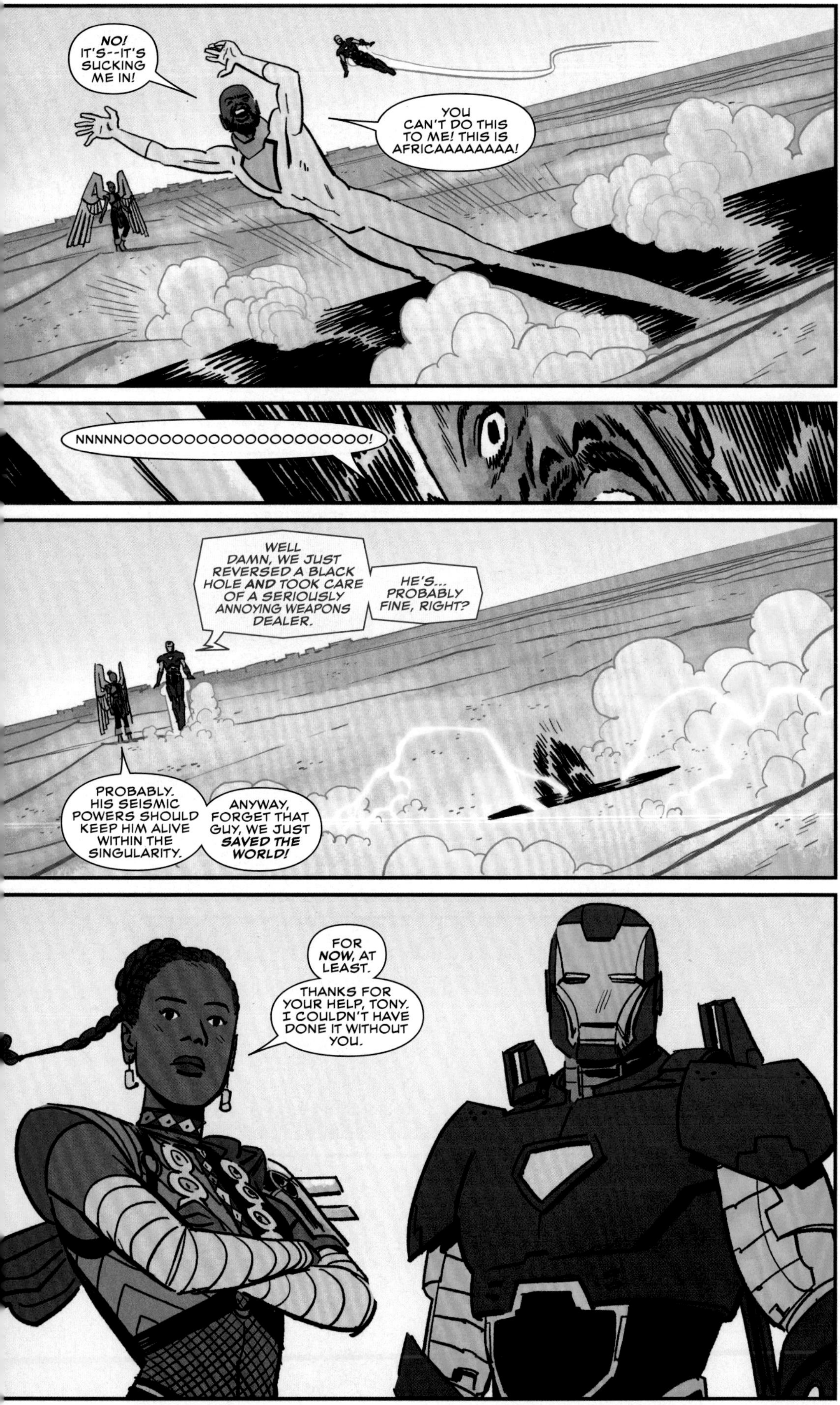
NO! IT'S--IT'S SUCKING ME IN!
YOU CAN'T DO THIS TO ME! THIS IS AFRICAAAAAAAA!
NNNNNOOOOOOOOOOOOOOOOOOOOOO!
WELL DAMN, WE JUST REVERSED A BLACK HOLE AND TOOK CARE OF A SERIOUSLY ANNOYING WEAPONS DEALER.
HE'S... PROBABLY FINE, RIGHT?
PROBABLY. HIS SEISMIC POWERS SHOULD KEEP HIM ALIVE WITHIN THE SINGULARITY.
ANYWAY, FORGET THAT GUY, WE JUST SAVED THE WORLD!
FOR NOW, AT LEAST.
THANKS FOR YOUR HELP, TONY. I COULDN'T HAVE DONE IT WITHOUT YOU.

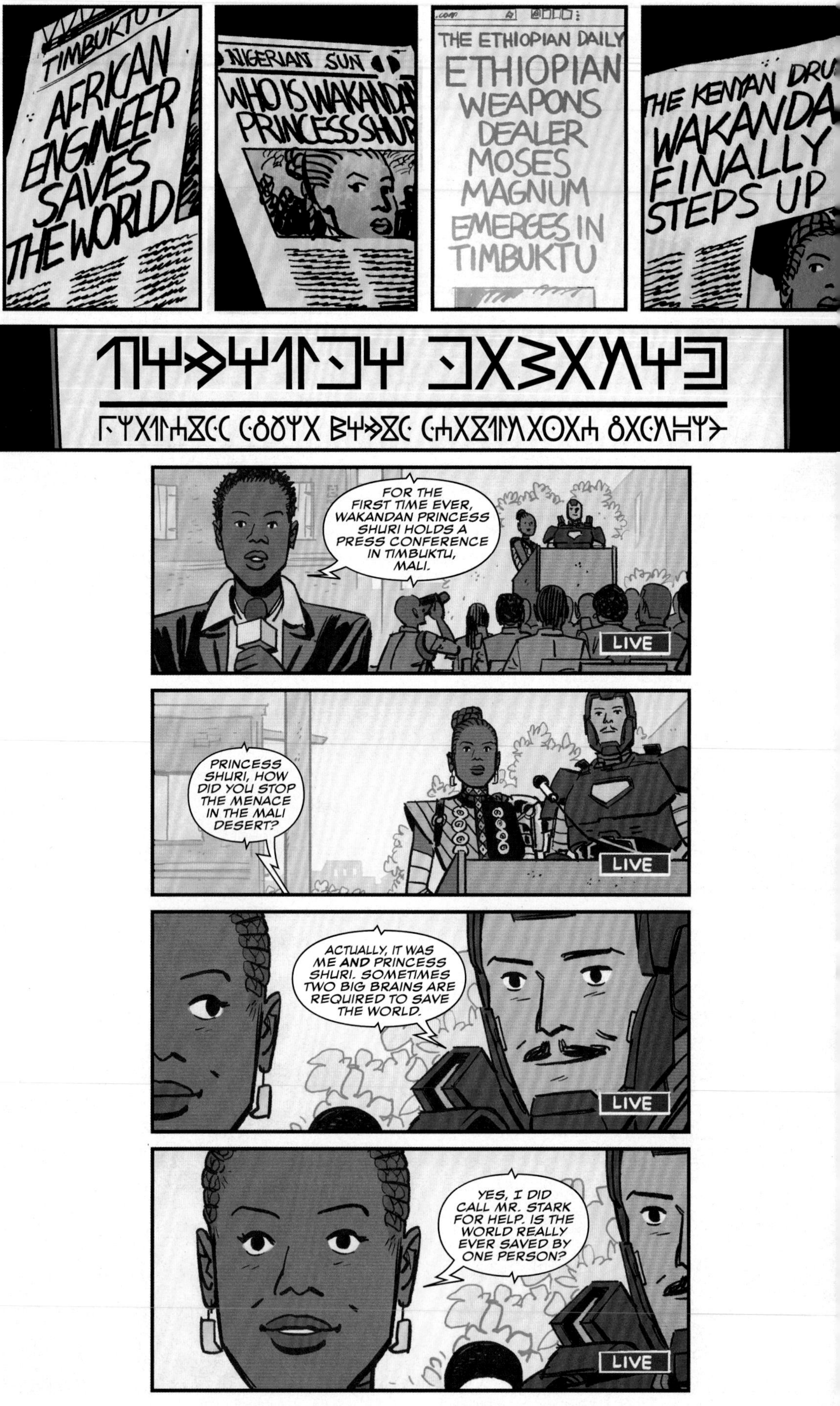
TIMBUKTU
AFRICAN ENGINEER SAVES THE WORLD
NIGERIAN SUN
WHO IS WAKANDA PRINCESS SHUR
THE ETHIOPIAN DAILY
ETHIOPIAN WEAPONS DEALER MOSES MAGNUM EMERGES IN TIMBUKTU
THE KENYAN
WAKANDA FINALLY STEPS UP
FOR THE FIRST TIME EVER, WAKANDAN PRINCESS SHURI HOLDS A PRESS CONFERENCE IN TIMBUKTU, MALI.
LIVE
PRINCESS SHURI, HOW DID YOU STOP THE MENACE IN THE MALI DESERT?
LIVE
ACTUALLY, IT WAS ME AND PRINCESS SHURI. SOMETIMES TWO BIG BRAINS ARE REQUIRED TO SAVE THE WORLD.
LIVE
YES, I DID CALL MR. STARK FOR HELP. IS THE WORLD REALLY EVER SAVED BY ONE PERSON?
LIVE

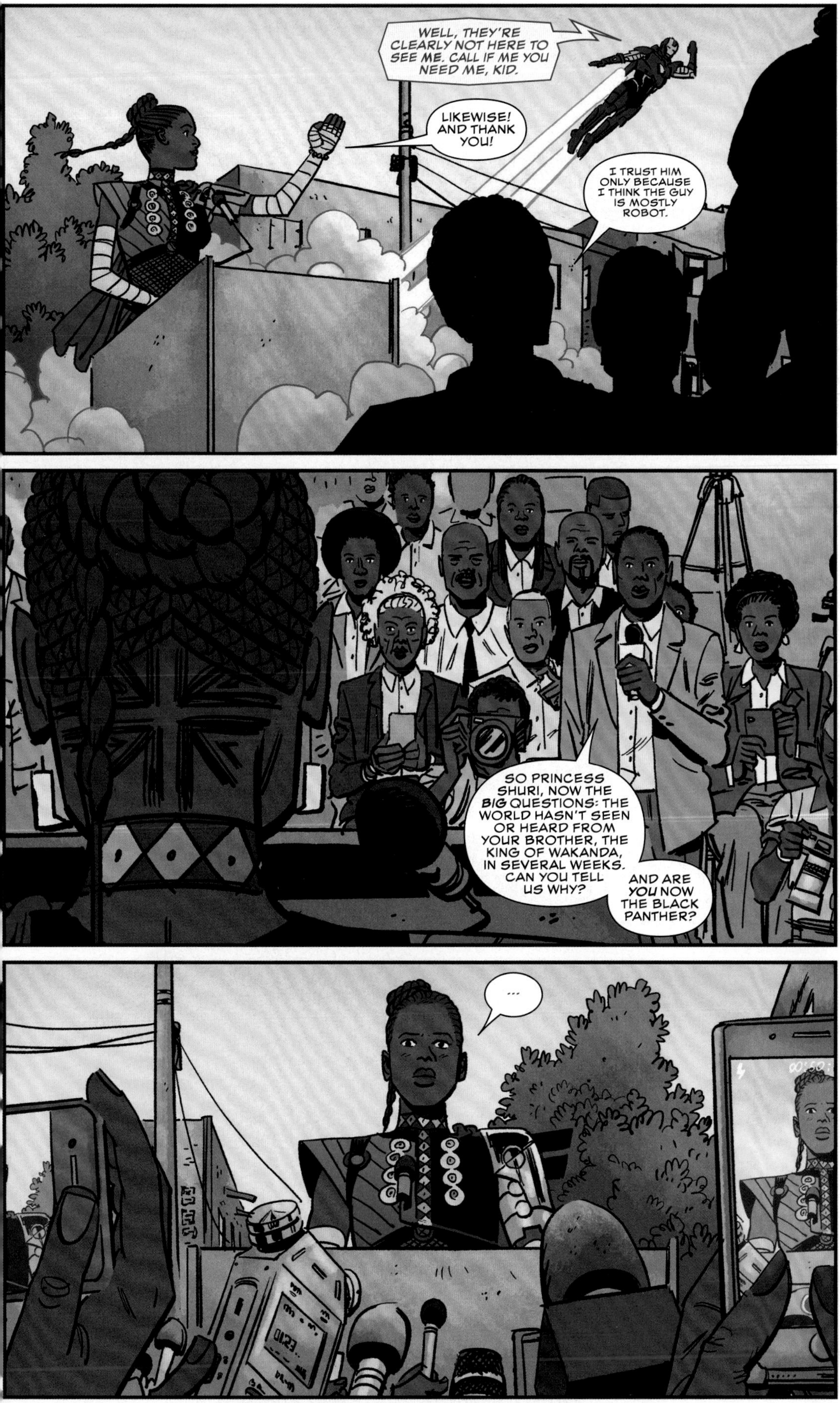
WELL, THEY'RE CLEARLY NOT HERE TO SEE ME. CALL IF ME YOU NEED ME, KID.
LIKEWISE! AND THANK YOU!
I TRUST HIM ONLY BECAUSE I THINK THE GUY IS MOSTLY ROBOT.
SO PRINCESS SHURI, NOW THE BIG QUESTIONS: THE WORLD HASN'T SEEN OR HEARD FROM YOUR BROTHER, THE KING OF WAKANDA, IN SEVERAL WEEKS. CAN YOU TELL US WHY?
AND ARE YOU NOW THE BLACK PANTHER?
...

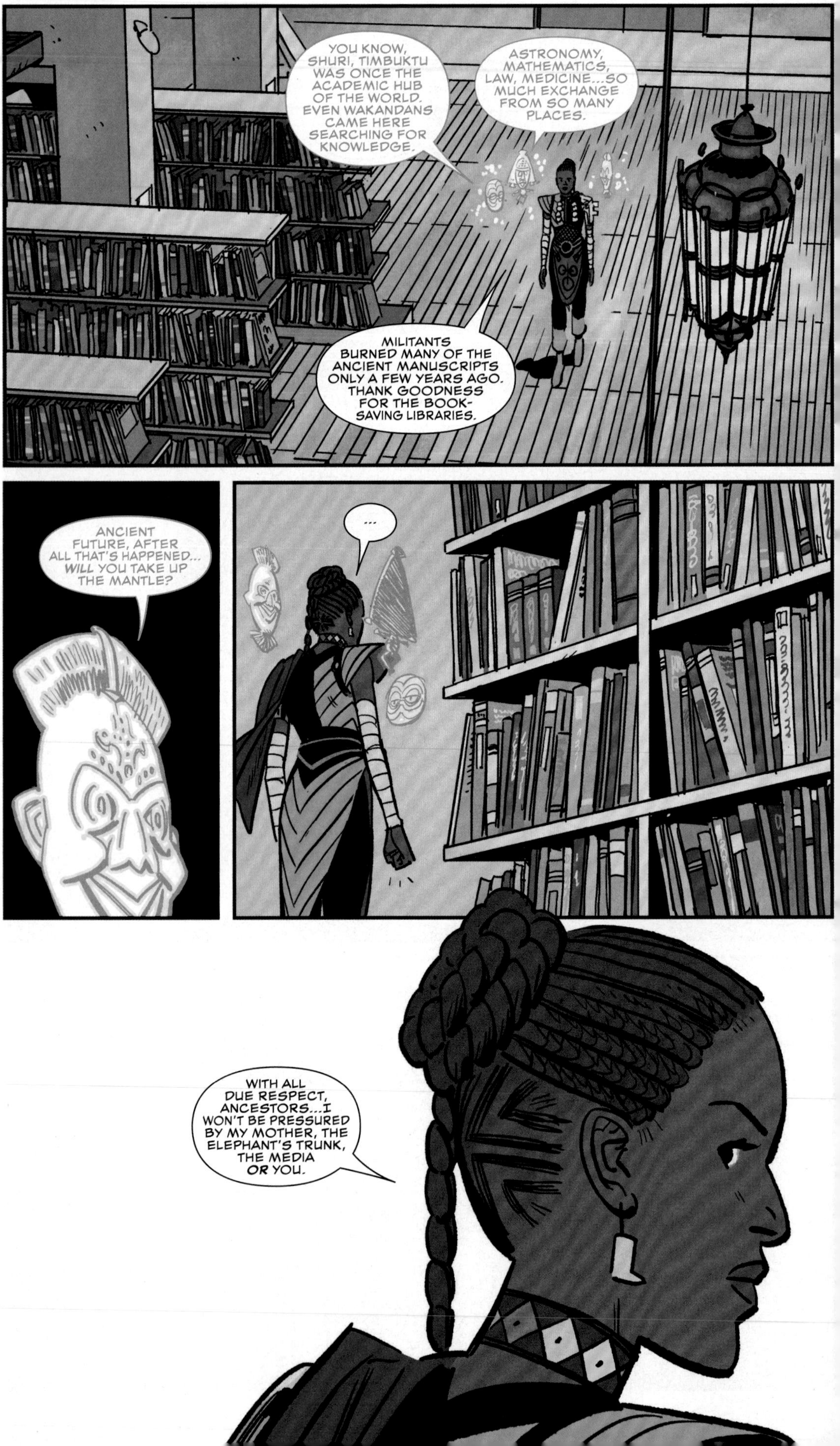
YOU KNOW, SHURI, TIMBUKTU WAS ONCE THE ACADEMIC HUB OF THE WORLD. EVEN WAKANDANS CAME HERE SEARCHING FOR KNOWLEDGE.
ASTRONOMY, MATHEMATICS, LAW, MEDICINE...SO MUCH EXCHANGE FROM SO MANY PLACES.
MILITANTS BURNED MANY OF THE ANCIENT MANUSCRIPTS ONLY A FEW YEARS AGO. THANK GOODNESS FOR THE BOOK-SAVING LIBRARIES.
ANCIENT FUTURE, AFTER ALL THAT'S HAPPENED... *WILL* YOU TAKE UP THE MANTLE?
...
WITH ALL DUE RESPECT, ANCESTORS...I WON'T BE PRESSURED BY MY MOTHER, THE ELEPHANT'S TRUNK, THE MEDIA *OR* YOU.

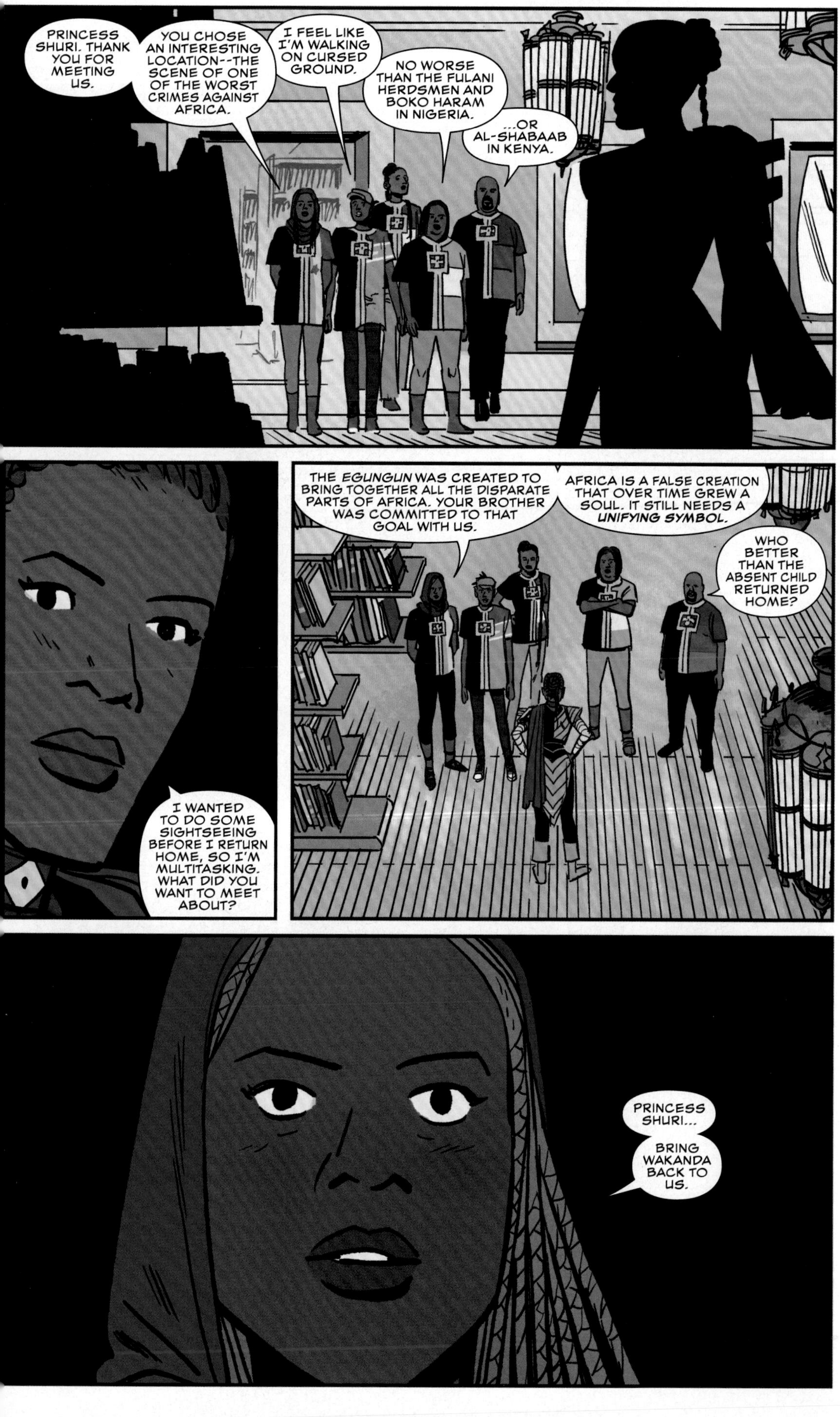

PRINCESS SHURI. THANK YOU FOR MEETING US.
YOU CHOSE AN INTERESTING LOCATION--THE SCENE OF ONE OF THE WORST CRIMES AGAINST AFRICA.
I FEEL LIKE I'M WALKING ON CURSED GROUND.
NO WORSE THAN THE FULANI HERDSMEN AND BOKO HARAM IN NIGERIA.
...OR AL-SHABAAB IN KENYA.
I WANTED TO DO SOME SIGHTSEEING BEFORE I RETURN HOME, SO I'M MULTITASKING. WHAT DID YOU WANT TO MEET ABOUT?
THE *EGUNGUN* WAS CREATED TO BRING TOGETHER ALL THE DISPARATE PARTS OF AFRICA. YOUR BROTHER WAS COMMITTED TO THAT GOAL WITH US.
AFRICA IS A FALSE CREATION THAT OVER TIME GREW A SOUL. IT STILL NEEDS A ***UNIFYING SYMBOL***.
WHO BETTER THAN THE ABSENT CHILD RETURNED HOME?
PRINCESS SHURI...
BRING WAKANDA BACK TO US.

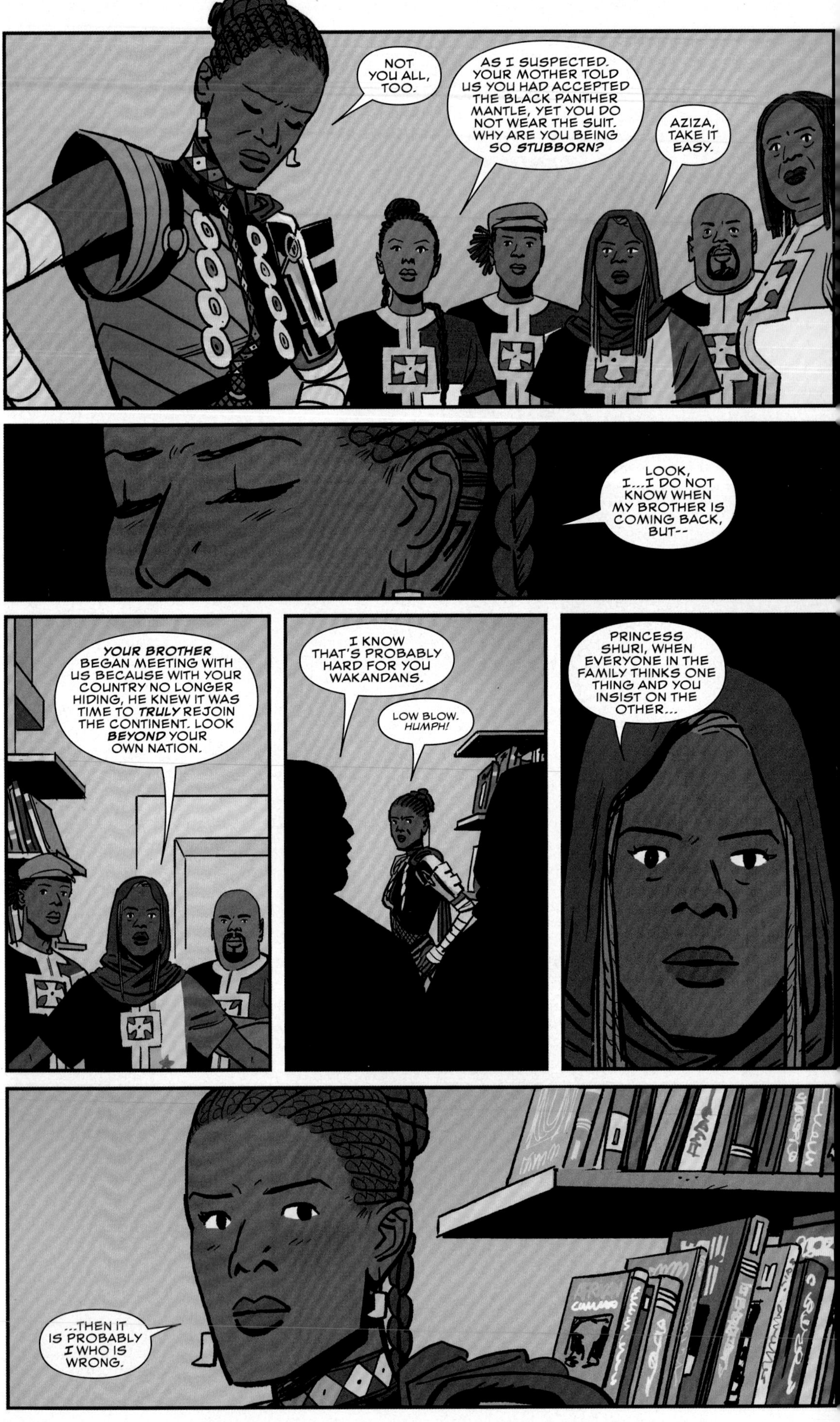
NOT YOU ALL, TOO.
AS I SUSPECTED. YOUR MOTHER TOLD US YOU HAD ACCEPTED THE BLACK PANTHER MANTLE, YET YOU DO NOT WEAR THE SUIT. WHY ARE YOU BEING SO STUBBORN?
AZIZA, TAKE IT EASY.
LOOK, I...I DO NOT KNOW WHEN MY BROTHER IS COMING BACK, BUT--
YOUR BROTHER BEGAN MEETING WITH US BECAUSE WITH YOUR COUNTRY NO LONGER HIDING, HE KNEW IT WAS TIME TO TRULY REJOIN THE CONTINENT. LOOK BEYOND YOUR OWN NATION.
I KNOW THAT'S PROBABLY HARD FOR YOU WAKANDANS.
LOW BLOW. HUMPH!
PRINCESS SHURI, WHEN EVERYONE IN THE FAMILY THINKS ONE THING AND YOU INSIST ON THE OTHER...
...THEN IT IS PROBABLY I WHO IS WRONG.

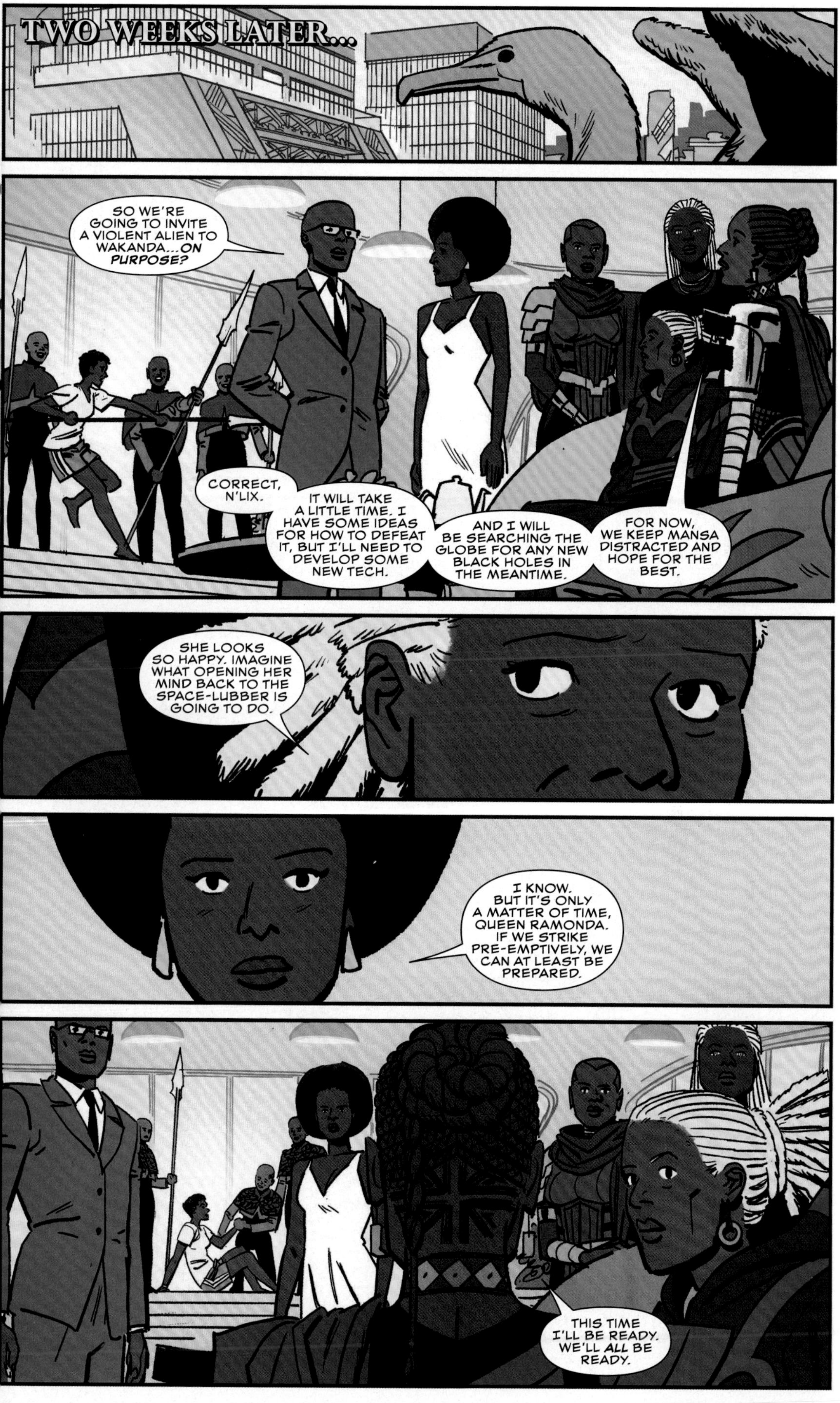
TWO WEEKS LATER...
SO WE'RE GOING TO INVITE A VIOLENT ALIEN TO WAKANDA...ON PURPOSE?
CORRECT, N'LIX.
IT WILL TAKE A LITTLE TIME. I HAVE SOME IDEAS FOR HOW TO DEFEAT IT, BUT I'LL NEED TO DEVELOP SOME NEW TECH.
AND I WILL BE SEARCHING THE GLOBE FOR ANY NEW BLACK HOLES IN THE MEANTIME.
FOR NOW, WE KEEP MANSA DISTRACTED AND HOPE FOR THE BEST.
SHE LOOKS SO HAPPY. IMAGINE WHAT OPENING HER MIND BACK TO THE SPACE-LUBBER IS GOING TO DO.
I KNOW. BUT IT'S ONLY A MATTER OF TIME, QUEEN RAMONDA. IF WE STRIKE PRE-EMPTIVELY, WE CAN AT LEAST BE PREPARED.
THIS TIME I'LL BE READY. WE'LL ALL BE READY.

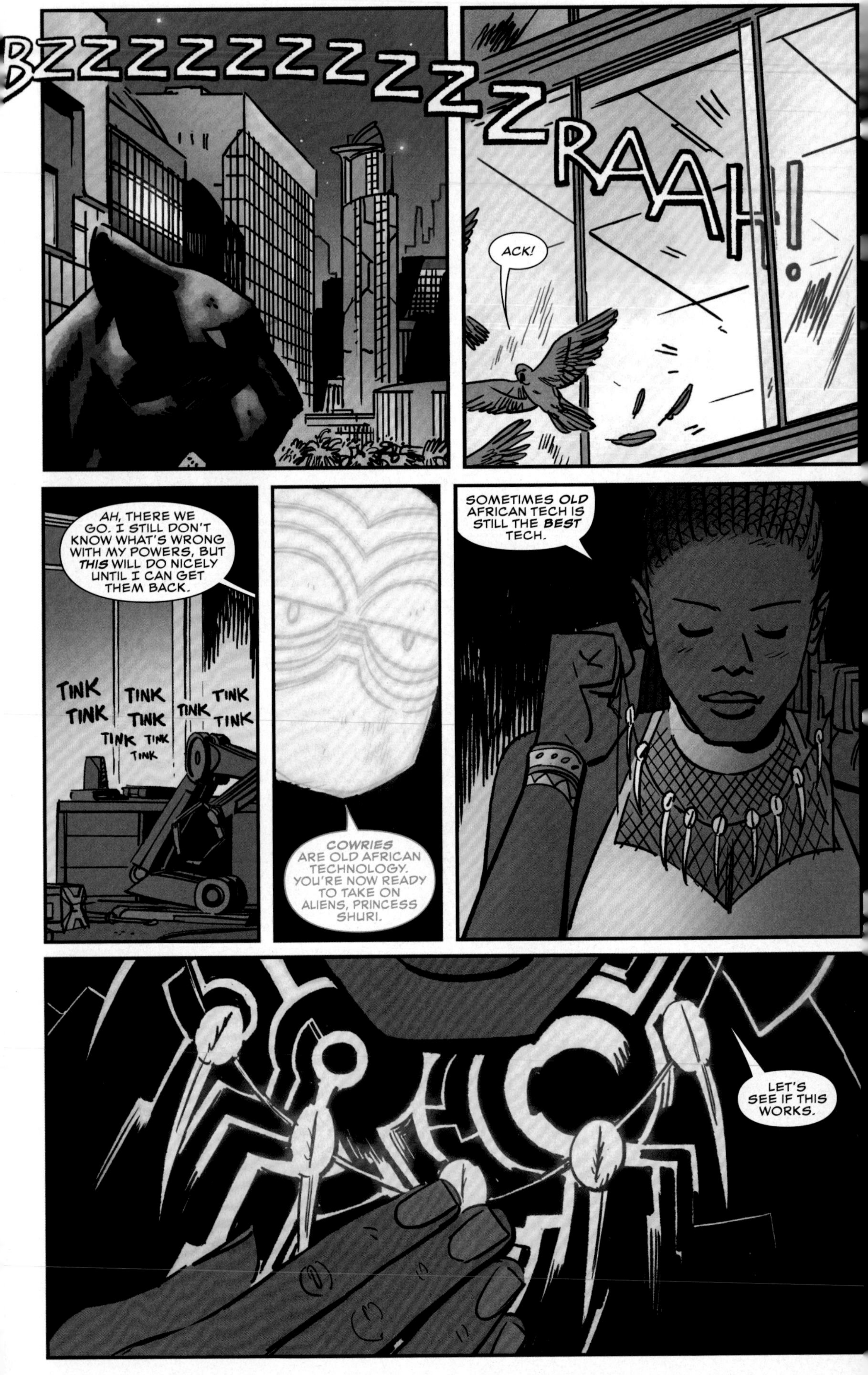

BZZZZZZZZZZZRAAH!
ACK!
AH, THERE WE GO. I STILL DON'T KNOW WHAT'S WRONG WITH MY POWERS, BUT THIS WILL DO NICELY UNTIL I CAN GET THEM BACK.
TINK TINK TINK TINK TINK TINK TINK TINK TINK TINK
COWRIES ARE OLD AFRICAN TECHNOLOGY. YOU'RE NOW READY TO TAKE ON ALIENS, PRINCESS SHURI.
SOMETIMES OLD AFRICAN TECH IS STILL THE BEST TECH.
LET'S SEE IF THIS WORKS.

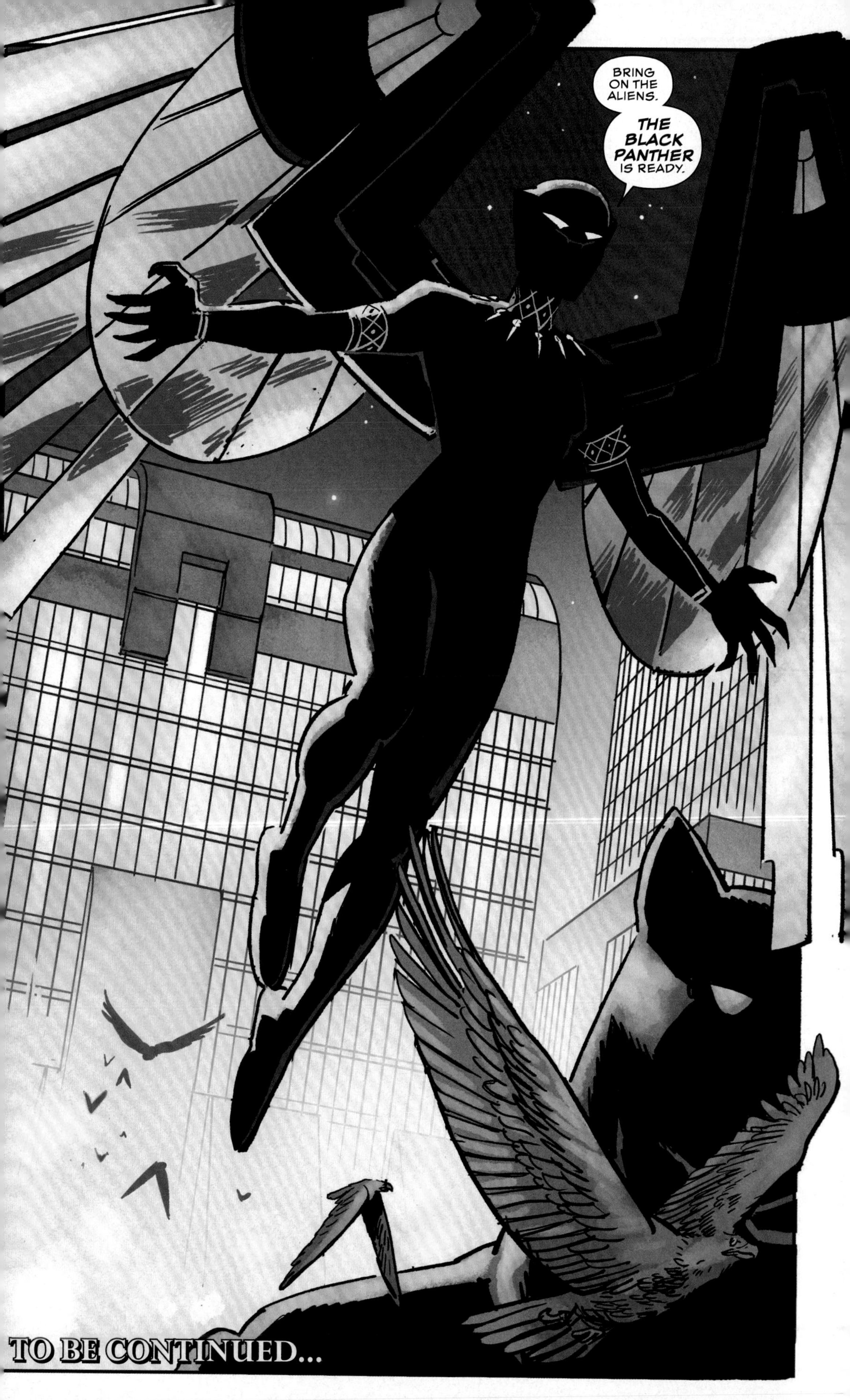
BRING ON THE ALIENS.
THE BLACK PANTHER IS READY.
TO BE CONTINUED...

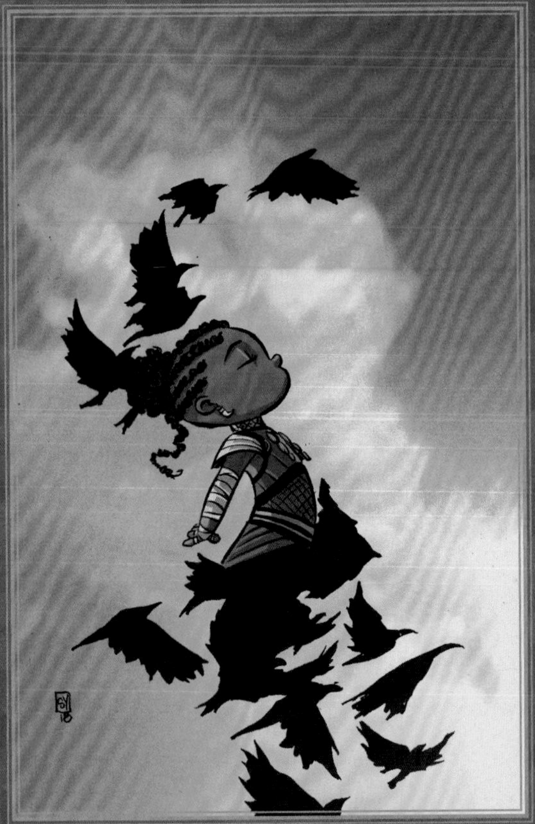

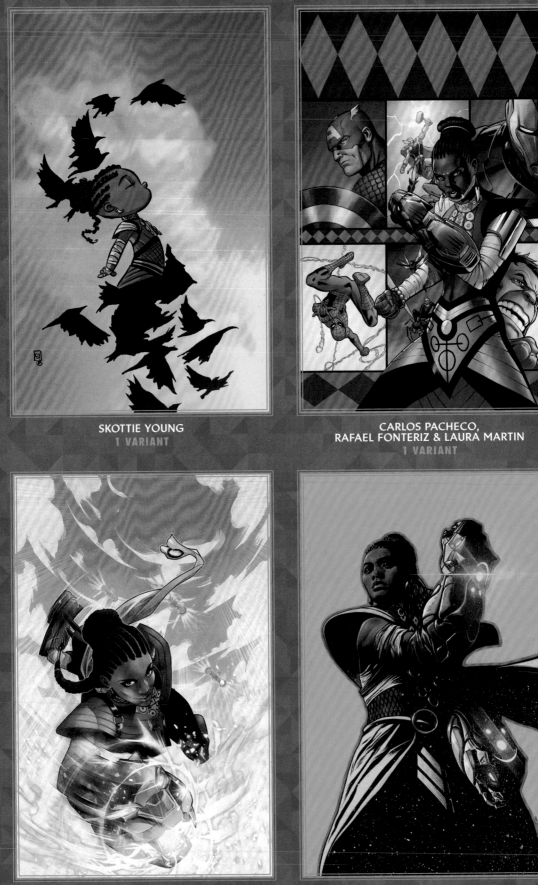

SKOTTIE YOUNG
1 VARIANT

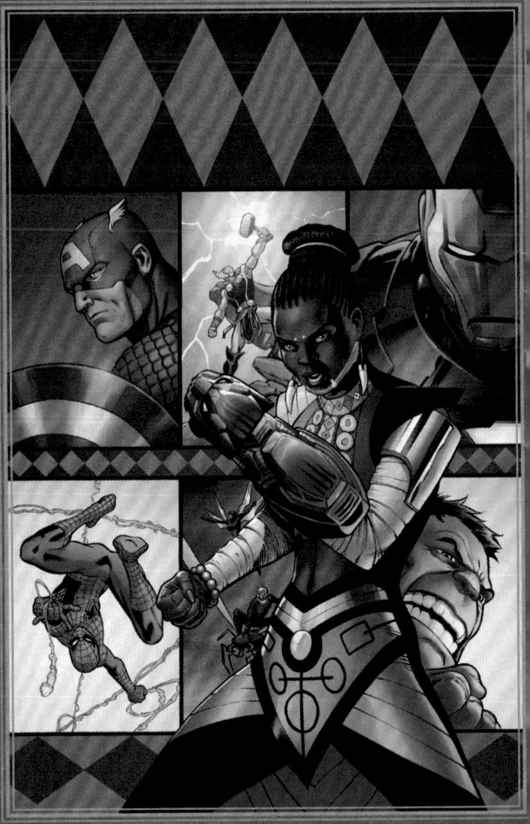

CARLOS PACHECO,
RAFAEL FONTERIZ & LAURA MARTIN
1 VARIANT

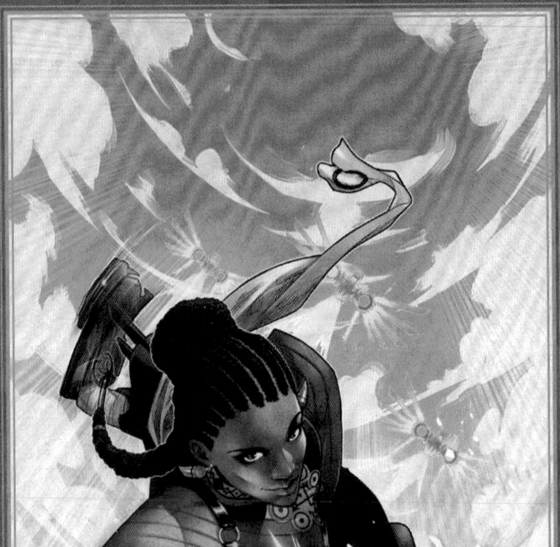

JAMAL CAMPBELL
1 VARIANT

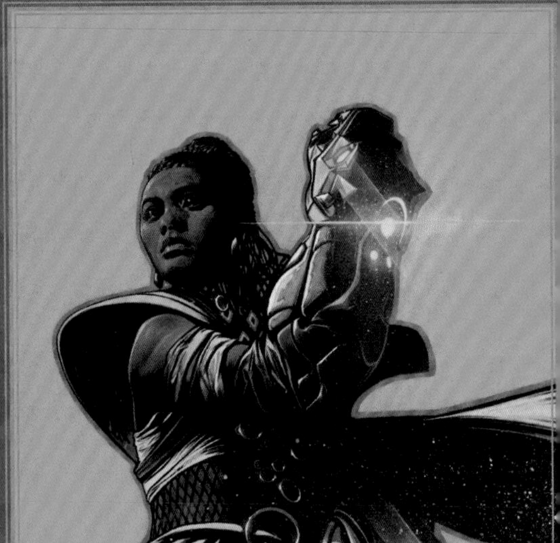

TRAVIS CHAREST
1 VARIANT

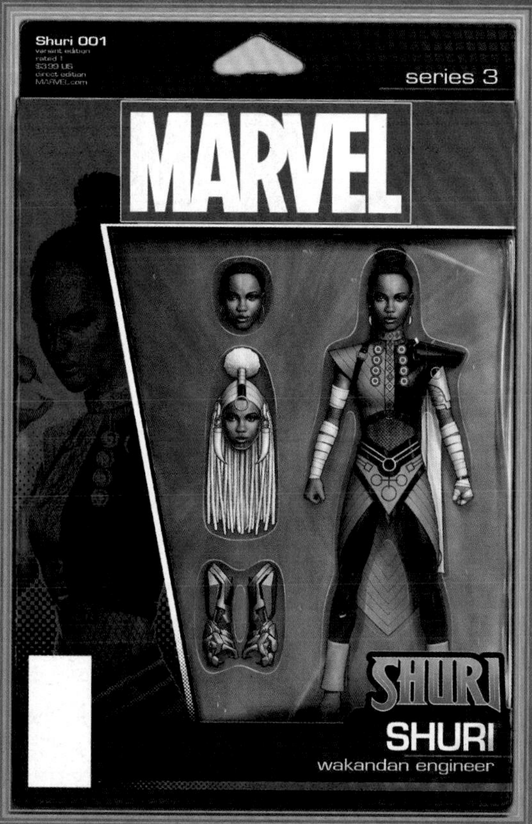
Shuri 001
series 3
MARVEL
SHURI
SHURI
wakandan engineer

JOHN TYLER CHRISTOPHER
1 ACTION FIGURE VARIANT

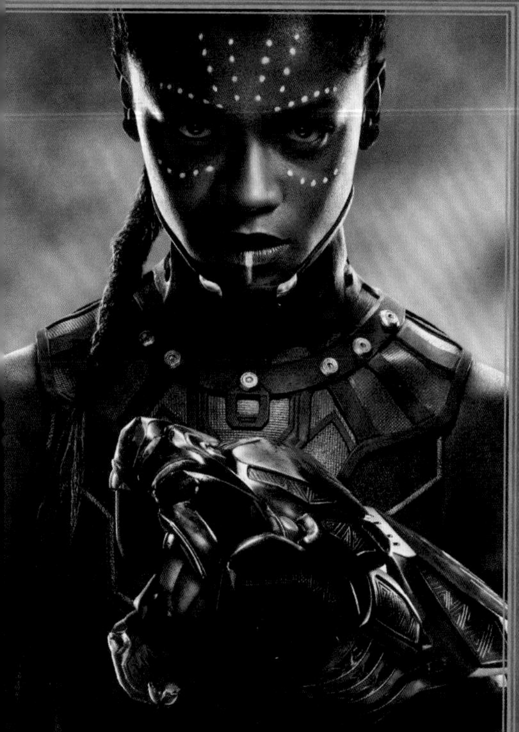

2 MOVIE VARIANT

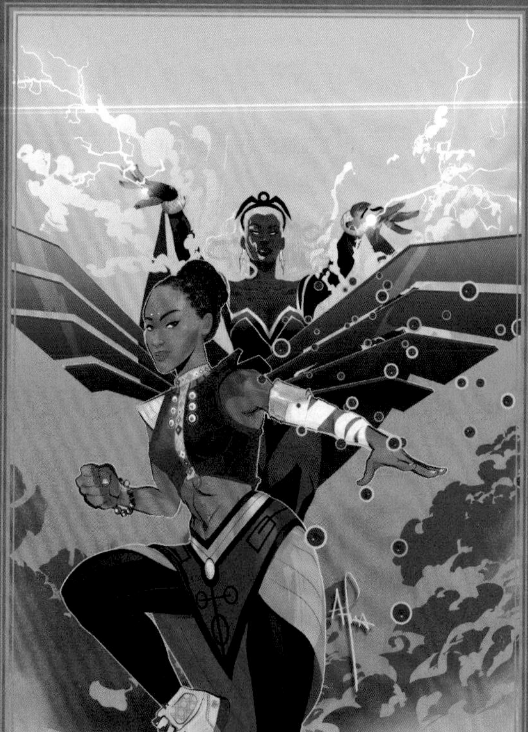

AFUA RICHARDSON
2 VARIANT

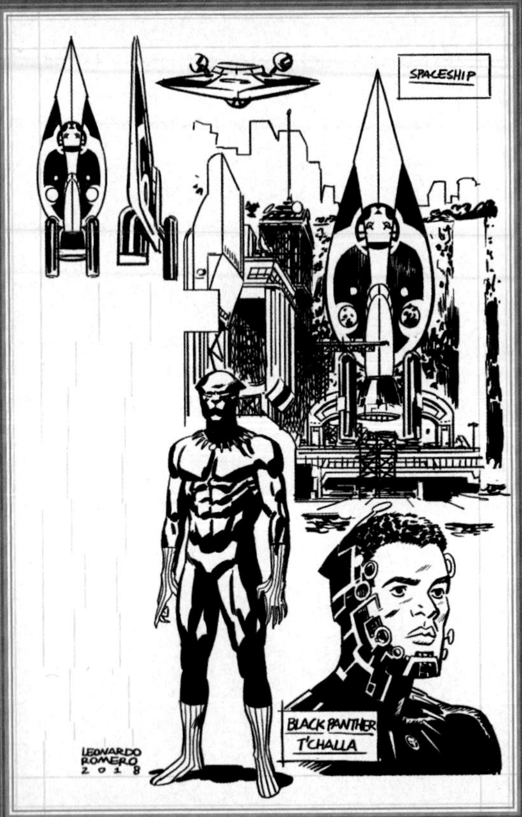
SPACESHIP
BLACK PANTHER
T'CHALLA
LEONARDO
ROMERO
2018

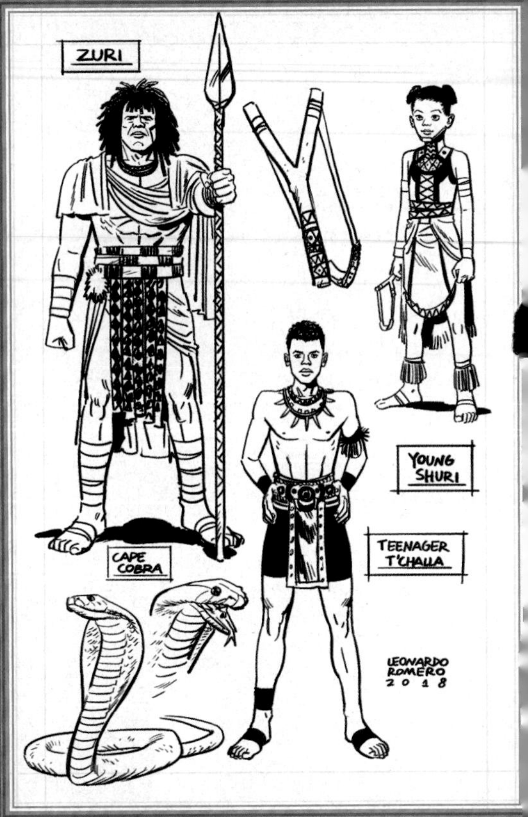
ZURI
YOUNG
SHURI
TEENAGER
T'CHALLA
CAPE
COBRA
LEONARDO
ROMERO
2018

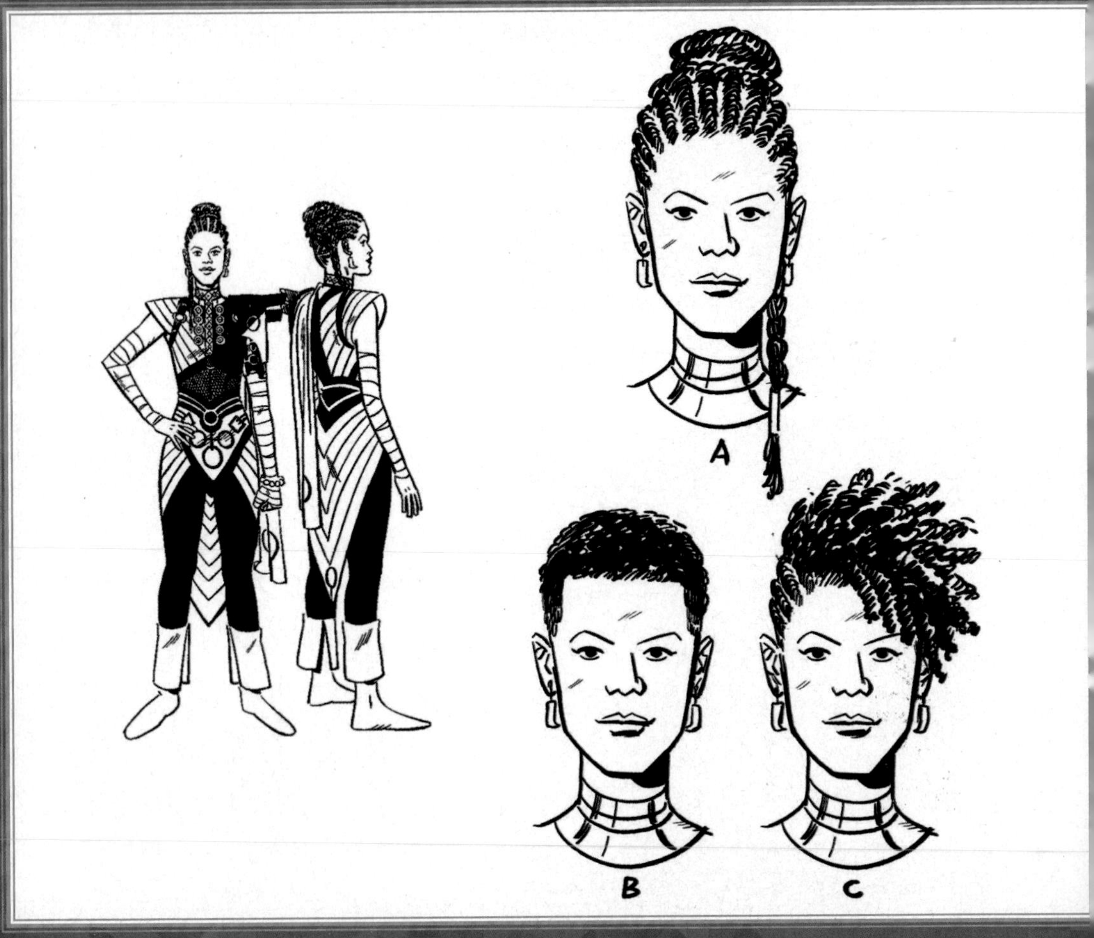
A
B
C

CHARACTER DESIGNS BY LEONARDO ROMERO